Women in the American Economy

Women in the American Economy

A DOCUMENTARY HISTORY, 1675 TO 1929

W. ELLIOT BROWNLEE
MARY M. BROWNLEE

New Haven and London, Yale University Press, 1976

Designed by Sally Sullivan.
Set in Caslon type and
printed in the United States of America by
The Colonial Press Inc., Clinton, Massachusetts.

Published in Great Britain, Europe, and Africa by
Yale University Press, Ltd., London.
Distributed in Latin America by Kaiman & Polon,
Inc., New York City;
in India by UBS Publishers' Distributors Pvt.,
Ltd., Delhi; in Japan by John Weatherhill, Inc., Tokyo;
in Australasia by Book
& Film Services, Artarmon,
N.S.W., Australia.

For Charlotte Louise,
who suggested that "Wonderwomen" would be a better title.

Contents

Introduction

At the beginning of this century, census takers found women employed in a myriad of diverse occupations. They worked as architects, chemists, engineers, lawyers, surveyors, shippers of farm products, railroad conductors, electricians, road machinery operators, blacksmiths, mechanics, metal molders, meat cutters, bartenders, law-enforcement officers, stevedores, and teamsters. However, the participation of women has been diverse throughout the history of the American economy, extending well beyond household tasks and the occupations traditionally considered women's work—occupations that seemed suited to the presumed physical, psychological, and intellectual inferiority of women and that *appeared* to extend logically from household responsibilities: nursing, elementary school teaching, manufacture of textiles and clothing, domestic service, and prostitution. Although such occupations have been statistically very significant, the employment of women has included the gamut of human enterprise, from the heaviest forms of low-skilled labor to the most sophisticated tasks associated with the exploitation of high technology.

Wide diversity of employment has long been accompanied by considerable depth—depth in terms of both the total labor force and the female population. Even before the rapid expansion in the employment of women resulting from the mobilization for World War II, women accounted for almost a quarter of all people in the labor force, and a quarter of all women above the age of 14 were working. (See table 1.) Thus, the direct contribution of women to the economic development of the nation has been consistently significant, and that participation has been a central part of the social life of American women. To enhance appreciation of the diversity and extent of that economic contribution and to explore the relationship between the marketplace life of women and their total social history are the tasks of this book. We wish to provide a historical sense of the striking variety of women's economic activities and to suggest the reasons for the precise forms that the participation in the marketplace assumed.

Recent interest in the work of women in the United States has been riveted on the years since World War II—an understandable focus in the light of the broad changes in women's economic and social position. During the decade that included World War II, both the character of women's work and the rate at which women participated in the labor force underwent exceptionally marked changes. Moreover, until the late 1960s, this rising participation by women occurred in the face of an intensifying cultural fixation on their virtues as housekeepers, child rearers, and husband custodians; the setting was a curious, almost paradoxical one for a dramatic transformation of women's economic life. But no explanation of why significant changes occurred at this time can be adequate if it lacks a grasp of the historical background of those changes. The recent emphasis on contemporary issues and the absence of any sustained analysis of women's work in general make it imperative that students of women's history become acquainted with source material that can stimulate understanding of the economic life of American women before 1929.

The documents selected for this book convey the diversity of women's attitudes toward work and the complexity of women's participation in the marketplace, particularly the ingenuity, flexibility, shrewd adaptation, aggressiveness, and persistent search for a "sense of self" that have characterized the contribution of women to the nation's economic life. Women's perceptions of their economic experience have a meaning and validity that transcend any need for interpretive gloss. The writing of representative women highlights

Table 1. Participation of Women in American Labor Force, 1800–1970

Year	(1) Women's Share of Labor Force (%)*	(2) Working Women in the Female Population (%)†
1800	4.6	4.6
1810	9.4	7.9
1820	7.3	6.2
1830	7.4	6.4
1840	9.6	8.4
1850	10.8	10.1
1860	10.2	9.7
1870	14.8	13.7
1880	15.2	14.7
1890	17.0	18.2
1900	18.3	21.2
1910	20.0	24.8
1920	20.4	23.9
1930	22.1	24.4
1940	24.3	25.4
1950	27.9	29.1
1960	37.1	34.8
1970	42.8	42.6

*Including, for 1800–80, females over age 10; for 1890–1950 females over age 14; and for 1800–60, only free women.

†Population of women defined on same basis as women workers.

SOURCES: Gertrude Bancroft, *The American Labor Force: Its Growth and Changing Composition* (New York: John Wiley, 1958), pp. 202–09; Stanley Lebergott, "Labor Force and Employment Growth, 1800–1860," in National Bureau of Economic Research, *Output, Employment, and Productivity in the United States After 1800, Studies in Income and Wealth*, vol. 30 (New York: Columbia University Press, 1966), pp. 134–46; id. *Manpower in Economic Growth, The American Record Since 1800* (New York: McGraw-Hill, 1964), pp. 56–62 and 519–20; U.S. Bureau of the Census, *Historical Statistics of the United States, Colonial Times to 1957* (Washington, D.C.: Government Printing Office, 1960), pp. 67–72; U.S. Bureau of the Census, *Occupational Trends in the United States: 1900–1950*, Bureau of the Census Working Paper No. 5 (Washington, D.C.: Government Printing Office, 1958); and U.S. Department of Commerce, *Statistical Abstract of the United States, 1971* (Washington, D.C.: Government Printing Office, 1971), pp. 211–12.

the general economic history of women as it documents the exploits of unusually accomplished individuals.

The remainder of this introduction is devoted to an exploration of the broad contours, potential as well as actual, of those experiences. In particular, we want to suggest a merger of insights derived from (1) the conventional history of the women's movement; (2) the improving definition of the changing social characteristics of the American population; and (3) the rapidly growing knowledge of the nation's economic development, including the nature of the labor force. Primary sources enable the reader to begin to evaluate the hypotheses we pose and to move beyond them by defining problems that appear more compelling. Consequently, we have included material that points toward divergent interpretations and distinctly different approaches to the study of women's work.

One of the best points of departure for probing of the economic, social, and cultural setting of women's work is the *rate* at which women have entered the work force. That rate reveals the highly significant extent to which women abandoned the constraints imposed by the household and submitted themselves to the conditions set by employer-employee relationships and, thereby, transactions involving the explicit exchange of services for money. Marketplace participation is, then, a potent measure of independence from sanctions of family. It is quite true that economic independence does not necessarily imply social independence. For example, women may work largely to satisfy economic aspirations set by the family and may exercise relatively little discretion over the disposition of earned income.[1] However, a significant number of married workingwomen have always been the primary breadwinners, and it is reasonable to assume that many more wives with working husbands have expanded their social independence along with their participation in the marketplace. Especially in a society so obviously committed to the cash nexus—to pecuniary income as a measure of worth—it is to be expected that as women have moved

1. For the suggestion that contemporary wives enter the labor force to help the family buy new appliances, see Stanley Lebergott, *Manpower in Economic Growth: The American Record Since 1800* (New York: McGraw-Hill, 1964), pp. 65–68.

out of the household into the market they have enhanced their autonomy.

The overall trend of the participation of women in the labor force is quite clear—refer to table 1. Even by 1930, three to four times as many women, relative to the total female population, participated in the labor force as had participated during the early decades of the nineteenth century. Yet it has often been claimed that such a change awaited the social disruption attending World War II. This claim has been made both by those who would stress the limitations on opportunities for women and by those who would, at least implicitly, attribute to women innate inferiority that was reflected in their social role. But to accept that conclusion one must deny the recorded evidence, based largely on that collected by census takers. One must claim either that the bias of observers distorted the results or that the rates of participation do not measure what they purport to measure. Both contentions require comment.

Those who charge observer bias assert that census takers only gradually became aware of the extent to which women worked— particularly women holding part-time jobs. Proponents of this claim usually cite the apparently high participation rate for women in 1910. They account for it by the fact that in that year census takers received unusually explicit instructions for counting women workers, particularly women employed on a part-time basis. To be sure, the 1910 census gives the best count before 1940. Still, it is probably less of an exaggeration than its critics would suggest, given four facts: (1) the census revealed no aberration in the women's share of the labor force; (2) even as late as 1890 a typical married woman made all the clothing for herself and her children as well as performing all the household chores with only minimal mechanical assistance; (3) the absolute number of women employed in agriculture declined sharply after 1910; and (4) the participation rate for 1930 was unusually low as a consequence of the onset of the Great Depression.[2]

2. For criticism of the reliability of trends revealed by census data on occupations before 1940, see A. J. Jaffe, "Trends in the Participation of Women in the Working Force," *Monthly Labor Review* 79 (May 1956): 559–65; Robert W. Smuts, "The Female Labor Force: A Case Study in the Interpretation of Historical Statistics,"

Criticism of census-derived data also questions the validity of the gainful-employment or labor-force concepts used to define women workers. Such criticism makes a central point that is certainly indisputable: women have performed socially useful work far beyond that which is measurable in the marketplace. In America prior to the rise of the factory system women contributed directly to the vast array and volume of manufactured (in the literal sense of hand-crafted) goods that were produced by household enterprise and that were usually consumed at home, bartered, or sold in local markets. It is a fact that the factory won its victory only gradually; household enterprise, although it diminished in relative importance as factory organization spread, survived into the twentieth century—most visibly on the family farm but in the city as well. There it both maintained its preindustrial character and evolved into the notorious sweatshops of the clothing industry. The sweatshop employed entire families and hordes of women, some of whom undoubtedly escaped the census even though the goods they made reached the market-place. Beyond household enterprise must be reckoned the work women did while performing the routines of homemaking. Un-counted in the official categorizations of occupations and members of society gainfully employed were all the women confined to the home and assigned strikingly diversified responsibilities for educa-tion, nursing, psychological counseling, management of consump-tion (which could be regarded as *investment*—in household enter-prise—rather than *consumption,* if one were to abandon orthodox income accounting), gardening, cleaning, and cooking.

But we feel that the fact of working outside the home was significant enough to justify the census-takers for excluding from their data those women who confined their work to the household. Furthermore, it is not true, as the critics of gainful-employment data tend to suggest, that as more women have joined the labor force

Journal of the American Statistical Association 55 (March 1960): 71–79; id., *Women and Work in America* (New York: Columbia University Press, 1959), chaps. 1 and 2 and pp. 157–59; and, initiating the questioning of census occupational figures, Isaac M. Rubinow, "Women in Manufactures: A Criticism," *Journal of Political Economy* 15 (January 1907): 41–47. But, the Jaffe-Smuts critique has been effectively questioned. See Sophia Cooper, "Comments," *Monthly Labor Review* 79 (May 1956): 566; and Lebergott, *Manpower in Economic Growth*, pp. 70–73.

society simply shifted work considered appropriate for women from the household to the marketplace. Except for factory work, the occupations that came to employ the largest numbers of women (such as teaching, nursing, and clerking) lacked functional counterparts in the preindustrial world, or had such counterparts filled by men, or, for a considerable part of even the industrial era, were pursued largely by men. Many women who had left their homes to work were displaced from their jobs by men who found the work attractive and who received preferential treatment from employers. In fact, the development of women's contribution in the marketplace has been no simple, direct transition from household work to gainful employment but a highly complex and variable one. The resulting patterns in the participation rates of women embody substantial information about the changing character of social opportunities for women.

Trends in the participation rate, if accurately defined as to their timing and extent, facilitate analysis of the historical circumstances altering working opportunities for women. Thus, explaining the overall upward trend must begin with the recognition that the long-run pattern is the cumulative creation of several discrete spurts. These spurts can be summarized as (1) a slow increase in the participation rate from the decade 1800–1810 until the 1850s when it began to decline; (2) a sudden, crisp increase during the decade of the Civil War—a growth that did not hold up after the 1860s; and (3) an increase, almost doubling the relative size of the female population in the labor market, from the 1870s through the 1930s, although probably climbing at a reduced rate during the last half of the period. The precise trend after 1910 is difficult to determine because 1930 rested in a period of depression and because 1940 followed the Great Depression during which the high rates of unemployment led to pervasive efforts to circumscribe the work of women, who appeared to be depriving male heads of households of their livelihoods.[3] Because it is very likely that before the onset of

3. See Grace Adams, *Workers on Relief* (New Haven: Yale University Press, 1939), and Lorine Pruette, *Women Workers Through the Depression, A Study of White-Collar Employment* (New York: Macmillan, 1934).

the Great Depression the participation rate for women had reached a level higher than that obtained in 1940, it is reasonable to conclude that the initial rate of participation continued to increase, although at a reduced pace, from 1910 until the 1929 peak.

It is on the problem of explaining these increases that our interpretive endeavor is focused, in contrast with the popular concentration of historical analysis on explaining why the participation rate for women was consistently lower than that for men. The recognition that the past experience of women has not necessarily been all of a piece is liberating. It permits us to explore the ambiguities in American culture that allowed significant variations in women's economic participation before World War II; it allows us to avoid sweeping condemnation of American institutions and historical figures; and it encourages us to develop a firmer sense of the contribution of those women who confidently seized new openings for expanding and deepening their social existence.

For the seventeenth and eighteenth centuries, before the forces of industrialization had begun to transform the nation's social fabric, the increasing economic participation of women can be documented only indirectly. Thus, it might seem hopeless to generalize about the patterns of economic participation displayed during the period, that is, before comprehensive data existed and before the labor force became specialized enough to allow us to invoke modern categories of employment. However, a recent spurt of scholarship designed to describe the demographic characteristics of the colonial population allows strong inferences to be drawn about the nature of women's work in that period.

Certainly the pivotal characteristic of the American population was its phenomenal rate of growth; during the eighteenth century, the population more than doubled every twenty-five years—a rate at least twice that prevailing in Europe at the same time. The transatlantic movement of people was important in creating that higher rate of increase, but it was the reproduction of the existing population that accounted for most of the differential between the American and the European rates. Behind the remarkable rate of natural increase are two central factors that directly affected the role of women in America: (1) colonists, in response to greater agricultural opportunities, married somewhat earlier and thereby tended to have more children during the course of their marriages than did Europeans; (2) as a result of the more favorable conditions of land and climate in America, mortality rates, particularly for infants and children, were lower, perhaps by as much as half.[4]

The typically larger size of the American conjugal group suggests that child-rearing responsibilities must have increased during the transplanting of European society. The low infant mortality rate undoubtedly eased the psychological anguish of child rearing, whereas in early modern Europe the infant death rate was so high that parents restrained themselves in their emotional commitment to their infant children. Not only did the investment in child rearing probably increase in North America, but it well may have become concentrated more in the hands of women. The latter conclusion is based on the strong attachment to the values of the marketplace that characterized colonial agriculturalists. The impulse to maximize pecuniary returns, the impressive profits to be made from expanding production, the acute scarcity of labor (including family servants), and the fact that the productivity of women working in the fields was less than that of men, all joined with the growing social emphasis the colonists placed on child rearing to tie women increasingly to the tasks of infant care and child training.[5] This is not to deny either that the work of women had grown more similar to that of men—which was the case because of the shortage of servants—or that there were slight regional variations. Thus, in New England, where financial returns from agriculture were generally less than elsewhere in the colonies, child rearing was somewhat less exclusively the province of women. But even in New England the trend toward the concentration of responsibilities for child nurture in the hands of women was beginning. For example, during New England's first generation, religious education was the

4. For a discussion of the demographic conditions underlying colonial society, see W. Elliot Brownlee, *Dynamics of Ascent: A History of the American Economy* (New York: Alfred A. Knopf, 1974), pp. 44–49.

5. For a discussion of the implications of male and female productivity differentials in primitive agricultural systems, see Ester Boserup, *Woman's Role in Economic Development* (London: George Allen and Unwin, 1970), pp. 53 ff.

responsibility of the household patriarch, but by the third generation, at the end of the seventeenth century, that obligation,
including the teaching of reading and writing, was beginning to shift
to his spouse.[6] At the same time, apprenticeship was on the wane.[7]
Apprenticeship had provided not only entry into a craft but also
rigorous religious preparation, and its decline signified increasing
confidence in the ability of the family to transmit cultural values.
That confidence, in turn, meant greater reliance on a specialized
role for women in the cultural integration of society.[8] One of the
probable results of the increasing specialization of New England
mothers in child rearing was an intensification of the conflict
between mothers and their daughters—a conflict perhaps expressed
in the intergenerational anguish of the Salem Witch Trials.[9]

Although attitudes attributing inferior capacities, intellectual as
well as physical, to women prevailed throughout the colonial era, the
definition of the nuclear family as the typical family group
(accomplished by the end of the seventeenth century in New
England) and the increasing absorption of women in child-rearing
responsibilities did not indicate, as yet, a hardening specification of

6. The strictures of Benjamin Wadsworth, pastor of Boston's Church of Christ,
against leaving family education in the hands of women suggest that such a transfer
was well underway by the beginning of the eighteenth century. Benjamin
Wadsworth, "The Well Ordered Family . . ." (Boston: B. Greve, 1712). By the
mid-eighteenth century women were often found as teachers in elementary schools.
Mary Sumner Benson, *Women in Eighteenth-Century America, A Study of Opinion and
Social Usage* (New York: Columbia University Press, 1935), p. 109.

7. Bernard Bailyn, *Education in the Forming of American Society* (New York:
Random House, 1960), pp. 29–36. (Bailyn emphasizes the significance of the decline
for the rise of public schools, whereas our interest is in the affirmation of the nuclear
family.)

8. On the educational functions of apprenticeship, see Marcus W. Jernegan,
Laboring and Dependent Classes in Colonial America, 1607–1783 (New York:
Frederick Ungar, 1960), especially pp. 157–71. For discussion of the significance of
the decline of apprenticeship for the emergence of the culture associated with the
modern family, see Philippe Ariès, *Centuries of Childhood, A Social History of Family*
(New York: Alfred A. Knopf, 1962), pp. 265 ff. Despite the Ariès coverage of a wide
range of interpretive ground, he offers little insight into the development of a more
specialized role for women within the concept of the modern family.

9. For suggestions of the implications of the witch trials for intergenerational
relationships, see John Demos, "Underlying Themes in the Witchcraft of Seventeenth-Century New England," *American Historical Review* 75 (June 1970):
1311–26.

an inferior social role for them.[10] Religious instruction was considered a deeply significant responsibility. The scarcity of labor enhanced appreciation for the economic contribution of women, despite the belief in female inferiority. Independent single or widowed women widened their economic roles during the eighteenth century, learning crafts and managing small businesses, and, simultaneously, daughters and helpmates participated to an increasing degree in the enterprises of their fathers and husbands.[11] Throughout the colonies, in the South as well as in New England, women tended gardens and worked in the fields at harvest time.[12] Thus, specialization of work by sex, although increasing, had not become sharply defined, and as a result of the general labor scarcity women may well have increased their relative participation in the labor force, especially in the expansion of the craft industry. Furthermore, the possibility for widened social opportunities for women was clearly present. With the entrenchment of the nuclear family (by the eighteenth century) came the relatively free choice of mates and an expansion of freedom before marriage. This colonial development created a potential, realized in the nineteenth century, for the massive employment of women who wanted an interval of independence before choosing familial confinement.

In the latter half of the eighteenth century the implication of the nuclear family in the expanded activity of women in the labor force became apparent. In New England, especially, household manufac-

10. An early statement of the hypothesis that the rise of the nuclear family preceded the industrial revolution in the United States and Great Britain, is Sidney M. Greenfield, "Industrialization and Family in Sociological Theory," *American Sociological Review* 28 (June 1963): 312–22. Confirmation of this hypothesis for American development has come most significantly from Philip Greven and Kenneth A. Lockridge. See, for example, Greven, "Family Structure in Seventeenth-Century Andover, Massachusetts," *William and Mary Quarterly* 23 (April 1966): 234–56; and Lockridge, "The Population of Dedham, Massachusetts, 1636–1736," *Economic History Review* 19 (August 1966): 318–44.

11. Elizabeth Anthony Dexter, *Career Women of America, 1776–1856* (Francestown, N.H.: Marshall Jones, 1950); id., *Colonial Women of Affairs* (Boston: Houghton Mifflin, 1931); and Alice Morse Earle, *Colonial Dames and Good Wives* (New York: Houghton Mifflin, 1895).

12. For the work of women in southern agriculture, see Julia Cherry Spruill, *Women's Life and Work in the Southern Colonies* (Charlotte: University of North Carolina Press, 1938).

turing enterprises multiplied as growing returns from trade stimulated town growth and the domestic market for manufactured goods. Indeed, after 1750, per capita incomes may well have risen significantly, causing the demand for manufactured goods to increase more rapidly than the population.[13] New England households, for the most part situated on inferior agricultural lands and cut off from easy access to new lands in the West, became the loci of what might be best described as "proto-industrialization."[14] With the extension of the market for the vast array of items of home manufacture, New England women turned their energies from the tasks of family-farm agriculture to those of domestic manufacture.[15] Consequently, if an effective census of occupations had been taken in 1760 and 1790, it would have found a marked increase in the extent to which New England women participated in the marketplace. This shift of female energies required no new social or cultural change as a prerequisite; the shift occurred simply in response to economic forces: the conjunction of a growth in the demand for manufactured goods and the greater availability of labor in New England than elsewhere in the colonies.

Although no fundamental social change caused women to join in the enthusiastic expansion of household industry, their participation created pressure for a widened social realm. As would be the case among the immigrants of the late nineteenth century, household manufacturing enhanced the value of children to their families and provided those children, including young women, with increased freedom from parental control. Such freedom even further weakened parental control over the arrangement of marriages and, along with the lack of economic opportunities on New England's inhospitable land, delayed the age of marriage and increased the period during which young women remained aloof from wifely chores. A well-documented indicator of this increase in the

13. Brownlee, *Dynamics of Ascent*, pp. 50–51.

14. For the explication of this term, in the context of European development, see Franklin F. Mendels, "Proto-industrialization: The First Phase of the Industrialization Process," *Journal of Economic History* 32 (March 1972): 241–61.

15. Rolla M. Tryon, *Household Manufactures in the United States, 1640–1860* (Chicago: University of Chicago, 1917), p. 75 ff.

independence of women and the delaying of marriage is a sharp rise in the rate of illegitimacy in the late eighteenth century.[16] Only when urbanization facilitated the practice of birth control would the rate of illegitimacy decline. Despite the fact that young working-women enjoyed greater freedom than housewives, the work they performed was held to be culturally inferior to the tilling of the land and the management of the most highly skilled trades, which women usually undertook only as widows of craftsmen.

The household manufacturing embraced by young New England women in the colonial period was shunned by their brothers; if young men were blocked by a lack of opportunity on the land, they usually sought their fortunes in other colonies or in the sea trades, rather than in manufacturing. Largely as a consequence, in the eighteenth century there was a net migration of unmarried young men out of New England, leaving a surplus of women. This migration increased even further the pool of labor available to household manufacture.[17]

Through the 1840s growing economic opportunity together with the increasing taste of young women for social independence continued to bring about a gradual increase in the rate at which women participated in the labor force. The modest character of the increase should be understood partly in terms of the slow growth in demand for women's labor. The emergence of the factory system was by no means dramatic; New England's textile mills gained sustained competence only in the 1820s, when they capitalized on lessons learned from the fierce British competition that followed the War of 1812. For many of the young women in the initial factory labor force, industrialization meant a relatively smooth passage from market-oriented, household spinning or weaving to small-scale factory textile production. The early organizers of factories modeled them on the forms of organization characteristic of proto-industriali-

16. See Daniel Scott Smith and Michael S. Hindus, "Premarital Pregnancy in America, 1640–1964: An Overview and Interpretation" (paper delivered at the annual meeting of the American Historical Association, New York, 29 December 1971), pp. 55–57.

17. J. Potter, "The Growth of Population in America, 1700–1860," in D. V. Glass and D. E. C. Eversley, eds., *Population in History* (Chicago: Aldine Publishing, 1965), pp. 648–49.

zation; the young women workers often had already won considerable social independence from their families; and the new factories were not set in an urban milieu, but located in the country at the only available waterpower sites. Factory owners sought to make the transition to factory labor as easy as possible by creating a social environment in the mills that was at once protective of young women and conducive to the development of intellectual independence from parental authority.[18] Thus, many young women working in the new factories, whether they lived at home or lived in dormitories such as those made famous at Lowell, Massachusetts, experienced little change in their work patterns. Those farm girls who had no previous contact with household manufacturing found the character and pace of work substantially new, but for them the shock of change was mitigated by the rural setting of the first factories and the fact that factory work was less demanding physically than farm chores had been.

The expansion of textile manufacture—the first locus of the industrial revolution—widened total work opportunities for women and, as a consequence, attracted more women than simply those who had devoted themselves to home manufacture. Increasing numbers of young women who probably would otherwise have remained tied to their parents or an early marriage joined the new factory labor force. Earlier, if such women had looked for employment outside the home they would have found little more than domestic service. Service to families in their household tasks remained almost as important as factory labor as a source of employment for women, throughout the early decades of the nineteenth century, but its relative significance declined rapidly in face of factory opportunities. White American women already had come to consider service in the homes of others degrading and took up such work only under the compulsion of sheer material necessity. Factory labor not only offered a larger measure of social freedom to such women, but it also paid higher wages—given the necessity factory owners faced of attracting the women employed in home textile manufac-

18. On the satisfactions from the social and intellectual independence from parental authority possible at Lowell, see Lucy Larcom, *An Idyl of Work* (Boston: James Osgood, 1876).

ture—and did not incur the stigma attached to domestic service.[19]

Until the 1840s the wages and status of factory employment attracted many women who were, or might have been, employed in domestic service, but the incentives were inadequate to lure significant numbers of men. Both the numerous highly skilled crafts that remained untouched by the advance of the factory system and the new agricultural opportunities on western lands proved more attractive to young men. The farms of New York and the Great Lakes territory enticed New England men frustrated by the obstacles created by overpopulation of their homeland. Their exodus began after the Revolution when those opportunities opened up in a dramatic way, and that exodus enhanced even further the employment of women (and children) in New England's new mills.

The rapid increase in the number of young women working in factories was not reflected in an obvious rise in the overall rate of women's participation. This was so mainly because the proportion of young women among all women began to decline in the nineteenth century. The source of the decline was a reduction in the fertility of American women that began during the first or second decade of the nineteenth century and that would continue throughout the century.

The preference of young women for work outside the home, including factory labor, continued through the 1840s and into the 1850s, but the combination of cultural barriers and changing economic opportunities brought a decline in both the rate at which women worked and the share they represented of the labor force. Powerful cultural factors limited the upward mobility of women factory workers into the ranks of skilled labor and the managerial class. Such mobility would have been a logical culmination of the years of experience acquired by many women if they and their employers had not been bound to the conventional persuasion that woman's appropriate social role lay in the home. In fact, young factory women rarely aspired to careers of any length, and the turnover rate of women factory workers was higher than that of

19. Although Stanley Lebergott has shown the large gap that existed between the wages of domestics and the wages of cotton textile workers in the early part of the century, his data leave the real earnings differential between factory work and *home industry* obscure. Lebergott, *Manpower in Economic Growth*, pp. 128–29.

men.[20] This fact justified the reluctance of employers either to train women for highly skilled tasks or to promote them into supervisory positions. But in large part this lack of ambition reflected lack of opportunity. Where women did extend their employment beyond the customary age for marrying and leaving the factory, they found no greater opportunity than younger women workers and discovered that their chances for advancement were far narrower than for men with comparable experience and abilities. Employers were not solely responsible for such limitation of opportunity. If they ventured to place a woman in the position of supervising men they invariably encountered the stern opposition of those male employees. Furthermore, beginning in the 1850s, male skilled workers resisted the addition of women to their order by fortifying themselves with modern craft unions. Such unions had marked strength even before the Civil War.[21] Although women had worked in factories for almost two generations and many had been supervisors in the first mills, by the 1850s they only occasionally served as supervisors and then almost always of other women.

Even with an artificially small number of skilled women workers, American manufacturers had an adequate supply of skilled labor for successful, sustained competition. But, by the 1840s, textile manufacturers were finding that children and young, single women formed an inadequate supply of unskilled labor for their buoyant production requirements. The resulting demand for unskilled labor initiated the first of the great waves of European immigration that would wash over American factories and cities during the next three

20. The Scottish women employed at the Lyman Mills during the 1850s exhibited mobility patterns typical for women factory workers; fewer than one-third remained as long as three years. Apparently most married and left the labor force. Ray Ginger, "Labor in a Massachusetts Cotton Mill," *Business History Review* 28 (1954): 83–85. For evidence that high turnover rates persisted into the early twentieth century, see Cornelia Stratton Parker, *Working with the Working Woman* (New York: Harper and Brothers, 1922), pp. 42 ff.

21. Elizabeth B. Butler, *Women and The Trades, Pittsburgh, 1907–1908, The Pittsburgh Survey*, vol. 1 (New York: Russell Sage Foundation, 1909), pp. 372–73; Helen Sumner, "History of Women in the Trade Unions," vol. 10, *Report on Condition of Woman and Child Wage-Earners in the United States*, Senate Document no. 645, 61st Cong., 2d sess. (Washington, D.C.: Government Printing Office, 1910 and 1911).

generations. Beginning in the 1840s and more rapidly during the 1850s, European immigrants, supplemented in New England by French Canadians, replaced native Americans in the unskilled factory labor force. Employers clearly preferred the immigrants from Ireland, Germany, and Canada to American women because the immigrants were willing to work for lower wages, for longer periods of time, and with fewer complaints about conditions of work—particularly the speeding up of production that employers had begun in the 1840s to maximize returns on their capital investment. Many young, native-American women went on strike or protested in response to the factory speed-up.[22] In contrast to the Irish immigrants who had been displaced from their rural homes, American women often could return to their families and resume a life on the land. Consequently, the labor of native women tended to be more expensive than that of immigrant women. Although many of the new factory workers were women, the immigrant population was predominantly male, and the ratio of men to women among the factory labor force increased sharply during the 1850s, contributing to the overall decline in the importance of women's employment recorded for the 1850s.[23]

The replacement of native-American women in the factory labor force, however, was not solely due to their being squeezed out by cheaper labor. The expansion of agriculture, in particular, and the rapid growth of urban, nonfactory employment for young native-American men enhanced the economic appeal of early marriage and thereby worked to reduce the supply of young women available for factory labor. The economic history is clear: agriculture in the Great Lakes states during the 1840s and 1850s pulled families from the New England and Middle Atlantic states to lands of high productivity. Beginning in the 1840s, the old Atlantic seaports rapidly created new opportunities for both immigrants and rural

22. On the protests of women textile workers in New England, see Hannah Josephson, *The Golden Threads, New England's Mill Girls and Magnates* (New York: Russell and Russell, 1949), pp. 228–85; and Norman Ware, *The Industrial Worker, 1840*–1860 (Chicago: Quadrangle, 1964), pp. 106 ff.

23. Edith Abbott, "History of the Employment of Women in the American Cotton Mills," *Journal of Political Economy* 16 (November–December 1908): 602–21.

native Americans. In that decade, those cities ended a generation of sluggish growth and grew more rapidly than the nation as a whole by developing expansive industrial structures that complemented their basic commercial strength. By the 1850s, most western opportunities could best be exploited by those families capable of the highly diversified efforts needed to work the land; the family had become well-established as the central economic unit in prairie agriculture.[24] Attractive opportunities were available to those who could devote some capital and a great deal of labor to the process of capital formation on the farm; consequently, the rates of marriage and birth were higher in new territories.[25]

The expansion of jobs for women in the rapidly growing cities and towns of the late antebellum period offered some compensation for the declining rate of participation of women in factory work. Hints of the new urban opportunities that would become statistically significant by the end of the century appeared by the 1850s. These opportunities would lie in the skilled service occupations that demanded relatively well-educated people for their performance. Ironically, the decline of household and factory manufacturing as an enterprise for women contributed to opening middle-class careers to women. Although many women responded to the closing off of manufacturing jobs by marrying earlier, others extended their common-school education—a possibility created by rising income levels that reduced young women's need to help support their families. Reinforcing the impact of rising incomes was a blossoming "cult of domesticity" that demanded education for women because of their value as the carriers of civilization—as child rearers who bore the prime responsibility for teaching democratic values to the young.[26] Many of the well-educated women that this impulse

24. See, in particular, Allan G. Bogue, *From Prairie to Corn Belt* (Chicago: Quadrangle, 1968), pp. 21–28; and Jack E. Eblen, "An Analysis of Nineteenth-Century Frontier Populations," *Demography* 2 (1965): 399–413.

25. Yasukichi Yasuba, *Birth Rates of the White Population in the United States, 1800–1860* (Baltimore: Johns Hopkins, 1962), pp. 52–53, 115, and 119.

26. Barbara Welter, "The Cult of True Womanhood, 1820–1860," *American Quarterly* 18 (1966): 151–74; id., "Anti-Intellectualism and American Women, 1800–1860," *Mid-America* 48 (1966): 258–70.

produced formed a labor pool that would drain into the marketplace when sufficient demand arose. The potential size of this skilled labor force of women was substantial. Its dimensions are suggested by the fact that in 1890 two-thirds of the nation's high school graduates were women.

It was the demand for teachers that first tapped the growing supply of skilled women. That demand accelerated most significantly during the 1880s and 1890s, when the contribution that formal education could make to economic progress became widely recognized.[27] But common schools had expanded early in the nineteenth century and, beginning in the late 1830s, had taken advantage of women who had completed elementary or secondary education. The preference for women as common-school teachers arose far less from an appreciation of their abilities than from the doubts of nineteenth-century Americans as to the benefits of a large public investment in education and from their consequent reluctance to divert resources from private purposes, even for education. Towns were predisposed to hire teachers at the lowest possible wages, and began, particularly after the Panic of 1837 had restricted public credit, to fill teaching positions with young women, rather than men. In so doing, school boards recognized both the extent to which the number of schooled women had increased and the degree to which the scarcity of outlets for their skills in the private sector had artificially depressed their wages. Subsequently, these trends intensified, and during the 1850s school employment of women increased even more rapidly. The expansion of teaching was accompanied by that of other urban, middle-class occupations, including the occasional literary or commercial roles filled by women who were both exceptionally gifted and willing to assault male bastions. Even so, the growth of these occupations was insufficient to offset the decline in the rate at which women worked. During the 1850s, for the first and perhaps for the last time in any sustained way, the general tendency was for women to find their appropriate economic roles increasingly within the context of care of home, husband, and children. That predilection suggests that the 1850s

27. Albert Fishlow, "Levels of Nineteenth-Century American Investment in Education," *Journal of Economic History* 26 (December 1966): 418–36.

ought to be seen as the high point of the Victorian family as a social fact, although its pinnacle as a cultural ideal was to follow a generation later.

The Civil War and the changing character of industrialization during the closing decades of the nineteenth century combined to widen work opportunities for women and to induce them to leave the households of their parents and husbands for the attractions of the marketplace. Most obviously, the Civil War released to the free market the 1.9 million black women who had toiled under slavery. Most of these women found their new situations unchanged from slave days even though they had acquired, in principle at least, ownership of their own earning capacity through emancipation. In spite of having gained the right to leave the countryside for new urban opportunities, relatively few did so until the decade of World War I. Instead, the vast majority of the ex-slave women continued to work as household domestics and field hands, either as wage laborers or alongside husbands who were sharecroppers or tenant farmers. As during slavery, a very high percentage of black women worked—now simply to maintain a near-subsistence level of earnings for their families and themselves.[28] No complex explanation is required to understand why black women, both single and married, worked at very high rates and continued to do so even when the incomes of black families rose in the twentieth century. Discrimination, particularly in hiring practices and in access to education, consistently forced black men to work for wages insufficient to maintain their families even on a par with immigrant families from Southern and Eastern Europe. Consequently, their wives and daughters worked at whatever jobs were available. No

28. In 1890, for example, well over a third of the black women over 10 years of age worked, in contrast to the little more than a tenth of the native white women over 10 years of age who worked. And, in further contrast with white women, the participation rate for black women did not vary a great deal by age. Clarence D. Long, *The Labor Force Under Changing Income and Employment* (Princeton: Princeton University Press, 1958), pp. 106–07. For documents illustrating the economic adjustments of ex-slave women, see Gerda Lerner, ed., *Black Women in White America, A Documentary History* (New York: Vintage Books, 1973), especially pp. 217 ff.

cultural change was necessary for black women to accept that role; slaveholders had always highly valued black women as field hands and servants. They had also prized black women as slave breeders, given the scarcity of slave labor created by the closing of the Atlantic slave trade early in the century. Not surprisingly, the fertility of black women declined markedly after emancipation: they chose to devote less of their lives to childbirth and child rearing and more to gainful employment.[29] Largely as a consequence, then, of the addition of nearly a million working black women to the labor force of 1870, the labor force participation rate for all American women went up sharply between 1860 and 1870.

The Civil War also expanded the participation of women in the marketplace by increasing the demand for them in two higher-status occupations—nursing and teaching. In both the North and the South, the reduction of the labor force by war drew women into these occupations at a sharply accelerated pace. The women entering nursing and teaching during the 1860s generally were single, had an above-average level of education, and would have remained at home had they not found those particular jobs open. Thus, the Civil War proved that women were ready to participate in the marketplace far beyond the opportunities previously available to them, despite the cultural force of the Victorian family.

Mobilization also widened the employment of women in North-

29. A recent study deemphasizes the value of slave breeding to slave owners but still attributes a substantial portion of the market value of female slaves during their childbearing years, in both the Old and New South, to the value of their childbearing capacity. See Robert W. Fogel and Stanley L. Engerman, *Time on the Cross: The Economics of American Negro Slavery*, vol. 1 (Boston: Little, Brown, 1974), pp. 78–86. Certainly the value of the childbearing capacity of female slaves appears great enough to have justified an elaborate reward structure designed to enhance fertility, although the incentives employed by slave owners were probably less extreme than those that abolitionists considered typical. (For examples of possibly typical incentives, see Kenneth M. Stampp, *The Peculiar Institution, Slavery in the Ante-Bellum South* [New York: Random House, 1956], p. 250.) The reliability of the Fogel-Engerman estimate of childbearing value remains undetermined because it includes values of a critical variable taken from a general population model, rather than from pertinent evidence. Fogel and Engerman, ibid., vol. 2, p. 84.

For the data on post–Civil War black fertility, see Reynolds Farley, *Growth of the Black Population: A Study of Demographic Trends* (Chicago: Markham Publishing, 1970).

ern factories, but the new factory jobs were not as numerous as those in teaching and nursing and most were closed off after 1865. Opportunities for women remained good in teaching and nursing because the employers of teachers and nurses were not willing or able to compete in labor markets for the services of men. Neither governments nor private charities (the primary supporters of wartime nursing services) could command resources sufficient to compete with farms, factories, and shops for the purchase of the labor of men. But well-educated women were available in large numbers for such work because they remained blocked from other occupations that could have utilized their abilities.[30] Moreover, the number of women working as nurses could grow rapidly because training for the most part was acquired on the job. Although women who took these jobs were exploited in the sense that their wages were held below the level that would have prevailed if general discrimination had not existed, they viewed these new employments as opportunities to be seized with little hesitation. These opportunities provided added freedom from household obligations, a means of delaying the age of marriage, a means of taking on a long-term career, and a means of satisfying intellectual and psychological needs stirred and awakened by education. In the case of nursing, women had to overcome an additional barrier: Victorian prudery. Although we have come to think of nursing as a logical transfer of women's duties from the home to the marketplace, American Victorians developed that concept only after nurses followed the Civil War armies and the bloodshed intensified enough to justify females in treating naked male bodies. Subsequently, cultural acceptance of women as nurses allowed impoverished private relief agencies to

30. Gerda Lerner has explained low wages for women in teaching and nursing in terms of the low status accorded to those professions as a result of women having filled those occupations. It is suggested here that she has reversed cause and effect. The low wage level in occupations with heavy female components resulted from an oversupply of women in those occupations which itself resulted from discrimination in other industries and the public or quasi-public character of employers in teaching and nursing that rendered those employers unable to continue to pay competitive wages. Only subsequently did the status of the work decline to reflect the low level of wages and become identified as women's work. See Lerner, "New Approaches to the Study of Women in American History," *Journal of Social History* 3 (Fall 1969): 57.

continue their employment practices born of wartime necessity and the insistence of middle-class women.[31]

Finally, Civil War casualties increased work for women by reducing the supply of men available for the labor force. At the same time it increased the supply of available women: women who were widowed, became spinsters, or had disabled husbands with inadquate pensions. The precise influence of Civil War mortality on women's participation in the marketplace remains undetermined. The impact appears to have been most pronounced in the South where, in the 1870s and 1880s, women enjoyed an expansion of opportunities that was considerably beyond what one might have predicted either for emancipated black women or for white women who were taking advantage of their superior position in a society ordered by a caste system.[32] However, for the nation as a whole, the long-run influence of the Civil War on women's work was slight in comparison with that of the accelerating industrial revolution.

The industrial revolution increased its pace during the closing decades of the late nineteenth century, and the social changes associated with that trend included a marked increase in the rate at which women chose to apply their abilities to earning incomes. The rates of labor-force expansion during the 1880s and the first decade of the twentieth century have never been exceeded in any census interval, and the voracious demand for skilled and unskilled labor resulting from that growth pulled an increasing percentage of women into gainful employment. Thus, partly as a result of the forces of demand, between 1880 and 1910 the proportion of women who were employed increased from 14.7 to 24.8 per cent.

Meanwhile demographic changes were increasing the number of women available for employment. Among the most basic changes was simply the continued progress of urbanization. The rate at which urban women joined the labor force was always greater than

31. Mary A. Livermore, *My Story of the War: A Woman's Narrative of Four Years Personal Experience* (Hartford: A. D. Worthington, 1888); and Mary Elizabeth Massey, *Bonnet Brigades* (New York: Alfred A. Knopf, 1966).

32. Anne Firor Scott, *The Southern Lady, From Pedestal to Politics, 1830–1930* (Chicago: University of Chicago Press, 1970), pp. 82–102.

that for rural women so increasing urbanization alone would have increased their numbers in the marketplace. Accelerated urbanization was accompanied by a hastened decline in the fertility of women. As a consequence of declining fertility, the women who passed childbearing age in about 1910 (i.e., those women who were 45 to 49 years old in 1910) had remarkably small families. More than one-quarter of all such women in the United States, and well over 40 per cent of all women in the Middle Atlantic and Great Lakes states, had no more than two children. This meant increasing freedom from the physical requirements of childbearing and child rearing. Furthermore, beginning in the mid-nineteenth century, the rate of marriage decreased steadily and both the age at first marriage and the proportion of women who had never married rose consistently until the 1890s. Then the tendency of the women born in the late 1860s and early 1870s (the women in the birth "cohort" of 1865–74) to marry at an earlier age stabilized the overall rate of marriage. The rising age of marriage freed women to take advantage of work opportunities or extended education.[33] More sustained than the increase in the age of marriage was the almost fivefold increase in the divorce rate between 1870 and 1930.[34] The fact that divorce became more common has often led to the suggestion that society had come to view more tolerantly women who satisfied individual aspirations at the expense of fulfilling customary familial obligations or orthodox social duty.[35] Consequently, one might expect a rising divorce rate to produce an increase in the economic participation of older women.

Augmenting the thrust of demographic change was the accelerating influx of Europeans—an influx whose peaks in the 1880s and

33. On the importance of urbanization to fertility trends, see Yasuba, *Birth Rates of the White Population*; on family size, see Wilson Grabill et al., *The Fertility of American Women* (New York: John Wiley, 1958), p. 65; on marriage rates, see Conrad Taeuber and Irene B. Taeuber, *The Changing Population of the United States* (New York: John Wiley, 1958), pp. 151–56.

34. Alfred Cahen, *Statistical Analysis of American Divorce* (New York: Columbia University Press, 1932), pp. 21–31; and Paul H. Jacobson, *American Marriage and Divorce* (New York: Rinehart and Company, 1959), p. 90.

35. See Donald Koster, *The Theme of Divorce in American Drama, 1871–1939* (Philadelphia: University of Pennsylvania, 1942).

during 1900–1910 coincided with the decades of the most rapid increase in the participation rate of women. The proportion of workingwomen was far higher for immigrant women than for native-American women who tended to be older and, more importantly, wealthier than immigrant women. It is true that immigrant women over 20 were less likely to work than native-American women over 20, probably because of the larger responsibilities of the former in child care. However, according to 1920 figures, the rate of participation was almost 50 per cent higher for young immigrant women than for their native-American counterparts, accounting for the greater participation rate of immigrant women as a whole.[36]

The changes that led to this greater participation of women—the increased demand for their labor, shifting demographic conditions, and the growth of the foreign-born population—were striking. Indeed, the changes were so extensive that the increase in women's participation between 1880 and 1910 ought to be regarded as really very modest in comparison to the increase that might have resulted. Because its actual growth failed to live up to the potential that would have been expected on the basis of economic and social changes, we must look for some explanations outside the realm of readily quantifiable trends. We might begin by asking why native women, unlike immigrant women, resisted the strong demand for their labor, particularly in offices, stores, hospitals, and schools, when it offered such high potential for freedom from family life.[37] At the same time we should ask why, despite stringent pressures to utilize the nation's human resources to their fullest, American society embraced with deepening enthusiasm an ideal family type that inhibited the individual development of women.

Behind the choice of native middle-class women to remain at home lay the value that Victorian culture in America attached to a

36. Long, *Labor Force*, pp. 105–10.

37. Long's data suggest that the participation rate for native white females, 14 years of age and older, only increased slowly between 1890 and 1900: from 16.3 per cent to 17.7 per cent. The urban contribution to that increase, however, remains undetermined (ibid., p. 295).

highly specialized, yet subordinate, role for women in the nuclear family. The nuclear family was, of course, a long-established social fact supported by a firm cultural foundation (the origins and sources of which lie beyond the scope of this discussion). But the late Victorians elaborated on the reality of the nuclear family to increase the specialization of household work and to emphasize the family's patriarchal quality. To an extent, the preferences of the Victorians were appropriate to the forces of economic modernization. The increased Victorian emphasis on education, within as well as without the family, represented an effort to increase society's investment in "human capital." Perpetuating a middle-class life style—the product of skills deemed valuable by the wider society—or raising lower-class children to middle-class status in fact required an increased diversion of society's energies to child rearing. But the Victorians' response to the need for an increased investment in children was predicated on an assumption that did not spring from the logic of the marketplace, was not necessarily embodied in the processes of modernization, and would leave a legacy of social cost to future generations: they assumed that divine design had assigned women the special function of nurturing children. Nothing inherent in the philosophy of capitalism restricted the role of women to that of raising children within the context of the nuclear family. That choice of the Victorians was a product of cultural assumptions they derived independently of the force of the market.[38]

The cultural restriction of women meant that the increasing divorce rate was not so much a vehicle for greater opportunity for women as a safety valve designed to protect the institution of marriage and mother-oriented processes of child nurture. No doubt

38. For suggestions of the content of late-Victorian family culture, see Ailenn S. Kraditor, *Up From the Pedestal* (Chicago: Quadrangle, 1968), pp. 189–203; Carroll Smith-Rosenberg and Charles Rosenberg, "The Female Animal: Medical and Biological Views of Woman and Her Role in Nineteenth-Century America," *Journal of American History* 60 (September 1973): 332–56; and Andrew Sinclair, *The Emancipation of the American Woman* (New York: Harper and Row, 1965), pp. 113–26. It should be noted that the Rosenbergs stress the growing force of medical thought that was emphasizing the presumed physical delicacy of women, suggesting that mental development during puberty would compromise the progress of sexual maturity, and urging that birth control would damage both women and unborn children, thereby weakening the nation's genetic strength.

some women, particularly those with creative talents and ambition in the arts, employed divorce as an instrument of liberation. The participation of a group of artistic women in an incipient bohemian subculture centered in Greenwich Village called nationwide attention to the rise of modern divorce.[39] But the pleas of Emma Goldman and, earlier, Victoria Woodhull to use divorce and free sexual expression as an alternative to marriage, as a means of placing men and women on equal social ground, proved meaningful to only a very few women.[40] Most who resorted to divorce soon remarried and limited their periods of employment to brief episodes. Consequently, the rate of participation of divorced women in the economy did not increase significantly between 1870 and 1930. Furthermore, even with the rate of divorce sharply increasing, the overall rate of marriage dissolution grew only slightly between 1870 and 1930. This was so because while the divorce rate was climbing, the mortality rate of marriage partners was declining dramatically, as a result of improvements in public health and in techniques of delivering babies.[41] Because death served less effectively to provide marital variety, protection of the institution of marriage (and the position of women within it) demanded greater toleration of divorce.

Despite the force of cultural norms that bore no necessary relationship to marketplace considerations, the marketplace did assist the Victorians in refining the restriction of women to the home. In an era of rapidly rising real incomes, middle-class families were able to satisfy their expenditure objectives more easily. They found it less essential to send women to work and could make the social choice of devoting that portion of the family's resources represented by the earning capacity of the mother to the rearing of children. Moreover, especially in the 1870s, they began to find

39. The oracle of this subculture was *The Masses*. See William O'Neill, ed., *Echoes of Revolt: The Masses, 1911–1917* (Chicago: Quadrangle, 1966).

40. On the fascinating career of Emma Goldman, see Richard Drinnon, *Rebel in Paradise* (Chicago: University of Chicago, 1961); Kenneth S. Lynn, *Visions of America* (Westport, Conn.: Greenwood Press, 1973), pp. 149–56; and, of course, Emma Goldman, *Living My Life* (Garden City, N.Y.: Garden City Publishing Co., 1934).

41. William L. O'Neill, *Divorce in the Progressive Era* (New Haven: Yale University Press, 1967), pp. 30–31; Jacobson, *American Marriage and Divorce*, pp. 141–43.

available an array of consumer durable goods (such as washing machines, wringers, iron clothespressers, egg beaters, and sewing machines) that promised to lighten household chores. With the electrification of the household that began after 1910, absorption with child rearing became even more fervent.[42] Ironically, the immediate effect of the technological revolution in the household was not to increase the size of the female labor force but, rather, to encourage even greater specialization of women in the tasks of child nurturing. (Women's concentration on professional consumerism emerged from the technological flux of 1910–30, but that interest was distinctly secondary to and supportive of the transcending absorption with investment in the future of children.) Similarly, the declining size of families, rather than immediately expanding work opportunities, only allowed mothers to devote themselves to their children more easily.

Could the Victorians have developed an alternative to the tasks of education by the family that would have offered greater possibilities for women? Certainly they could have supported formal schooling, both public and private, with greater resources; day-care centers for working mothers (or fathers) were quite possibly feasible; and at least one political economist, Simon N. Patten (in *The Theory of Prosperity* [1902]), proposed public subsidies to women to insure their economic independence. Such alternatives did not bear the onus of socialism; indeed, their objective of enhancing the nation's stock of privately-owned human capital was eminently capitalist. But, given the traditionally modest support for formal schooling and the fact that the share of the national product diverted for education was increasing very rapidly in the 1880s and 1890s, one ought to be

42. On the economic changes that allowed a vast increase in the resources devoted to the purchase of consumer durables in the mid-nineteenth century, see Dorothy S. Brady, "Relative Prices in the Nineteenth Century," *Journal of Economic History* 24 (June 1964): 175–88. For an attempt to measure that increasing resource commitment, see Robert Gallman, "Gross National Product in the United States, 1834–1909," in National Bureau of Economic Research, *Output, Employment and Productivity in the United States After 1800* (New York: Columbia University Press, 1966), p. 18. For an identification of the entire period 1840–80 as the era of "mechanization of the household," see Harold G. Vatter, "Has There Been a Twentieth-Century Consumer Durables Revolution?" *Journal of Economic History* 27 (March 1967): 1–16.

hesitant about criticizing the Victorians for ignoring that alternative to increasing emphasis on the family. The size of the population also was growing phenomenally, particularly during the 1880s and the first decade of the twentieth century, as the nation experienced the cresting of the massive waves of immigration. Not only was the expense of educating the new millions staggering, but the task of assimilating the highly heterogeneous masses was enormous as well. Thus, the concern for cultural homogenization, coupled with the expense of formal schools, led American Victorians to become absorbed—with an intensity unique in modern industrial nations—in the mission of raising children within the context of the patriarchal nuclear family.

Although the effort of American political and social leaders to achieve cultural homogenization might be construed as an economic undertaking insofar as it was an effort to create a disciplined modern labor force, their concerns—and certainly those expressed by a fearful native-American middle class—were broader than that. Indeed, during this critical period, 1880–1910, middle-class Americans began a multifaceted program to promote cultural uniformity. It is clear that prohibition, restriction of immigration, and the 100 per cent Americanism movement during and after World War I constituted the climax of this program of cultural homogenization. It has been less obvious that the promotion of the Victorian family was a part of the same movement. The campaign to restructure American social life along the mythical lines of orderly preindustrial communities, founded on the rock of the nuclear family, included institutionalizing the ideal of womanhood through motherhood as the central ingredient in the civilizing of modern industrial society. When American men extended the suffrage to women in 1919, they did so to mobilize the nation's child rearers behind a wide-ranging program of social control.

Ironically, for their part, new immigrants found the Victorian family ideal compelling. Lacking a coherent lower-class culture with which to identify—a possibility precluded by the diversity of the new lower class emerging in the late nineteenth century—immigrants emulated middle-class standards far more than did their contemporaries in Europe's lower classes. For example, immigrant lower-class single women, in contrast with their European cousins, lacked a subculture of young women embracing sexual freedom with which they could associate and thus more easily prolong a period of economic independence outside of marriage.[43] Middle-class America, as part of its response to new immigration, expressed shock at the liberated sexual values of the new European lower class and vigorously upheld the ideal of confining sex to marriage. Correspondingly, the suspicion that economic independence bred sexual licentiousness and the conviction that low wages bred prostitution partly motivated the attack that middle-class women reformers waged against the exploitation of immigrant women in sweatshops and factories.

More generally, middle-class analysis of the character of industrial poverty, culminating with the report of the 1907 Immigration Commission, saw poverty as the outcome of the failure of individuals to repress sexual impulses. Only marriage, which placed sex at the service of child rearing, could apply sexual energies to the improvement of the race. And, because of the disorganized quality of urban life for new immigrants, the power of this message proved irresistible; in the face of bewildering social flux, the search for internal salvation through intense family life (not to mention traditional religion) became an overwhelming social objective. When men's wages rose sufficiently, immigrant women withdrew from the marketplace to pursue the goal, often illusive, of equipping their children to join the middle class. As witness to the economic success of their husbands, the participation rate for foreign-born white women remained constant between 1890 and 1900 (while it declined for immigrant women between the ages of 20 and 24) and then decreased between 1900 and 1920.[44] Consequently, the proportion of factory workers who were women continued to decline into the twentieth century, and the total number of women factory

43. For a suggestion of this comparison, see Edward Shorter, "Female Emancipation, Birth Control, and Fertility in European History," *American Historical Review* 78 (June 1973): 616, n. 15.

44. Long, *Labor Force*, pp. 106–07.

workers grew only slowly, at a rate of less than 4 per cent between 1910–30.[45]

Reinforcing the decline of immigrant women in factory work were the efforts of employers and women reformers to promote home life among immigrants (and thus conservatize them) and the exertions of male-dominated unions of skilled workers to exclude women from the ranks of the more highly paid. Thus, particularly at the level of skilled work, women faced decided discrimination in the form of restricted opportunity. Such discrimination was economically irrational and thus is difficut to understand simply in marketplace terms. However, it was part of a conscious policy, embraced by almost the entirety of American society, to lend the nuclear family an even more critical role in integrating conflicting cultures. Although the industrial revolution of the nineteenth century was the occasion for a more pronounced focus on the role of the family, and within the family for a narrowing of the role of women, that transformation in the United States was due not to the power of the nation's commitment to capitalism but to the tension at the core of urban culture that was a reaction to massive European immigration. At the same time, the cultural position of women was eroded further by a self-feeding process inherent in the specification of certain roles as "women's work." That is to say, during the Victorian era, there existed a rigorous stereotyping of women as suited for only narrow social capacities that restricted their access to social opportunity and both limited the development of career models and reinforced the wider belief in female inferiority.[46]

By the late nineteenth century, then, the marketplace for labor was highly segmented with respect to sex. In other words, to a very significant extent the labor market for women was segregated from that for men; in effect, the markets were divided into distinct sexual components. During the late nineteenth and early twentieth

45. Mary Elizabeth Pidgeon, *Women in the Economy of the United States of America* (Washington, D.C.: Government Printing Office, 1937).

46. Although he has underestimated the extent to which women have participated in the market, William Chafe has recently reminded us of the way in which allocation of certain social functions to women has reinforced cultural images of women. See Chafe, *The American Woman, Her Changing Social, Economic, and Political Roles, 1920–1970* (New York: Oxford University Press, 1972).

centuries, as the pattern of segmentation was becoming firm, fewer manufacturing tasks were being defined as women's work and a greater variety of jobs within the service sector were being seen as appropriate to the supposed unique attributes of women.[47] Between 1910 and 1930, for example, when the employment of women in manufacturing increased only very sluggishly (by less than 10 per cent), the employment of women in clerical occupations more than tripled, in trade more than doubled, and in professional service also more than doubled.[48] Consequently, by 1930, fully 15 per cent of all women employed were professional workers (including teachers and nurses) and 31 per cent were clerical and sales workers. In the same year, in sharp contrast, only 5 per cent of the men employed were professional workers and only 17 per cent were clerical and sales workers. At the same time, while as many as 12 per cent of male workers were proprietors, managers, and officials and 22 per cent were skilled workers and foremen, only 2 per cent of women employees filled the first class of jobs and only 1 per cent the second.[49]

The most rapidly growing sectors of women's employment were office and sales work. Employers in both sectors were taking advantage of the relatively higher level of formal education attained by women and the cheapness of the labor of women who could do arithmetic or acquire secretarial skills with ease and meet the public in an articulate fashion. The late nineteenth century witnessed a uniquely rapid multiplication of bureaucratic organizations and a concomitant demand for staffs of paper-moving technicians and a work force that would market their products. In the latter category of employment the rise of modern department stores created a particularly large demand for women. These palaces of consumption in the nation's major cities grew rapidly as entrepreneurs in the services acted on their realization that the productivity of American

47. Useful analysis of the separation of male and female labor markets since 1890 is found in Valerie Kincade Oppenheimer, *The Female Labor Force in the United States, Demographic and Economic Factors Governing Its Growth and Changing Composition* (Berkeley: Institute of International Studies, 1969), pp. 64–120.

48. Pidgeon, *Women in the Economy*, p. 18.

49. The National Manpower Council, *Womanpower* (New York: Columbia University Press, 1957), p. 114.

manufacturing had outstripped the ability of American manufacturers to reach the consuming public. To sell the abundant goods to the middle-class urban woman, department stores used young, attractive women as salesclerks. In so doing, the managers were influenced by and, indeed, reinforced the Victorian definition of domesticity that attributed the role of consumer specialist to women. These stores, aware of the necessity of presenting a positive, appealing front to the consumer public, incidentally made their premises attractive places to work, much as firms that recognized the benefits of creating an environment with the trappings of prosperity for male professionals provided their secretaries and female clerks with pleasant offices and favorable working conditions. Consequently, store and office work became even more attractive to young women, and the shift of women workers to new service jobs meant a considerable improvement of the conditions of women's employment in general.

The decline of industrial employment continued two trends begun during the 1840s: (1) the replacement of women factory workers with immigrant men and (2) a solidification of the barriers against women in skilled positions within the factory work force. In addition, the period 1880–1910 marked the surge to industrial dominance of heavy industry—industry with labor requirements that precluded the widespread employment of women because of the increasingly pervasive presumption that they were physically delicate. This presumption was lent legal force by legislation regulating the hours, wages, and conditions of women's work.

To be sure, certain traditional industrial employments for women grew rapidly during the period. Needlecraft sweatshops proliferated particularly rapidly because garment manufacturers had an unusually abundant source of cheap labor—women (and children) of "new" immigrant families from Southern and Eastern Europe.[50] These women often faced barriers of language, dress, custom, and

50. The literature on this work, often pursued at home, is extensive. See, for example, Edith Abbott, *Women in Industry*, Commonwealth of Massachusetts, *Report on the Statistics of Labor, Home Work in Massachusetts*, part 5 (1914), pp. 71 ff.; and Caroline Manning and Harriet A. Byrne, *The Employment of Women in the Sewing Trades of Connecticut* (Washington, D.C.: Government Printing Office, 1935). For a suggestion that the extent of homework has been exaggerated, see Lebergott, *Manpower in Economic Growth*, pp. 72–73.

racism that blocked entry to the ranks of salesclerks and office workers. They were, therefore, available in large numbers for manufacturing employment. They found the employment attractive, not only as a way to supplement meager family incomes, but because working at home was a relatively unstressful way of adapting to a modern industrial society.[51]

The women of these "new" immigrant families may well have thought of their income as only supplemental to that of the family and, in any case, they often preferred to work at home rather than to enter a factory. In general, however, these women probably received low wages less because their work was only "moonlighting" for the family than because the labor market was segregated.[52] But it is too easy to exaggerate the cheapness of their labor and its impact. For example, it is tempting to make a causal connection between the low cost of home labor and the persistence, even into the 1970s, of very small-scale enterprise in the fashion industry. But a far more basic cause is the preference of consumers for diversity in clothing, which sharply limits demand for any single item of production.

The clothing industry, of all the industries employing women, offered workers the greatest chances of success in unionization. The inability of manufacturers to convert their small-scale operations into a more capital-intensive format, coupled with the ethnic solidarity of Jewish garment workers, particularly in New York, brought about the successful unionization of most women in the needle trades.[53] In general, however, the organization of women into unions could not overcome the hostility of male-dominated unions, the temporary character of women's industrial careers, and the tendency of sex discrimination to create an overabundance of women in those occupations open to them.[54]

51. Herbert Gutman has most recently reminded us that we should recognize the power of household enterprise to ease assimilation of peasant cultures: "Work, Culture, and Society in Industrializing America, 1815–1919," *The American Historical Review* 78 (June 1973): 531–88.

52. For a statement of the traditional moonlighting explanation, see Butler, *Women and the Trades*, pp. 345–46.

53. On the successes of the ILGWU, see Louis Levine, *The Women's Garment Workers Union* (New York: B. W. Huebsch, 1924).

54. Perhaps the best survey of the obstacles to the organization of women is Sumner, "History of Women in Trade Unions," pp. 140–52.

It was a realistic recognition of these central barriers to class organization that led Socialists who were concerned with increasing opportunities for women to turn to political solutions. It was their belief that the Socialist redemption of workingwomen could come only through Socialist electoral victories, which, in turn, would be made more likely by the enfranchisement of women. Socialist support for women's suffrage thus reinforced that given by those of capitalist persuasions, including such pragmatic leaders as Carrie Chapman Catt, who hoped—probably more realistically, from a long-range vantage point—that achieving suffrage was essential to the task of removing the discriminatory barriers that depressed women's wages.

The closing of new opportunities to women in the dynamic manufacturing sector, particularly in skilled categories, meant that there was an artificially large pool of highly competent women available for other employment, even after taking into consideration the growing attraction of the hallowed ideal of spiritual service to husband and children within the context of the nuclear family. Thus, although the participation rate for middle-class and native-American women may not have increased dramatically during this period, the strongly rising demand for services rapidly increased the number of educated women employed. This was so largely because women could be employed more cheaply than men with comparable education. It is true that the average period of employment of women in service jobs tended to be shorter than that of men because women's employment continued to be restricted largely to that interval of social freedom before marriage. But there is no evidence that the relative brevity of employment had any bearing on the productivity of women and, consequently, on their wages. Moreover, it should be kept in mind that the period of formal schooling was shorter on the average than is the case in contemporary America, and that the age at first marriage tended to be considerably higher than was the case until the 1970s. Thus, at the beginning of this century the period of work for women who later married was considerably longer than it is today. Given the generally low productivity prevailing in most of the nineteenth-century service sector, the period of women's employment was long enough to justify the employer's investment in training and the payment of wages equal to those they would have had to offer men.

As early as the 1880s the employment of women in offices and stores gave employers a large supply of labor at wages lower than productivity justified. Women who were skilled (in the sense of being literate in English and able to do arithmetic), willing to be exploited, and not blocked by restrictive craft unionism replaced the men who had predominated previously in clerical and sales jobs.

For middle-class women, the period between the Civil War and World War I was marked by increasing enthusiasm for the cultural position of the nuclear family and a consequent stagnation of the labor-force participation rate. At the same time, however, the oppressive obligations of homemaking and child rearing fueled the determination of a small group of highly educated women to widen social opportunities for women.[55] Building on organizational successes they had enjoyed during the Civil War, particularly in opening nursing to women, that group exerted crucial influence in opening higher education, the professions of medicine and law, and scientific occupations to women.[56] The number of women who took advantage of the new professional and educational opportunities, though still small, expanded rapidly. To pursue these careers with long-term success in the midst of a society that extolled the virtues of the family, a growing proportion of these women not only postponed marriage but rejected it altogether. However, the dim view that American men and women took of this experiment led the women's movement in the 1890s to turn away from any serious attempts to liberalize the ties of marriage and family in favor of single-minded concentration on winning the suffrage.[57]

55. Thus, we would agree with Gerda Lerner in attributing the origins of the women's movement to the status problems of well-educated women: see "New Approaches to the Study of Women," pp. 53–62. For a divergent view, emphasizing the loss of economic and educational functions of the family, see William R. Taylor and Christopher Lasch, "Two 'Kindred Spirits': Sorority and Family in New England, 1839–1846," *New England Quarterly* 36 (March 1963): 311–29.

56. For the opening of medicine, see Richard H. Shryock, *Medicine in America, Historical Essays* (Baltimore: Johns Hopkins, 1966), pp. 187 ff. No comparable discussion exists describing the penetration of the legal profession.

57. On the turning away of the women's movement from a search for alternatives to the Victorian family and the subsequent absorption with suffrage campaigns, see

By World War I, women's work had become set in a pattern that would prevail for more than a generation. Wartime mobilization induced a brief spurt in the demand for women in factories, but it declined again during the 1920s, even though the end of immigration brought a shortage of unskilled workers. Indeed, in the decade of World War I, sluggish demand for women factory workers and declining immigration, which had brought so many working women to America, caused the participation rate of women to drop for the first time since the 1850s.[58] Contributing further to the declining participation rate was the rising level of income being earned by foreign-born families, allowing increasing numbers of immigrant women to remain at home. Also, during the 1920s, changes in styles of clothing undermined the demand for women's labor in the needle trades.

Although jobs for women in factories expanded only slightly between 1910 and 1930, jobs in the vast array of services continued to increase rapidly, with an intensification of the demand for services requiring few skills and without any significant shift of women toward highly skilled occupations. The development of inexpensive typewriters allowed the demand for secretaries with only typing skills to increase, and many native-born daughters of immigrant families, most often from Ireland and Germany, began to take advantage of these new jobs, as well as those in clerking, rather than enter factories.[59] However, as women in the services acquired skills

Eleanor Flexner, *Century of Struggle, The Woman's Rights Movement in the United States* (Cambridge, Mass.: Harvard University Press, 1968), pp. 142–55; and William L. O'Neill, ed., *The Woman Movement, Feminism in the United States and England* (Chicago: Quadrangle, 1971), pp. 15–32.

58. It should be noted, however, that the end of immigration in the long run expanded employment opportunities for women. But as a consequence of both the cultural barriers to women's participation that prevailed during the 1920s and the tendency of the Great Depression crisis to accentuate preferences for male over female workers, the employment potential created by the end of immigration was not realized in a significant way until the 1940s.

59. On the slightly earlier predominance of native-born daughters of German and Irish parents among Pittsburgh salesclerks, see Butler, *Women and the Trades*, p. 22. Because of the proclivity of young women of Irish parentage to join the sales force, by 1910 only 16.5 per cent of the female textile-mill labor force was Irish or of Irish parentage, whereas 40.5 per cent were French-Canadian. See also, W. B. Palmer, "Women and Child Workers in the Cotton Mills," *Journal of the American Statistical Association* 12 (June 1911): 607–08.

that should have won them higher-status jobs, they found their way opposed by employers reluctant to place them in supervisory capacities. More often than not, those women ultimately returned to the nuclear family.

During the 1920s, women who might have been disposed to pursue social independence encountered not only the old arguments on behalf of the nuclear family but also an increasingly widespread vulgarization of Freudian psychology. It stressed that women ought to strive for the fullest expression of sexuality, defined as a concentration on bearing and rearing children.[60] The force of this theory dissuaded many women from seeking independence outside the family for fear that it would mean a denial of sexual expression. The new Victorianism discouraged them from embracing celibacy, as the independent women of the late nineteenth century had often done, or finding sex outside of marriage, as independent European women were able to do in a more liberal cultural setting.

The crisis of the Great Depression only reinforced the cultural forces that tended to confine women to the family, as the high rates of unemployment caused government, private employers, and unions to restrict opportunities for women. The cultural reaction following World War II to the massive employment of women necessitated by mobilization only reinforced the "feminine mystique" and kept the participation rate of women from rising dramatically until the 1960s.

Ironically, however, the cultural crisis of World War I and the 1920s, which had reinforced the inferior position of women within the family, contained the seeds of disruption. The coupling of the Freudian enthusiasms of the 1920s with rising incomes resulted in a baby boom in the 1940s and 1950s (delayed by the Great Depression). That baby boom, in turn, caused a demographic crisis during the 1960s: young middle-class people found that their great numbers were retarding the pace of upward economic mobility that their parents had known. In the 1960s, the age of marriage began to rise dramatically, and young people, aware of an ecological crisis

60. Andrew Sinclair has aptly described the Freudian enthusiasts as the "New Victorians"; see *The Emancipation of the American Woman* (New York: Harper and Row, 1965), pp. 343 ff.

that their numbers had helped to create, restricted family size sharply. Reinforced by these trends and supportive intellectual developments that emphasized the need for personal fulfillment outside the home, dramatically larger numbers of women, young and old, single and married, moved outside the home to broaden their lives. It appeared that the demographic trends that had first appeared in the nineteenth century and had created a potential for vast increases in the extent of women's roles (but were reversed during the 1940s and 1950s) would resume once again. This time, however, the cultural restrictions that earlier had blunted the impact of demographic change were far weaker. There had been little immigration in over a generation; Americans had recovered from the shocks of the Great Depression and World War II that had led them to embrace family "togetherness" during the 1950s; and the greater economic participation of married women during the 1940s had provided helpful examples for their daughters. Indeed, in the 1970s, a new culture may be emerging that will support a variety of social forms that will equalize the opportunities open to men and women.

The removal of cultural constraints on the full economic participation of women promises potent results, for it should allow the forces of marketplace capitalism to hold sway unmodified by assumptions of female inferiority. The premium attached by capitalism to the optimal use of human resources, unchecked by cultural restrictions, should lead to institutional innovations. Designed to take full advantage, both social and private, of women's work, such innovations might well feature child-care programs and the placing of household maintenance within the ambit of the marketplace. Perhaps, then, at long last, the promise for revolutionizing the social roles of women that the participants in the Seneca Falls convention of 1848 found inherent in American democratic idealism, and the promise that the play of market forces on a skilled population can offer, will be fulfilled.[61]

61. For a similarly optimistic assessment of the potential of the market place, see Juanita Kreps, *Sex in the Marketplace: American Women at Work* (Baltimore: Johns Hopkins Press, 1971), pp. 106 ff. To the extent that institutional innovation within American society is responsive to income-maximizing incentives, one has to be

confident about the prospects for American society developing ways of most fully employing the human capital embodied in its female population. For recent efforts to emphasize the contribution of the market place to institutional innovation in the American past (but one that ignores the massive, historic social costs of sex discrimination), see Lance Davis and Douglass C. North, *Institutional Change and American Economic Growth* (Cambridge: Cambridge University Press, 1971).

I

Women in Preindustrial Society

At the social pinnacle of those women who participated in the colonial marketplace was the handful who managed great wealth. The careers of such women as Maria van Rensselaer, Eliza Lucas Pinckney, and Hannah Penn (who administered the vast Penn estates from England between 1712 and 1726) all testify to the potential of independent women. But these stellar examples found opportunities in the face of widely held assumptions of female inferiority not only because they were highly capable but because they were part of far-flung subempires in the Atlantic basin that were held together by the cohesion of particular families that had proved deficient in male leadership. During the eighteenth century, under the dynamic, growing pressures of European capitalism on North America, such opportunities gradually withered and the accomplishments of the women whose power stemmed from traditional family connections ultimately proved to be, in large part, ephemeral.

The prevailing attitudes attributing inferiority to women did not change markedly during the eighteenth century, but there was some change, largely as a result of the demands created by a labor-scarce environment. As the pragmatic Benjamin Franklin recognized, this labor scarcity, characteristic everywhere except New England and most pronounced in the Middle Atlantic colonies, argued for a larger involvement of women in the marketplace, if only as helpmates for their husbands. However, the expansiveness of the eighteenth-century marketplace, the shortage of skilled people, the lack of coherent cultural restrictions on women's opportunities, and a high mortality rate (at least by modern standards) created opportunities for women who were full-fledged owners of mercantile establishments (often in partnership with other women), members of skilled trades, and widows who were able to carry on their husband's enterprise as a consequence of the informal training they had acquired.

No estimates exist as to how many of these independent women there were, but impressionistic evidence suggests that their numbers were greater, relative to the total size of the urban labor force, than was the case during the nineteenth century. Advertisements, announcements of changes in business addresses or of deaths, and notices of estate settlement in the newspapers of Baltimore, Philadelphia, New York, and Boston suggest the large number of independent women, particularly those who were merchants and shopkeepers. They sold not only dry goods but also seeds, tea, china, glass, tobacco, books, pharmaceuticals, and groceries. Independent women in the skilled trades were particularly outstanding in printing. In the middle colonies, Anna Zenger, Cornelia Bradford, Elizabeth Holt, and Elizabeth Oswalt established themselves prominently in printing and publishing. In New England, Ann Franklin, Sarah Goddard, Mary Draper, and Mary Crouch were among the most eminent eighteenth-century printers.

A large, but indeterminate, percentage of these women were widows. In an era in which a division of labor within the household was only beginning to become pronounced, a helpmate acquired a thoroughgoing knowledge of a husband's craft and thus was well equipped to continue her spouse's work after his death. Only later, when the line of distinction between work and home life became firm would such transfers become uniformly difficult. American men valued the contribution of these women and placed no significant obstacle in the way of their continuing their husbands' crafts. Most craftsmen and tradesmen commonly willed their property to their wives and the courts respected those transfers. Moreover, antenuptial contracts that were commonly drawn up between remarrying widows and their new husbands also found respect before the courts; these contracts guaranteed protection of the widows' property. Although historians have neglected these independent women, it should be remembered that they, like all eighteenth-century people of middle-class means, controlled only a small proportion of the total wealth of the colonies. At the middle of the eighteenth century in Boston, for example, the middling group of artisans, shopkeepers, and traders owned only about 10 per cent of the city's wealth. With the flowering of transatlantic trade during that century, a compact group of international traders, among whom virtually no women were to be found, had drawn apart from other urban people of wealth.

It should be added, with emphasis, that most colonial women—in fact, more than 90 per cent—pursued their economic lives on the countryside rather than in the city. These women labored either under slavery, to be discussed in the next chapter, or in an agricultural system in which male and female roles overlapped. Women shared extensively in the highly diversified labor of the colonial farm, engaging in both household manufacturing and, to a lesser degree, field work (planting, helping with harvesting, caring for livestock, and tending gardens). To only a limited degree was their role specialized in child rearing and household chores. Marked departures toward specialization for women in agriculture, as for women in all sectors of the economy, would come primarily during the era of industrial revolution.

A COLONIAL PROPRIETOR

The following correspondence is from the letters of Maria van Rensselaer (1645–89) who, for an extended and extremely difficult period of time, administered the patroonship of Rensselaerswyck, which, centered on Albany, New York, included some 700,000 acres on both sides of the Hudson River. By birth a van Cortlandt (whose family patroonship included 140,000 acres), at age 17 Maria married, quite possibly for political and business reasons, Jeremias van Rensselaer, who in 1658 had become director of his family's estate. When Jeremias died in 1674, only Maria was available to protect the family interests in the New World because her and Jeremias's children were too young and Richard van Rensselaer, the only surviving son of the first Rensselaer patroon, was occupied in the more important task of conducting the family's affairs in Holland. Consequently, Maria administered the patroonship from 1674–76; acted as the treasurer of the patroonship from 1676–78 (when Nicolaes van Rensselaer, the younger brother of Jeremias and favored by the Duke of York and Governor Edmund Andros, assumed leadership); and, after the death of Nicolaes in 1678, resumed administration of the patroonship because the technical director, her brother, Stephanus van Cortlandt, resided in New York. Throughout her direction of van Rensselaer affairs, which continued until her death, she displayed not only competence in managing the day-to-day operation of her estates but also great adroitness in maneuvering around a constellation of unsettling circumstances: the tightening of English rule of New York after 1674; continuing Indian problems relating to the conduct of the Albany fur trade; rivalries among the families of van Rensselaer, van Cortlandt, and Livingston (Robert Livingston having married the widow of Nicolaes van Rensselaer and made claims on the Rensselaer estate); persistent quarrels between the town of Albany and Rensselaerwyck; and the lack of a sufficiently large settling class to develop the potential of the patroonship's landed resources. As a consequence of her finesse, Maria had the pleasure before her death of witnessing the securing of Rensselaer title to almost all of the old patroonship and the succession to the title of lord of the manor by her eldest son, Kiliaen.

FROM THE CORRESPONDENCE OF MARIA VAN RENSSELAER

To Richard van Rensselaer

[December 1675]

Reygart van Rensselaer

Dear Brother: Your agreeable and long awaited letter of July 5th, stating that you were heartily sorry to learn of the death of your

From A. J. F. van Laer, trans. and ed., *Correspondence of Maria van Rensselaer, 1669–1689* (Albany, N.Y.: University of the State of New York, 1935), pp. 16–21 and 37–39.

brother, my husband, was duly received by me on the 18th of November, new style. I doubt not but it has caused a great sorrow, but as it has pleased the Lord to afflict me with such a great sorrow, I must put my [trust] in God's will. May He make me patient and strengthen me in all adversity and in my infirmity, from which at present I suffer great pain, through Jesus Christ, who gives me strength and who through His mercy will further [sustain] me.

As to the coming over of brother Nicolaes, you will have learned about that from my preceding letter. I had expected more from him. If it had pleased God to spare my husband, deceased, a while longer, things would not go so [badly]. And as to the colony, matters still stand as they did when my husband, deceased, was living. Could he have spoken with his Excellency, it would have gone better. I trust that before the receipt of this letter you will already have learned everything from my letter to brother Jan Baptist, to which I refer. That I should have liked to see you come over, is true, as you know the situation better than a stranger [and also know] the circumstances in which I am placed. I doubt not but you would have helped me in everything. But as it has pleased God to provide you with a family there, I can not advise you in the matter, as the situation of the country is well known to you.

As to the government here in this country [it is, as far as I know] good. Trade is carried on as heretofore to Boston and the West Indies and the trading with the Indians goes on as while you were here. The past summer there was a lively trade. As to agriculture, it has during the last two years become so much worse on account of high water and the increase of weeds that the farmers demand a reduction [in the rent]. The honorable governor has prohibited the exportation of wheat flour for six months, but allowed that of bread.

As to my house and the land across [the river], they are in the same condition as when my late husband was living. May it please the Lord that we may [possess] them in peace and have the grist-mill and sawmill also, in order that I may be able to support myself. But we live here in great fear on account of the great war between the English and the Indians around the north and of New England, although, thank God, we do not yet hear of any calamities. The Indians have plundered many villages and killed many [people].

It seems that it pleases the Lord to visit us also in this region. May God Almighty preserve us and prevent that they receive reinforcement from other nations, for they are very bold, and that they may not proceed farther. The state of religion in this country is still the same, for which mercy we can not sufficiently thank God Almighty. Wherewith, with hearty greetings from myself and my son Kiliaen and Anna to you and your wife, I commend you to God.

From Stephanus van Cortlandt

[June 1677]

Juff' Maria van Cortlandt

Worthy and dear Sister: I received your two letters, but having been very busy I have until now not been able to answer them. I have written at length to Domine Rensselaer. I hope that he will take everything into consideration and will see how matters stand. If you should happen to speak to him about it, offer to leave everything in love and friendship to impartial persons and show him that the fault is not yours but his and that you will always inform him of everything you receive, provided he does the same on his part, and that you will help each other in the household with whatever is received from the mill, one advising, assisting, and consoling the other. Give him full measure, without loss or detriment to yourself in any way. Consult some one and do your best to arrange matters on a firm basis. Should he at times talk somewhat extravagantly, let it pass unnoticed, for it is only provisionally and will apparently not last long. But if he will not allow you to do anything, whether to receive anything, or to enjoy any revenue from the mill to live on, you must see what is best to be done, but you need not abstain [from doing anything], even if he will not allow it, but may go on [according to the instructions] from Holland. . . . Since May I have had no time to do anything about your affairs. When the busiest time is past I shall take the matter up again to make an end of it. Meanwhile, I hope to hear better tidings from above than heretofore, which may God grant. Commending you to His protection, I remain, after greetings.

Your affectionate brother
S. V. Cortlandt

If possible, I would ask you to send me 60 good floor boards to repair the rear part of the house, whereby you will do me a favor.

To Richard van Rensselaer

[June 1678]

Sr Reygart van Rensselaer

Dear Brother: I can not refrain from letting you know that we are all well. I hope that the same is true of all the friends. In the year 1676, I sent over an order of Jan Gaue on one Willem Verspeck, in the sum of fl.51:15, which you were to receive, but as I have no letter from you, I do not know whether the order was accepted. Be pleased to let me know, otherwise Jan Gaue must pay here. But if you received the money, I would ask you kindly to send me a good piece of linen for it, as that which you left with us has been stolen and I am in need of it. Also two intelligent market gardeners.

I had planned to send over Kiliaen, but as the war still rages so severely I have on the advice of the friends apprenticed him here in this country to a silversmith to learn that trade and meanwhile to see what God may grant with respect to the war.

Enclosed herewith goes a letter from Thunis de Metselaer. He asks you kindly to be pleased to deliver this letter to Paeus Cornelisz, as he sailed before he [Thunis] knew it. And in case he should already have left, he asks you to be pleased to forward the letter to his friends, taking off the cover of the letter.

We are longing very much for the arrival of . . . governor [Andros], in the hope that something may have been done in the matter of the colony.

I received a letter from brother Nicolaes, stating that one Dirck Wesselse and Mr. Cornelis had bought a piece of land with a swale, situated on the east side, directly opposite the land of Broer Cornelis, although they were told and it was proved to them that it was purchased land. Nevertheless they go ahead, so that we do not understand how it is with the colony, whether . . . it is again for sale. Gerrit Slechtenhorst bought . . . land, which land has already been surveyed for him. It lies close to Klaverack. Barent, the

shoemaker, has 38 morgens of land, lying near Bere island. So it
goes, one piece after another.

Be pleased to give my hearty greetings to uncle van Wely and to
tell all the friends that they must excuse me this time for not writing
to them. The reason is that I should like to send their account with
it, which I hope will be sent over [at the next opportunity]. . . .

Brother, be pleased to remember what you promised me when
you took leave of me. Brother will also remember what my husband,
deceased, wrote to you about the piece of gold of 28 gl. That was
given to me as a christening gift *[pillegift]* and I should therefore like
to keep it as a remembrance and also because my daughter is
growing up.

As there is no further news here, I shall break off and commend
you and your wife and the children to God's keeping. May He grant
to all of us what will save our souls and bless our bodies.

Your faithful and affectionate sister
Maria van Rensselaer

To Richard van Rensselaer

[September 1680]

Sʳ Reygart van Rensselaer

Dear Brother: Your favor of the 12th of July came duly to hand
and from it I saw that you duly received the account of my husband,
deceased, your brother, regarding the colony, and that you and your
sister were quite shocked when you saw the balance of the account.
In answer thereto I shall say that if my husband, deceased, had made
up the account himself, there would have been quite a bit more due.
Do not think, dear brother, that it is an account which is made up
out of my head. God preserve me from doing that. We have taken it
from his own writings and if I should include all the expenditures
which have been made and charge for all the extraordinary meals, a
great deal more would be coming to me. Dear brother, you well
know yourself how it went, first upon the arrival of the English,
then upon the arrival of the Dutch, and then again upon the arrival
of the English, and how, whenever anyone of importance came from
New York, he had to be entertained to keep up the dignity of the

colony. You also well know that brother Jan Baties[t] wrote that one should not be particular about 1000 gl. or two. For whom, then, was it done except for the colony? For ourselves we did not need it; we could have got along very well with one authority.

And as to what brother writes about loss on grain, seawan, etc., you also know how the grain has gone up in schepels, to 5 and 6½ schepels to the beaver, which is a great loss to the colony, and the seawan from 20 to 25, 30 and 36 gl. to the beaver. What would have become of us, then, if we had not had something else besides? If you examine the receipts of the colony, you will see that one year with another it could not produce enough to cover the expenses. One has to pay the schout, the secretary, the governor, the councilors, and in addition pay all expenses. If brother will take that into consideration, he can only say that it is true.

And as to what you write about my deceased husband's [capital] having been great when he went to New Netherland and that [the business] which he afterwards did on commission [as well] as in brewing did not leave anything, I will not deny it, and therefore, brother, be pleased to consider also how the goods sent to him by [Jan] Batiest, deceased, and others have dwindled in the colony and . . . how little [is left] to me. . . .

That the friends in Holland through the war have suffered great loss makes us heartily sorry, God knows, but consider, dear brother, whether to lose my health and in addition to lose my property and my dearest partner and to be left with six children and such an encumbered estate is not hard on me either, especially, to sit here and not to know what I have and to get further and further into debt, for as long as I remain thus in possession of the undivided estate it will be nothing but loss to me and to the friends. And as to there being some items in the account which, as you write, have been entered twice, I shall in the spring write about it to my brother and find out what there is to it and if there is anything that is not right I shall be glad to see it straightened out. Therefore, dear brother, do me the favor to examine the account and talk it over with the friends and if, please God, you intend to come over, we can inform each other of everything and settle all accounts as to one thing and another, in order that for once we may know where we stand. And if the friends do not at the same time resolve to do something about the colony, things will run entirely wild.

You also complain that nothing is being sent over. How can anything be sent over when so many outlays had to be made and must still be made? On the farm called Turckeyen a new house has been built. On the farm of the Vlaming a new house must be built. On the farm of Thunis Dircx a new house must be built. Gerrit Gysbert, at Bettlem, will in the spring build a barn. Jonge Jan must build. Hen[drick] Mase must build. Hendrick van Nes must build a dwelling house and the old grist-mill must be completely torn down. One hears of nothing but expenses and at present there is such a poor harvest that many will not have any grain for bread. Furthermore, much money has been spent on the new mill, as I thought that it would produce some revenue, but now bolting [of flour] is also prohibited, so that I am at a loss to know where a stiver is to come from to be sent over. Yes, if 700 schepels of wheat did not have to be paid and if they were private farms, every one would sell his grain with a profit and send over his. I shall keep all the farmers waiting as long as I can, in order that I may learn whether it is possible for you to come over so that you may see things for yourself sometime. . . .

A PLANTATION MANAGER

The readings that follow are from two periods in the correspondence of Eliza Lucas Pinckney (ca. 1722–93). (Some of the excerpts are letters and others are notes or abstracts of correspondence, including some undated items.) The first, written in the 1740s, concern her management of her father's plantations in South Carolina. The second, a letter written in 1760, treats her conduct of her husband's plantations after his death in 1758. Her successes were undoubtedly exceptional. During her first career in the years 1739 to 1743 when she was only a very young woman she rapidly augmented the value of the assets she managed. She is commonly regarded as responsible for the introduction of West Indian indigo to South Carolina to supplement rice production. She was the first to grow the crop there and persuaded her neighbors to follow suit. In her second career, she innovated in the culture of silkworms and the manufacture of silk. But her significance extends beyond these remarkable accomplishments. Her careers exemplify the wide opportunities available to young women, wives, and particularly widows to manage property where there were an abundance of land and a scarcity of labor. In the case of the Lucas family, there were few mature individuals to manage the family's enterprises, which had become far flung under Eliza's grandfather and father, who was lieutenant-governor of Antigua. While taking up plantations in South Carolina he remained in the West Indies to conduct military operations against the French, so Eliza was necessarily impressed to manage the family's Carolina interest. Such opportunities for the management of agriculture were particularly great in the South, given the fact that white women directing black men were viewed more tolerantly than white women directing white men. And one might speculate that such opportunities were greatest in South Carolina, among all the colonies, because of the unique proportion of the black population (some 70 per cent of the total by the end of the colonial period) and the unusually large social role of a compact elite of white plantation owners.

FROM THE CORRESPONDENCE OF ELIZA PINCKNEY

[To Colonel Lucas]

[1740]

Hon'd Sir

Your letter by way of Philadelphia which I duly received was an additional proof of that paternal tenderness which I have always Experienced from the most Indulgent of Parents from my Cradle to this time, and the subject of it is of the utmost importance to my peace and happiness.

As you propose Mr. L. to me I am sorry I can't have Sentiments

From Elise Pinckney, ed. *The Letterbook of Eliza Lucas Pinckney, 1739–1762* (Chapel Hill: University of North Carolina Press, 1972), pp. 5–8, 15–17, 40–42, 44–45, 58–59, and 142–46, by permission of the publisher.

favourable enough of him to take time to think on the Subject, as your Indulgence to me will ever add weight to the duty that obliges me to consult what best pleases you, for so much Generosity on your part claims all my Obedience, but as I know 'tis my happiness you consult [I] must beg the favour of you to pay my thanks to the old Gentleman for his Generosity and favourable sentiments of me and let him know my thoughts on the affair in such civil terms as you know much better than any I can dictate; and beg leave to say to you that the riches of Peru and Chili if he had them put together could not purchase a sufficient Esteem for him to make him my husband.

As to the other Gentleman you mention, Mr. Walsh, you know, Sir, I have so slight a knowledge of him I can form no judgment of him, and a Case of such consequence requires the Nicest distinction of humours and Sentiments. But give me leave to assure you, my dear Sir, that a single life is my only Choice and if it were not as I am yet but Eighteen, hope you will [put] aside the thoughts of my marrying yet these 2 or 3 years at least.

You are so good to say you have too great an Opinion of my prudence to think I would entertain an indiscreet passion for any one, and I hope heaven will always direct me that I may never disappoint you; and what indeed could induce me to make a secret of my Inclination to my best friend, as I am well aware you would not disaprove it to make me a Sacrifice to Wealth, and I am as certain I would indulge no passion that had not your aprobation, as I truly am

Dr. Sir, Your most dutiful and affecte. Daughter

E. Lucas

To my good friend Mrs. Boddicott

May the 2nd [1740]

Dear Madam

I flatter myself it will be a satisfaction to you to hear I like this part of the world, as my lott has fallen here—which I really do. I prefer England to it, 'tis true, but think Carolina greatly preferable to the West Indias, and was my Papa here I should be very happy.

We have a very good acquaintance from whom we have received much friendship and Civility. Charles Town, the principal one in this province, is a polite, agreeable place. The people live very Gentile and very much in the English taste. The Country is in General fertile and abounds with Venison and wild fowl; the Venison is much higher flavoured than in England but 'tis seldom fat.

My Papa and Mama's great indulgence to me leaves it to me to chose our place of residence either in town or Country, but I think it more prudent as well as most agreeable to my Mama and self to be in the Country during my Father's absence. We are 17 mile by land and 6 by water from Charles Town—where we have about 6 agreeable families around us with whom we live in great harmony.

I have a little library well furnished (for my papa has left me most of his books) in which I spend part of my time. My Musick and the Garden, which I am very fond of, take up the rest of my time that is not imployed in business, of which my father has left me a pretty good share—and indeed, 'twas inavoidable as my Mama's bad state of health prevents her going through any fatigue.

I have the business of 3 plantations to transact, which requires much writing and more business and fatigue of other sorts than you can imagine. But least you should imagine it too burthensom to a girl at my early time of life, give me leave to answer you: I assure you I think myself happy that I can be useful to so good a father, and by rising very early I find I can go through much business. But least you should think I shall be quite moaped with this way of life I am to inform you there is two worthy Ladies in Charles Town, Mrs. Pinckney and Mrs. Cleland, who are partial enough to me to be always pleased to have me with them, and insist upon my making their houses my home when in town and press me to relax a little much oftener than 'tis in my honor to accept of their obliging intreaties. But I some times am with one or the other for 3 weeks or a month at a time, and then enjoy all the pleasures Charles Town affords, but nothing gives me more than subscribing my self

Dear Madam,

Yr. most affectionet and

most obliged humble Servt.

Eliza. Lucas

Pray remember me in the best manner to my worthy friend Mr. Boddicott.

July [1740]

Wrote my Father a very long letter on his plantation affairs and on his change of commissions with Major Heron; On the Augustine Expedition; On the pains I had taken to bring the Indigo, Ginger, Cotton and Lucerne and Casada to perfection, and had greater hopes from the Indigo (if I could have the seed earlier next year from the West India's) than any of the rest of the things I had tryd.

June the 8th, 1741

Wrote again to my father on the subject of the Indigo, Cotton, &c. Also concerning the fall of bills of Exchange. Lamenting the death of his worthy friend Captain Fleming. Acquaint him with Mr. Manigault's great Civility with regard to Lushers taking in his goods.

To my Father

June the 4th, 1741

Hon'd Sir

Never were letters more welcome than yours of Feb. 19th and 20th and March the 15th and 21st, which came almost together. It was near 6 months since we had the pleasure of a line from you. Our fears increased apace and we dreaded some fatal accident befallen, but hearing of your recovery from a dangerous fitt of Illness has more than equaled, great as it was, our former Anxiety. Nor shall we ever think ourselves sufficiently thankful to Almighty God for the continuance of so great a blessing.

I simpathize most sincerely with the Inhabitance of Antigua in so great a Calamity as the scarcity of provisions and the want of the Necessarys of life to the poorer sort. We shall send all we can get of all sorts of provisions particularly what you write for. I wrote this day to Starrat for a barrel [of] butter.

We expect the boat dayly from Garden Hill when I shall be able to give you an account of affairs there. The Cotton, Guiney corn, and most of the Ginger planted here was cutt off by a frost. I wrote you in [a] former letter we had a fine Crop of Indigo Seed upon the ground, and since informed you the frost took it before it was dry. I picked out the best of it and had it planted, but there is not more than a hundred bushes of it come up—which proves the more unluckey as you have sent a man to make it. I make no doubt Indigo will prove a very valuable Commodity in time if we could have the seed from the west Indias [in] time enough to plant the latter end of March, that the seed might be dry enough to gather before our frost. I am sorry we lost this season. We can do nothing towards it now but make the works ready for next year. The Lucern is yet but dwindlering, but Mr. Hunt tells me 'tis always so here the first year.

The death of my Grandmama was, as you imagine, very shocking and grievous to my Mama, but I hope the considerations of the misery's that attend so advanced an age will help time to wear it off.

I am very much obliged to you for the present you were so good to send me of the fifty pound bill of Exchange which I duely received.

We hear Carthagene is taken.

Mr. Wallis is dead. Capt. Norberry was lately killed in a duel by Capt. Dobrusee, whose life is dispaired of by the wounds he received. He is much blamed for querreling with such a brawling man as Norberry who was disregarded by every body. Norberry has left a wife and 3 or 4 children in very bad circumstances to lament his rashness.

Mama tenders you her affections and Polly joyns in duty with

My Dr. Papa
Y.m.obt. and ever D[evoted] D[aughter]
E. Lucas

[To Miss Bartlett]

[ca. June 1742]

Dr. Miss B.

After a pleasant passage of about an hour we arrived safe at home as I hope you and Mrs. Pinckney did at Belmont. But this place appeared much less agreeable than when I left it, having lost the agreeable company that then enlivened it. The Scene is indeed much changed for instead of the easey and agreeable conversation of our friends I an engaged with the rudiments of the law to which I am yet but a stranger. And what adds to my mortification, I soon discovered that Doctor Wood wants the politeness of your Uncle, who with a graceful ease and good nature peculiar to himself is always ready to instruct the ignorant. But this rustic seems by no means to court my acquaintance for he often treats me with such cramp phrases I am unable to understand him; nor is he civil enough to explain them when I desire it. However, I hope in a short time with the help of Dictionarys French and English we shall be better friends, nor shall I grudge a little pains and application if that will make me useful to any of my poor Neighbours. We have some in this Neighborhood who have a little Land and few slaves and Cattle to give their children that never think of making a will till they come upon a sick bed and find it too expensive to send to town for a Lawyer. If You will not laugh too immoderately at me I'll Trust you with a secrett. I have made two wills already. I know I have done no harm for I coned my lesson very perfect and know how to convey by will Estates real and personal and never forget in its proper place, him and his heirs for Ever, nor that 'tis to be signed by 3 Witnesses in presence of one another. But the most comfortable remembrance of all is that Doctor Wood says the Law makes great allowance for last Wills and Testaments presumeing the Testator could not have council learned in the law. But after all what can I do if a poor creature lies a dying and their family takes it in to their head that I can serve them. I cant refuse; but when they are well and able to employ a lawyer, I always shall.

A Widdow here abouts with a pretty little fortune teazed me intolerable to draw her a marriage settlement, but it was out of my depth and I absolutely refused it so she got an abler hand to do it. Indeed she could afford it. But I could not get off from being one of her trustees to her settlement and an old Gentleman the other. I shall begin to think my self an old woman before I am well a young one having these weighty affairs upon my hands.

I have just heard the meloncholy and shocking storry of Mrs. Le

Brasures shoting herself. It surprizes me so much I must conclude.

Yr.m.o.st

E. Lucas

Mama and Polly desire their Compliments to Colo. Pinckney and Lady and [are] much obliged to them for their friendly vizet.

[To George Lucas]

[1742]

My Dear brother

The account my father lately gave us of your going soon on service has been the subject of my thoughts almost ever since. Among that variety of objects which press upon the mind in its most serious intervals this never fails to make one. I cant help reflecting on the dangerous situation of a soldiers life, continually exposed to accidents and fatigue, and the melencholy consideration of a beloved father and brother being in great danger depresses me to the greatest degree and prevents my proceeding any farther—

I have recollected my self and will endeavour to banish a train of thinking fitter for a Sceptick than a Xtian. But what subject shall I write on. I am quite at a loss. Apropo, I was lately thinking how valueable a Virtue fortitude is and I stand in great need of it just now my self, and have also a mind to indulge the vanity of dictateing to you.

Remember then, My dear brother, that fortitude, a Virtue so Necessary in all stations of life and to all people, seems more particularly so to a Soldier, and I believe the generallity of that profession think so; but I doubt the younger sort dont always distinguish rightly between true fortitude and that which too often passes for it, and often decieves even the possesors them-selves. I mean heat of temper and a certain fierceness to encounter an Enemy which, as I said, often passes under the name of courage, but in which some of the brute Creation Equals if not exceeds the greatest Hero of you all. But, how deferent from that is the truely aimable Virtue fortitude or Strength of mind, which is hardened against evil upon rational principles, that is so guarded with reason and Consideration that no outward event is able to raise any violent disturbance in it, that has such a Constant power over its passions as not to be very timerous in danger, Envious in want, impatient in suffering, or revengeful under injuries. This composed [state] of mind in the midst of dangers and evil accidents is what I would have my dear brother endeavour to attain in as great a degree as this state of imperfection will permit.

Pardon my dear brother the liberty I take with you. I am a little older than you are and therefore assume on that account, or advise rather from the tenderest regard for your happiness, as I am truely

Your most affecte Sister

E. Lucas

Mama desires I will tell you her blessing and prayers attend you wherever you go.

Feb. the 3rd, 1743/4

Wrote to my Aunt concerning Mr. Smith.

The same day wrote to my father concerning his affairs in England and of my brother Tommy.

Thanks for all the things he sent. Sent him by the return of the Vessel. 2 barrels Rice, ditto Corn, 3 ditto peese, 1 pickled pork, 2 keggs Oysters, one of Eggs by way of Experiment put up in salt; in case they answere, my scheme is to supply my fathers refineing house in Antigua with Eggs from Carolina.

Concerning settleing a plantation to the North with the Woppo slaves, &c., &c.

To My Father

Feb. 10, 1742/3

I am at a loss where to write to my Dear and Honoured Father, but am determined not to omit this pleasing duty while I am able to perform it. I shall therefore send this to my brother to forward it to you. Possibly the expedition may be over and you returned in safety. Happy indeed shall I be when this grateful news reaches us; sufficiently thankful I never am to the great Author of all my happiness for a blessing like this, for more than the utmost gratitude I can pay is due.

I received the friendly congratulations of Miss Dunbar on your being made Lieut. Col. and Gov. of Antigua with a very gentile present to Polly and another to myself. My brother seems mortified at being left behind and not suffered to attend you on this expedition. His going would doubtless have improved him in military affairs, but I hope his staying will be no disservice to his morrals as it may teach him to bear disapointments and curb too ambitious aspireings in his young tho' good mind—a useful piece of knowledge in human life and perhaps requires as much true fortitude as faceing an enemy.

But to cease morrallizing and attend to business. The [rice] crop at Garden Hill turned out ill, but a hundred and sixty barrels; and at Wappo only 43. The price is so very low as thirty shillings per hundred. We have sent very little to town yet for that reason. People difer much in sentiment about the number of ships we are still to have.

We have not heard from England for more than three months. What can keep the shiping? We conjecture 'tis an imbargo.

In my letter of the 3rd of Feb. I desired to know if you aproved of settleing a plantation to the North near Major Pawly. Please to let us know in your next if we have your approbation and it shall be done in the fall.

We expect a Vizet from the Spainards this Summer. Mr. Oglethorp harrases them much at their forts at St. Augustine. He has lately killed some and took two prisoners.

Mama tenders you her affections, and blessing to my brother, and I am

Hond. Sir
Y.m.o.[bedient] and D[utiful]
D[aughter]
E. Lucas

My dear Children

March [1760]

The fleet being just upon sailing (and I lately so hurry'd about other matters that I began late to write to England) will prevent my writing to you so fully as my inclination leads me to do and as your pretty letters of the [blank] demand. Be asured I shall answer them more particularly very soon. In the meantime I hope my dear Charles will readily acquiesce in changing his school as the air of Camberwell does not agree with his dear little brother. I know your grateful and affectionate temper and know it will give you a good deal of pain to leave Mr. Gerrard, but your affection to your brother and the defference you will, I know, always pay to the judgment of our friends in England who advise it and can more properly judge of matters than I can at this distance. Rely intirely on their friendship and judgement in the case—which I hope will make you the more readily give up your own judgment and inclination to theirs.

I dont yet know where you are fixt or would write to your Master to whom pray pay my Compliments and inform him so. My Lady Carew was so good to inform me you wrote to me the day before she did in Dec. last, but your letters are not yet come to hand. I impatiently expect them. You know, my dearest boys, how near my heart you lie, and that all the happiness I have upon Earth is centered in you and your dear Sister. Let me then hear from you as often as possible if 'tis but 2 lines to say you are both well.

And now, my dear little Tomm, your Mama has one petition to make to you. 'Tis to think of her frequently when you are tempted to eat unripe or too much fruit. If you knew how much anguish I suffer upon every apprehension of your want of health I am sure you would punish your self to give me this consolation. You and your dear brother are the dayly—almost hourly—subject of my prayer and thoughts. Do not therefore forget to take care of your selves and joyn with me in imploring the Divine blessing upon you.

Your Sister is, I thank God, well and will write to you if the ships stay a day or two longer. Be good children, mind your learning, and love one another; and that the Almighty will bless you both with your dear Sister, protect and guide you and make you his children is the most devout petition that is put up to Heaven by, my dear boys,

> Your ever effectionate Mother
> Eliza. Pinckney

By Mr. T. Smith [to Mr. Morly]

March 14th, 1760

Dear Sir

Since mine of the 3rd o' Nov. by the Brig Spy, Capt. Lyford, to Bristol inclosing 3 letters, one to Sir Richard Lyttleton, one to Miss McCartney, and one to Mr. Onslow, I received your favour of the 31st of Aug. inclosing Coppys of 3 I had before received dated the 29th May, 5th June, and 17th July, for all which pray accept my most grateful thanks.

I was in hopes to have inclosed you a bill for a hundred pound sterling by the last ships but could not prevail on the person I was to have them from to draw before the fleet sailed. I now inclose them and beg the favour as soon as you receive it to present Doctor K with 6 Guineas for his attendance on my children, and Mr. Gerrard with the value in lieu of a barrel of Rice which he ought to have had long ago, and Miss Bartlett the remainder of the Legacy of ten pound. I am very much obliged to you for what you advanced her of it before. It was very kind and you may be sure what I must approve.

The beginning of this Year there was such a fine prospect on our plantations of a great Crop that I was hopeful of clearing all the mony that was due upon the Estate, but the great drought in most parts of the Country, such as I never remember here, disapointed those expectations so much that all that we make from the planting interest will hardly defray the charges of the plantations. And upon our arrival here we found they wanted but every thing and [were] every way in bad order, with ignorant or dishonest Over Seers.

My Nephew had no management of the planting interest, and my brother who, by a stroak of the palsey, had been long incapable of all business. I thank God there is now a good prospect of things being deferently conducted. I have prevailed upon a conscientious good man (who by his industry and honesty had raised a fine fortune for 2 orphan children my dear Mr. Pinckney was guardian too) to undertake the direction and inspection of the overseers. He is an excellent planter, a Dutchman, originally Servant and Overseer to Mr. Golightly, who has been much solicited to undertake for many

Gentlemen; but as he has no family but a wife and is comfortable enough in his circumstances, refuses to do it for any but women and children that are not able to do it for themselves. So that if it please God to prosper us and grant good Seasons, I hope to clear all next year.

I find it requires great care, attention, and activity to attend properly to a Carolina Estate, tho' but a moderate one, to do ones duty and make it turn to account, that I find I have as much business as I can go through of one sort or other. Perhaps 'tis better for me, and I believe it is. Had there not been a necessity for it, I might have sunk to the grave by this time in that Lethargy of stupidity which had seized me after my mind had been violently agitated by the greatest shock it ever felt. But a variety of imployment gives my thoughts a relief from melloncholy subjects, tho' 'tis but a temporary one, and gives me air and excercise, which I believe I should not have had resolution enough to take if I had not been roused to it by motives of duty and parental affection.

I have not yet proved the Will and am advised not to do it as it would be attended with much trouble in taking particular Inventory of every thing, the most minute, which must be returned upon oath; and the proving of it 'tis said is unnecessary as there is but little due from the Estate and no body to call me to account. And the Will it self must remain good and in force as it is a record. However if you think it best, I shall not mind the trouble but will still do it, as I would perform the Sacred trust to the utmost of my ability in every Tittle in the best manner I can.

I hope you received mine of the 19th Septr., acknowledging the receipt of yours that inclosed several from my other friends, the answers to some of which and some former ones I have last month and now trouble you with.

The long experience I have—and still daily have—of the friendly part you take in our concerns has occationed you the trouble of so long a letter. Be so good to pay my Compliments and thanks to Mr. Chatfield for his management of our little affairs at Riply and for the trouble he and Mrs. Chatfield are so good to give themselves to indulge my dear boys. I am really ashamed to give Mr. Chatfield so much trouble about the house. I should be much obliged to you to do for me what you think I should do in the case either to make him, as he is a man of business, an acknowledgment for the trouble by way of commissions or in what way you think best.

I wrote you a short letter in Febr. last in such a hurry that I kept no coppy by Capt. Cramp, and Coppy by Lambert Tree, inclosing several letters in each packet, Viz: one to Miss Lyttelton, 3 in two packets to Miss Mackartney, one to Mrs. King, one to Miss Varier, one to Mr. Keat, one to Dr. Kirkpatrick, and one to Mr. Gerrard.

Your favour of the 19 Novr. by way of Bristol gave me great pleasure as it informed me of my dear boys health. Indeed, Sir, 'tis not only friendly but really charitable to let me hear as often as you can from them. My heart bleeds at our separation but it must be so for a time.

The day after I wrote the foregoing I received your favour of the 31st of Decr. by Capt. Rains and another from my friend Mrs. Evance by the same opportunity; but none from Dr. Kirkpatrick or my children as you imagined I should. You may be sure, My good Sir, that I acquiesce in every thing you and my other friends do with regard to my children. You are upon the spot and must be better judges of their care than I possibly can be at this distance. The prospect of the change of air's establishing my dear little babes health is of it self a sufficient reason for removing him and I should not chuse to have the brothers separated if I could help it. I have always heard a great character of Harrow school, but if that at Kensington is equally good as there is fewer scholars and 'tis nearer London and the air aproved for tender constitutions I should think that would be to be prefered.

You are very good to have given your self so much trouble about the 30 £ bill on Mr. Davison. My poor brother has been very ill many months, so that matter must rest for the present.

My best Compliments to the D. and Mrs. E.

I received Lady C. letter

Sent this letter by Mr. T. Smith, inclosing bills for a hundred pound, and the Coppy by the Trent with a 2nd Set of bills.

THE INHERITANCE OF PROPERTY

The following readings consist of abstracts of wills recorded in the New York Surrogate's office during the period 1754–60. They suggest the variety of means by which wives and daughters could function independently as a result of the death of husbands and fathers. The wills indicate the rather substantial estates that had been accumulated largely by middle-class families by the end of the colonial period, by both men and women. The women benefiting from these wills often were able to embark on independent careers or new marriages with considerable financial backing.

ABSTRACTS OF NEW YORK WILLS

In the name of God, Amen. I, James Cooper, of Southampton, in Suffolk County, yeoman, being well in health. "All debts and duties that I do owe in Right and Conscience, to be paid." I leave to my four sons, James, Zebulon, Stephen, and Moses, each 20 shillings. To my daughter Elizabeth, 20 shillings. To my son Selah, 10 shillings. I leave to my wife Mary the use of my dwelling house, and the land adjoining, "and the use of my part of the sloop 'Dolphin,' " so long as she remains my widow. "Only my part of the sloop I do give her to dispose of as she thinks fit." After her death or marriage I leave the said house and land to my son, Ezekiel Cooper, but if he dies under age, then to my son, Silas Cooper, and if he dies under age, then to my sons Benjamin and Philip. I leave to my sons Benjamin, Silas, and Philip, and to my daughter Abigail, each 10 shillings. My wife is to take care of my son Selah and provide for him during her life, and after that my son Ezekiel is to provide for him. After payment of debts and legacies, I leave the rest of movables to my wife Mary, and make her executor.

Dated February 24, 1753. Witnesses, Mehitabel Mackie, Anne Mackie, John Mackie. Proved, January 25, 1754.

From *Collections of the New York Historical Society, 1896* (New York: New York Historical Society, 1897), pp. 10–11, 24–25, 30–31, 58–61, 76–83, 356–59, 365–67, and 398–400.

In the name of God, Amen. I, Garrit Harsin, of New York, gunsmith, being weak in body, this May 15, 1753. I leave to my well-beloved son Bernardus £5, and my Large Dutch House Bible, after the decease of my wife, in full bar of all claim as eldest son. I leave to my wife Engeltie all real and personal estate during her widowhood, with full power to sell any one of my dwelling houses and lots in New York. If she marries, she is to have 1/3 of my estate. After her death, all my estate to my children, Bernardus, George, and Engeltie, wife of Peter De Wint; my sons to have each £50 extra. I make my wife and sons executors.

Witnesses, Abraham Van Gelder, Francis Sylvester, Simon Johnson. Proved, August 29, 1754.

In the name of God, Amen. I, John Vreeland, of New York, ship wright, being sick. My body is to be decently interred at the discretion of my wife Elenor. I leave to my son, Enoch Vreeland, ship wright, £5, in bar of all claims. I leave to my grand daughter, Mary Pelletreau, daughter of my daughter Mary Pelletreau, widow, £25. I leave to my wife's grand daughter, Elizabeth Louttritt, a new suit of mourning and a gold ring. I leave to my wife Elenor all household stuff and furniture, brass and pewter, and my negro woman "Betty." I leave to my wife all that my house and lot of ground where I now live, during her widowhood, and then to my son Enoch and my daughter, Mary Pelletreau, and I also leave them all the rest of my estate. I make my wife, and my daughter, Mary Pelletreau, and my friend, Hendrick Vandewater, executors.

Dated August 18, 1744. Witnesses, Sarah Griffith, Frederick Becker, Lancaster Green. Proved, September 4, 1754.

Know all men by these Presents, that I, Conrad Ten Eyck, of New York, cooper, do make my wife Rebecca my true and lawful attorney. And considering the uncertainty of this transitory life, do make this my last will, and I bequeath to my wife all the rest of my estate and make her executor.

September 4, 1746. Witnesses, John Marschalk, Jr., Charles McNeil, Peter Van Norden. Proved, September 17, 1754. [The widow was then Rebecca King.]

I, Edmond Titus, of Wheatly, in the bounds of Oyster Bay, in Queens County, yeoman, being this 5 day of the 3d month, called March, in the year 1754, in a feeble condition of body, and willing to set my house in order before my final change. I leave to my wife Sarah one of the choicest of my beds, with full furniture, and one of the choicest of my horses, and her riding saddle, and my cupboard and oval table, and my Great Bible, and all bed linnen. I will that all my lands and meadows, both divided and undivided, lying in the Town of Hempstead, be sold by my executors, and the money to go towards payment of debts. My executors are to set apart so much of my household goods and utensils of husbandry as they shall find expedient for my wife and family to keep house with, and the rest to be sold. My will and desire is that my wife is to have liberty to carry on farming for the support of herself and family so long as my wife shall think it profitable, and my executors may sell lands at discretion. My 4 daughters, Sarah, Martha, Mary, and Hannah, shall each have so much money as to be equal to what I have given to my eldest daughter, Phebe Pryer, and when my youngest daughter is of age or married, then the estate to be divided between my wife and my 5 daughters. I make my brother in law, Jacob Titus, and my cousin, Samuel Willis, of Jericho, and Thomas Seaman, of Westbury, executors.

Witnesses, William Laton, Simon Losee, John Laton, David Laton. Proved, September 18, 1754.

In the name of God, Amen. I, Jeronimus Rapelye, of Flushing, in Queens County, yeoman, being now sick. I leave to my wife Ann my best bed, my silver teapot, and my riding chair, and a horse suitable to draw the same, and my cabinet and £350. I leave to my son John all that certain messuage, dwelling house and farm or Plantation which I lately purchased of Samuel Farrington, and where my son John liveth, situate in the township of Flushing, also a negro woman, and also the horses, cattle, and utensils I have already given to him, and which with the farm I value at £850, I also leave him my silver tankard for his birth right, and my wife shall have the use of it so long as she continues my widow. I leave to my son Richard £800, and a negro man. I leave to my daughter Ann £200, which with £100 lately given to her by her grandmother, and a negro wench which I value at £50, also given by her grand mother, makes her portion £350. I leave to my daughter Idagh £330, and a negro girl which I value at £30. To my daughter Elizabeth £330, and a negro girl which I value at £30. I leave to my son Stephen £890 when he is 21. I leave to my wife and chidren all the rest of my wrought plate. My son John is to have the care of the portions of my two eldest daughters, Ann and Idagh. I order that as soon as convenient my executors shall sell the farm and lands whereon I now live in Flushing, and all my other lands and meadows (except the farm which I have given to my son John), together with my dwelling house and buildings, and all the rest of my movable estate. The proceeds to be applied towards payment of debts and legacies, and the rest to my wife and children. I make my wife Ann, and my nephew, Garrit Rapelye, of New York, and my trusty friend and brother in law, Elbert Hoogland, of Flushing, executors.

Dated August 28, 1754. Witnesses, Thomas Willitt, Thomas Willitt, Jr., Benjamin Hinchman. Proved at Jamaica, September 23, 1754.

On the 7 day of April, 1755. I, John Johnson, of Hempstead, in Queens County, yeoman, do make this my last will and testament. I leave to my wife 2 cows and my mare and all household goods. To my son William my loom and weaving tackling. I give my guns and swords to my three sons, John, Jacob, and William. The rest of my movable estate to be sold by my executors, and from the proceeds I give to my two sons, Jacob and Samuel, each £4, and the rest to all my sons and daughters [not named], to the sons when 21 and to the daughters when 18. I leave to my wife the use of my mill and all real estate during her widowhood. And my wife is to find my mother [not named] her bread corn as long as she keep the mill. After my wife's marriage or death, my executors are to sell the mill and farm, and divide the money between my children. I make James Wood and Isaac Balding executors.

Witnesses, Joseph Burtis, Cornelius Jackson, Patrick Mott. Proved, April 25, 1755.

In the name of God, Amen. I, Elizabeth Hodgins, widow of Thomas Hodgins, of New York, "leather dresser," being sick and indisposed. I leave to Mary Robins, daughter of John Robins, £12, and to his daughter Sarah £12. To Elizabeth, wife of John Robins, a silver tankard. To James Hill £20 and a Bible when he is of age. All the rest of my estate I leave to Elizabeth Mesyer and make her executor.

Dated November 13, 1752. Witnesses, John Ellsworth, Peter Montanye, blacksmith, Abel Hardenbrook, merchant. Proved, May 6, 1755.

In the name of God, Amen. I, Elizabeth Sands, of the Borroughtown of Westchester, by and with the advice and consent of my husband, Samuel Sands, and my Trustee, Elisha Barton, Jr., do make this my last will. As to my dwelling house and lot of land in the said Borrough town of Westchester, I devise the same to my sister, Keziah Glover, and her daughter, Elizabeth Lynch, during their lives, provided Elizabeth Lynch pay to my niece, Rebecca Barnes, £40, and in case of the death of Rebecca Barnes, 1/2 of this is to go to her sister Sarah, wife of Benjamin Palmer, and the other 1/2 to my three sisters, Miriam, Dorcas, and Abigail. In case of the death of my sister, Keziah Glover, then to her daughter Elizabeth I leave the house and lot, and she shall pay to my two nieces, Sarah De Lancey and Elizabeth Cleeves, £35. I leave to my sister, Keziah Glover, 2 negro women and a negro boy, "and the bed that formerly was in the Parlor," and a blue and white calico quilt, and my cow and swine. I leave to my niece, Elizabeth Lynch, a negro girl, and to my niece, Elizabeth Cleeves, my Gold chain and a bed. To Elisha Barton £10. To Thomas, son of Augustine Baxter, £5. To Charles Warner's wife Jane £5. To Dorcas, wife of Samuel Berrian, £5. To William Tippett £5. To Marcus, son of Thomas Baxter, £5. To Ann, daughter of Benjamin Palmer, £5. To Joseph Palmer £5. To Michael, son of Oliver Baxter, £5. To Bathsheba, daughter of Thomas Palmer, a set of gold buttons "to the value of a Pistole." To Mary, daughter of Oliver Baxter, 1/2 dozen silver spoons. To Keziah, daughter of Oliver Baxter, 1/2 dozen spoons, and the same to Catharine, daughter of Benjamin Baxter. . . . To my brother,

Thomas Baxter, my looking glass. To my sister, Keziah Glover, my riding chair, and she is to pay to Phebe, wife of Arnot Cannon, £5. To Elizabeth, daughter of John Oakley. . . . I make John Oakley and Cornelius Willett executors.

June 4, 1759. Signed by Elizabeth Sands, Samuel Sands, and Elisha Barton. Witnesses, Israel Honeywell, Henry Charlick, Thomas Allen. Proved, January 15, 1760.

"I, Wright Frost, of the town of Oyster Bay, being through the Mercy of God in enjoyment of Health." All just debts to be paid, "and in order to it, it is my will that my wife Prudence and my sons, Zebulon, Penn, and Daniel Wright, shall carry on all their business jointly, as we have done heretofore," and support their families, and pay debts as soon as they can. I leave to my wife all movable estate within doors, and a negro man, a horse, 6 sheep, and her choice of rooms in my house, and the use of 1/3 of meadows and Creek Thatch. I leave to my son Daniel my 2 lots of land lying in Mosquito Cove Patent, one of which I had of my father, Wright Frost, being 50 acres, and the other I bought of Jacob Furman, 30 acres, with all appurtenances. I leave to my daughter Jemina so much of my out door movables as will make her equal to the outsetting I have given to my daughters, Mary Thornycroft and Phebe De Milt. I leave to my sons Penn and Daniel so much utensils of husbandry as will make them equal to what I have given to my son Zebulon. My sons and my daughter Mary, if she shall be a widow, are to have the privilege of living in my house with my wife. I leave to my daughters, Phebe De Milt and Jemina Frost, each £100. These legacies are to be paid by my 3 sons. My executors are to put £95 at interest for my daughter, Mary Thornycroft. I make my sons Zebulon and Penn, and my cousins, Daniel Underhill and Thomas Pearsall, executors. I leave to my son, Penn Frost, all my right on Pine Island, and to my 3 sons all my right in the Great Plains.

Witnesses, Joseph Latting, George Townsend, Thomas Frost. Proved, March 5, 1760.

In the name of God, Amen, February 5, 1760. I, Adam Ireland, of North Castle, in Westchester County, innholder. My executors are to sell the farm where I now live, and pay all debts. I leave to my eldest son John my young black mare, and new saddle, gun, sword and belt, cartridge box, and wearing apparell. To my daughter, Hannah Searle, three sheep. To my daughter Mary a bed and £7. All the rest I leave to my wife Martha. I make my brother in law, Caleb Fowler, and my son in law, John Searle, executors.

Witnesses, Caleb Haight, Daniel Tompkins, John Harris. Proved, March 1, 1760.

In the name of God, Amen, November 10, 1759. I, Ferdinand Cure, of New York, shoemaker. I make my wife Mary and Charles Beekman, Jr., executors. I leave to my wife all estate and the use of house until my daughter Elizabeth is of age, and after my wife's decease my daughter is to have all my estate.

Witnesses, Henry Croo, mason, Thomas Bokas, laborer, James Davis. Proved, March 15, 1760.

In the name of God, Amen, October 18, 1755. I, Jacob Ferdon, of Schralenburgh, Bergen County, New Jersey. My wife Marritje shall possess and enjoy all my estate during her life, but in case of a second marriage to be utterly excluded therefrom. "I will that in case of a second marriage, so it may Please God to continue her in the land of the living here on Earth after the decease of her second husband, then she is to possess what is willed to her as above." I leave to my son Jacob for his birth right or prerogative, my negro man Will. I leave to my son Jacob all that land or Plantation whereupon I am now dwelling, except 18 acres which I bought of Arie Demarest, with house and barn, and he is to pay to my daughter Maria, wife of Thomas Moore, £200. I leave to my daughter Maria 18 acres of land at Schralenburgh, which I bought of Arie Demarest by deed May 20, 1752. All that piece of meadow which I bought of Hendrick Bartholf, lying at Tien Neck, is to be sold to pay debts. All the rest I leave to my two children, Jacob and Maria.

Witnesses, Peter S. Demarest, Margarite Durent, Robert

Sweezy, schoolmaster. Proved in New York, June 3, 1760. Confirmed, June 10, 1760, and wife Maria appointed executor.

In the name of God, Amen. I, Alice Ratsey, of New York, widow. My executors are to sell, "as soon as conveniently they can," all my shop goods at public auction vendue, and pay all debts and funeral charges. I leave to my son Robert £20 when he is 21. I leave to my daughter Alice, in order to make her equal with her sisters already married, £200 as an outset. When my son Robert is of age my executors are to sell all the rest of estate, including the house and lot where I now live, and a lot near the Tan Yards, in or near the Cripple Bush, in New York, and pay the money to my children, Elizabeth, wife of Peter Goelet, Esther, wife of William Weymans, Alice, and Robert. The two last, being under age, are to be brought up. I make my son in law, Peter Goelet, and my daughter Alice, executors.

Dated September 14, 1760. Witnesses, William Tailor, brass founder, Ann Stocton, widow, Peter Silvester. Proved, June 3, 1760.

In the name of God, Amen. I, Richard Ayscough, of New York, Practitioner in Physick and Chirugeon, being weak in body. I leave to my daughter, Sarah Ayscough, £500 current money of N.Y. I leave to my brother, John Ayscough, Jr., £100 Stirling. To my brother Thomas £50. I leave to my wife Anne all that my house and lot of land where I now live in Hanover Square, in New York, in the East Ward, To her for life, and then to be sold at Publick vendue by my executors. From the proceeds they are to pay to my mother in law, Anne Langdon, widow of Richard Langdon £500. I leave to my wife 1/3 of my personal property. I leave the rest to my son, Richard Ayscough, and to such other children as my wife may bear. I make my wife, and my uncle, Rev. Dr. Francis Ayscough, and my friend, Charles Williams, Esq., executors.

Dated May 22, 1760. Witnesses, John Burnet, attorney at law, Cornelius C. Van Horn, Isaac Goelet, merchant. Proved, June 9, 1760.

LABOR UNDER APPRENTICESHIP

Contracts of apprenticeship ordered the work of many young women throughout the colonial period and throughout the colonies. The contracts, and abstracts of contracts, presented here are typical for New York in about 1700. Apprenticeship served a wide variety of purposes: it assured reliable instruction in religion and reading; it gave training in particular skilled crafts; it provided for a servant class; it allocated responsibilities for the care and upbringing of orphans and the children of the very poor or the very incompetent; and it mobilized European immigrants for a labor-scarce economy.

The contracts included provide examples of all these objectives (except the last), but because they are taken from a fairly narrow slice of time they do not give an adequate impression of the trends under way by 1700. For one thing, immigrants increasingly arrived as free persons, although for the colonial period as a whole about one-half arrived under some form of voluntary servitude, pledging, typically, four to five years of labor in order to have their way paid and their future secured. For another, the reliance on indentures to obtain a labor supply came to become more common in the Middle Atlantic colonies than in the colonies in the South and in New England. In the South planters found it more profitable to rely on the importation of African slaves; in New England the relative lack of opportunities on the land and a high rate of natural increase guaranteed a large supply of family labor. Furthermore, religious instruction and rudimentary education, particularly in New England, increasingly became considered the responsibility of parents and the common schools.

Finally, the abundant opportunities for labor reduced the supply of native people willing to engage in servitude and often those bound into domestic service broke their contracts, fleeing the household and seeking employment in another region. Thus, by the middle of the eighteenth century apprenticeship was largely a means to develop a skilled labor force and to protect homeless children, in the absence of public or private institutions for sustaining children on the margin of the market place. Young women participated extensively in apprenticeships for craft training, but apprenticeships opened only a relatively small area: millinery work, dress and mantua making, hairdressing, embroidery, and midwifery. Women learned a wide variety of other crafts as well but usually within the context of their immediate families: as daughters sharing in home manufacturing, as wives assisting the master craftsman in the shop or handling his accounts, and as widows assuming the craft formerly practiced by their husbands. In the nineteenth century, barriers to the entry of women into skilled crafts would heighten, but the use of involuntary servitude to support orphaned and indigent children would become relatively more common and, in fact, would persist into the twentieth century.

INDENTURES OF APPRENTICESHIP, 1698

Recorded for Mr. Anthony Farmer, y[e] 17th day of December, Anno. Dom. 1698

Indenture, dated May 15th, 1693, of Frances Champion, daughter of Frances Champion, with consent of Mother, to Anthony Farmer and Elizabeth Farmer, his wife, as an apprentice and servant, for nine years from date. Said Master and Mistress in addition to other Matters "to Instruct the said Frances to Reade and to teach and Instruct her in Spining, Sewing, Knitting or any other manner of housewifery" etc.

Signed in the presence of Frances Champion, Jno. Eldridge, Jno. Basford.

Acknowledged, December 17th 1698, before

Jacobus V: Cortlandt, Esq[r], Alderman.

Recorded for Capt. Peter Matthews, the 17th day of July, Anno. Dom. 1699.

Indenture of Sarah Baker, Daughter of Marietta Damean, a free

From *New York Historical Society Collections*, vol. 18, 1885 (New York: New York Historical Society, 1886), pp. 578–619.

Indian Woman, with the Consent of her Mother, to Capt. Peter Matthews Gent, & Bridgett, his wife, as a Servant for seven years from date, with usual covenants.

"And also shall teach or Cause to be taught & Instructed the Said Apprentice to Read the English tongue and to worke plain worke And att the Expiration of the S^d Terme to Give and Supply to their Said Apprentice two good Suits of Apparell." Provided allways that the Said Apprentice Shall not be Obliged to her Apprenticeship or any parte thereof out of the Province of New Yorke without the Consent of her S^d Mother. Any thing Above Mentioned to the Contrary Notwithstanding.

Signed &c. May 5th 1699.

her

Sarah X Baker

marke

her

Marietta X Damean

marke

In the presence of K. V. Renslaer, Will Sharpas.
Acknowledged before Jacobus V: Cortlandt Esqr, Alderman.

Recorded for Mr. Jacob Dekey, the 4th day of December, 1699

Indenture of Richard Buckmaster, aged 14 years, with consent of his parents, to Jacob Dekey, Baker and Bolter, for six years from date. [Usual form.]

Signed September 7th. 1699 by Richard Buckmaster, Elizabeth Buckmaster.

In the presence of Richd Willett, Will. Sharpas.
Acknowledged before J. V. Cortlandt.

Recorded for Joseph Latham & Jane his wife, ye 4th December Anno. Dom. 1699

Indenture of Hannah Buckmaster, aged 12 years, with the consent of her Mother, to Joseph Latham, Shipwright, and Jane, his wife, Seamstriss and Manto Maker, for five years from date, Said Hannah to be taught "to make Mantos, Pettycoats, Sew and marke plain worke" etc, With usual Conditions and proviso that in case of the death of Jane Latham these Indentures shall be void.

Signed October 9th 1699, by Hannah Buckmaster, Eliz^th Baldrydg.

In the presence of, Elizabeth Farmer, Will. Sharpas.

Acknowledged before J. V. Cortlandt.

Recorded for Peter White, ye 4th day of December, Anno. Dom. 1699

Indenture of Mary Buckmaster, aged 13 years, with the Consent of her Mother, to Peter White, Joyner, and Catherine, his wife, Taylor woman, for four years from date, With usual conditions and proviso that in case of the death of Catherine White these Indentures shall be null and void. .

Signed October 9th 1699, by Mary Buckmaster, Eliz^th Baldrydg.

In the presence of, Adam Baldrydg, Margrette Duncan.

Acknowledged before J. V. Cortlandt.

Recorded for Mr. Richard Stoaks the 8th day of January Anno Dom. 1700

Indenture of Mary Moore, aged 11 years with consent of her father and mother as apprentice to Richard Stoaks and Margarett his wife, for four years from date. [Usual form.] Said apprentice to be taught "to Sew Plaine worke and Read the English Tongue."

Signed December 11th 1700 by Mary Moore.

In the presence of John Moore, Will Sharpas.

Acknowledged before J. V. Cortlandt.

Recorded for John Shepard, the third day of February 1701/2

Indenture of Ann Skreen, aged 10 years, a poor fatherless and motherless child, with the consent of Rachel Graham, widow, to whose care she was left by her parents, deceased, before Thomas Noell, Esqre Mayor, to John Shepard, Cooper, and Mary, his wife, for 8 years from date.

[In usual form.] Said apprentice to be taught housewifery; also "to Read the English tongue."

Signed February 3d 1701, by Ann Skreen.

In the presence of Tho. Noell, Mayor, Rachel Graham, Will.
Sharpas.

*Recorded for Maude, a Negro Woman, ye 9th day of July, Anno. Dom.
1702*

This Indenture Wittnesseth that Col° Lewis Morris of New York
in America and Mary his wife for the Real Love kindness and
Affection that they bear unto Ann the Daughter of Thomas
Rudyard of New East Jersey of their Own Voluntary good Will doe
give freely unto the Said Ann Rudyard the use & Service of One
Negro maid Named Maude for and during the Space and Terme of
Eighteen Years from the day of the Date hereof During all which
time the Said Maude is faithfully to Serve the Said Ann Rudyard as
her Mistriss in all things Obeying and performing her just
Commands to her utmost Endeavoer as becometh And the Said Ann
Rudyard doth hereby Covenant & promise for her Selfe her Heirs
Executors and Administrators att the Expiration of the Said Terme
of Eighteen Years to give unto the Said Maude three Suits of
Apparell Either of Searge or Stuff with Lynen answerable and then
to Sett her the Said Maude at Liberty giving her freedom from any
and all manner of Service Whatsoever to goe and dwell where Shee
the Said Maude Shall think fitt and in the mean time to find her
with Sufficient Meat drinke lodging and Apparrell fitt for Such a
Servant to have and in due manner to Chastize her According to
desert.

In Wittness to all wch the parties Aforesaid to these presents have
Interchangeably Sett their Hands and Seals the Eighth day of the
third Month Caled May. . . .

                                                      Ann Rudyard

Signed Sealed & Delivered in the presence of Joⁿ Lawrence
Junio^r, John Pett, Wm. Bickley.

Recorded for John Crooke, the 27th day of July Anno. Dom. 1702

Indenture of Margarett Colly, daughter of James Colly, with the consent of her father, to John Crooke, Cooper, and Guartery, his wife for seven years from date.

[Usual form.] Apprentice "Shall be taught to read English with Such Other Needle worke and Other matters fitting for a good housewife of her ability."

Signed July 13th 1702. Margarett Colly.

In the presence of Tho. Noell, Mayor.

Recorded for Mr. David Vilant, the 29th day of August, Anno. Dom. 1705

Indenture made August 3d 1705 between David Vilant and Elizabeth his wife, and Mary Berry, by which Mary Berry apprentices herself as a Servant for seven years from date.

[Usual form.] A supplementary clause provides that all clothing given to Mary Berry shall not be taken from her at the expiration of the term.

Signed August 3d 1705 by David Vilant, Mary Berry.

In the presence of Geo. Duncan, Barth. Feurt.

Acknowledged August 29th 1705, before William Peartree, Mayor.

Recorded for William Horsewell, the 16th day of April, Anno. Dom. 1707

New York ss.

Indenture of Francis Bassett, son of Francis Bassett late of this Province, with the consent of his Mother Marie Magdelen, to William Horsewell, Pewterer, and "Hannah his wife if She Shall Survive him and Continue in the State of Widdowhood and also shall think fitt to prosecute and Carry on the Said Trade" as "An Apprentice within the Province of New York and in no Other place" for seven years from date.

[Usual form, with additions as above.] Also additional provision by Master and Mistress as follows: "And the Said William

Horsewell and Hannah his wife doth hereby promise that in Case of
Mortality of Either of them the Survivor will not for any Cause or
under any pretence whatsoever without the Consent of him the Said
Apprentice and Such of his Relations as he the Said Apprentice
Shall think fitt to take Advice from."

Signed, May 1st 1706, by Francis Bassett.

In the Presence of Barth. Feurt, Edward Pennant.

Acknowledged April 15th 1707, by Francis Bassett, and his
mother Maria Magdelen Bassett, before William Peartree, Mayor.

Recorded for Henry Swift, the 18th day of April, Anno. Dom. 1707

Indenture of Anne Swinney, daughter of Anne Davis, as
Apprentice to Henry Swift, Vintner, for ten years from date.

[Usual form.] Signed, April 15th 1706, by Anne Swinney.

In the presence of J. Stevens, Thomas Hooton, Anne Davis.

Acknowledged April 18th 1707, before William Peartree,
Mayor.

WOMEN AND REVOLUTIONARY IDEOLOGY

The correspondence of Abigail Smith Adams (1744–1818)
indicates that educated women of the Revolutionary generation were
aware of the potential of Revolutionary ideology for enlarging their
legal rights. Although her husband, John Adams, responded
frivolously to her initiatives, Abigail's letter to Mercy Otis Warren
suggests the seriousness and strength of her conviction.

Abigail Adams had no formal education but on her own she
became literate, taught herself French, and read widely in history.
Beginning with John's departure in 1774 for the First Continental
Congress, she spent almost ten years alone as mistress of the
household, educator of the children, and manager of the family's
farm and modest business affairs, applying rigid economy. After
1790, she continued to direct these affairs first from New York,
then Philadelphia, and finally Europe.

FROM THE CORRESPONDENCE OF ABIGAIL SMITH ADAMS

To John Adams

Braintree, March 31, 1776

I wish you would ever write me a Letter half as long as I write you; and tell me if you may where your Fleet are gone? What sort of Defence Virginia can make against our common Enemy? Whether it is so situated as to make an able Defence? Are not the Gentery Lords and the common people vassals, are they not like the uncivilized Natives Brittain represents us to be? I hope their Riffel Men who have shewen themselves very savage and even Blood thirsty; are not a specimen of the Generality of the people.

I am willing to allow the Colony great merit for having produced a Washington but they have been shamefully duped by a Dunmore.

I have sometimes been ready to think that the passion for Liberty cannot be Eaquelly Strong in the Breasts of those who have been accustomed to deprive their fellow Creatures of theirs. Of this I am certain that it is not founded upon that generous and christian princical of doing to others as we would that others should do unto us.

Do not you want to see Boston; I am fearfull of the small pox, or I should have been in before this time. I got Mr. Crane to go to our House and see what state it was in. I find it has been occupied by one of the Doctors of a Regiment, very dirty, but no other damage has been done to it. The few things which were left in it are all gone. Cranch has the key which he never delivered up. I have wrote to him for it and am determined to get it cleand as soon as possible and shut it up. I look upon it a new acquisition of property, a property which one month ago I did not value at a single Shilling, and could with pleasure have seen it in flames.

The Town in General is left in a better state than we expected, more oweing to a percipitate flight than any Regard to the inhabitants, tho some individuals discovered a sense of honour and justice and have left the rent of the Houses in which they were, for the owners and the furniture unhurt, or if damaged sufficient to make it good.

From L. H. Butterfield, ed., *Adams Family Correspondence*, vol. 1 (Cambridge, Mass.: Harvard University Press, 1963), pp. 369–70, 381–83, 396–98, and 401–03, by permission of the publisher.

Others have committed abominable Ravages. The Mansion House of your President is safe and the furniture unhurt whilst both the House and Furniture of the Solisiter General have fallen a prey to their own merciless party. Surely the very Fiends feel a Reverential awe for Virtue and patriotism, whilst they Detest the paricide and traitor.

I feel very differently at the approach of spring to what I did a month ago. We knew not then whether we could plant or sow with safety, whether when we had toild we could reap the fruits of our own industery, whether we could rest in our own Cottages, or whether we should not be driven from the sea coasts to seek shelter in the wilderness, but now we feel as if we might sit under our own vine and eat the good of the land.

I feel a gaieti de Coar to which before I was a stranger. I think the Sun looks brighter, the Birds sing more melodiously, and Nature puts on a more chearfull countanance. We feel a temporary peace, and the poor fugitives are returning to their deserted habitations.

Tho we felicitate ourselves, we sympathize with those who are trembling least the Lot of Boston should be theirs. But they cannot be in similar circumstances unless pusilanimity and cowardise should take possession of them. They have time and warning given them to see the Evil and shun it.—I long to hear that you have declared an independancy—and by the way in the new Code of Laws which I suppose it will be necessary for you to make I desire you would Remember the Ladies, and be more generous and favourable to them than your ancestors. Do not put such unlimited power into the hands of the Husbands. Remember all Men would be tyrants if they could. If perticuliar care and attention is not paid to the Laidies we are determined to foment a Rebelion, and will not hold ourselves bound by any Laws in which we have no voice, or Representation.

That your Sex are Naturally Tyrannical is a Truth so thoroughly established as to admit of no dispute, but such of you as wish to be happy willingly give up the harsh title of Master for the more tender and endearing one of Friend. Why then, not put it out of the power of the vicious and the Lawless to use us with cruelty and indignity with impunity. Men of Sense in all Ages abhor those customs which treat us only as the vassals of your Sex. Regard us then as Beings placed by providence under your protection and in immitation of the Supreem Being make use of that power only for our happiness.

From John Adams

Ap. 14, 1776

You justly complain of my short Letters, but the critical State of Things and the Multiplicity of Avocations must plead my Excuse.— You ask where the Fleet is. The inclosed Papers will inform you. You ask what Sort of Defence Virginia can make. I believe they will make an able Defence. Their Militia and minute Men have been some time employed in training them selves, and they have Nine Battallions of regulars as they call them, maintained among them, under good Officers, at the Continental Expence. They have set up a Number of Manufactories of Fire Arms, which are busily employed. They are tolerably supplied with Powder, and are successfull and assiduous, in making Salt Petre. Their neighbouring Sister or rather Daughter Colony of North Carolina, which is a warlike Colony, and has several Battallions at the Continental Expence, as well as a pretty good Militia, are ready to assist them, and they are in very good Spirits, and seem determined to make a brave Resistance.—The Gentry are very rich, and the common People very poor. This Inequality of Property, gives an Aristocratical Turn to all their Proceedings and occasions a strong Aversion in their Patricians, to Common Sense. But the Spirit of these Barons, is coming down, and it must submit.

It is very true, as you observe they have been duped by Dunmore. But this is a Common Case. All the Colonies are duped, more or less, at one Time and another. A more egregious Bubble was never blown up, than the Story of Commissioners coming to treat with the Congress. Yet it has gained Credit like a Charm, not only without but against the clearest Evidence. I never shall forget the Delusion, which seized our best and most sagacious Friends the dear Inhabitants of Boston, the Winter before last. Credulity and the Want of Foresight, are Imperfections in the human Character, that no Politician can sufficiently guard against.

You have given me some Pleasure, by your Account of a certain

House in Queen Street. I had burned it, long ago, in Imagination. It rises now to my View like a Phoenix.—What shall I say of the Solicitor General? I pity his pretty Children, I pity his Father, and his sisters. I wish I could be clear that it is no moral Evil to pity him and his Lady. Upon Repentance they will certainly have a large Share in the Compassions of many. But let Us take Warning and give it to our Children. Whenever Vanity, and Gaiety, a Love of Pomp and Dress, Furniture, Equipage, Buildings, great Company, expensive Diversions, and elegant Entertainments get the better of the Principles and Judgments of Men or Women there is no knowing where they will stop, nor into what Evils, natural, moral, or political, they will lead us.

Your Description of your own Gaiety de Coeur, charms me. Thanks be to God you have just Cause to rejoice—and may the bright Prospect be obscured by no Cloud.

As to Declarations of Independency, be patient. Read our Privateering Laws, and our Commercial Laws. What signifies a Word.

As to your extraordinary Code of Laws, I cannot but laugh. We have been told that our Struggle has loosened the bands of Government every where. That Children and Apprentices were disobedient—that schools and Colledges were grown turbulent— that Indians slighted their Guardians and Negroes grew insolent to their Masters. But your Letter was the first Intimation that another Tribe more numerous and powerfull than all the rest were grown discontented.—This is rather too coarse a Compliment but you are so saucy, I wont blot it out.

Depend upon it, We know better than to repeal our Masculine systems. Altho they are in full Force, you know they are little more than Theory. We dare not exert our Power in its full Latitude. We are obliged to go fair, and softly, and in Practice you know We are the subjects. We have only the Name of Masters, and rather than give up this, which would compleatly subject Us to the Despotism of the Petticoat, I hope General Washington, and all our brave Heroes would fight. I am sure every good Politician would plot, as long as he would against Despotism, Empire, Monarchy, Aristocracy, Oligarchy, or Ochlocracy.—A fine Story indeed. I begin to think the Ministry as deep as they are wicked. After stirring up Tories, Landjobbers, Trimmers, Bigots, Canadians, Indians, Negroes, Hanoverians, Hessians, Russians, Irish Roman Catholicks, Scotch Renegadoes, at last they have stimulated the [women] to demand new Priviledges and threaten to rebell.

To Mercy Otis Warren

Braintree, April 27, 1776

I set myself down to comply with my Friends request, who I think seem's rather low spiritted.

I did write last week, but not meeting with an early conveyance I thought the Letter of But little importance and tos'd it away. I acknowledg my Thanks due to my Friend for the entertainment she so kindly afforded me in the Characters drawn in her Last Letter, and if coveting my Neighbours Goods was not prohibited by the Sacred Law, I should be most certainly tempted to envy her the happy talant she possesses above the rest of her Sex, by adorning with her pen even trivial occurances, as well as dignifying the most important. Cannot you communicate some of those Graces to your Friend and suffer her to pass them upon the World for her own that she may feel a little more upon an Eaquality with you?—Tis true I often receive large packages from P[hiladelphi]a. They contain as I said before more News papers than Letters, tho they are not forgotton. It would be hard indeed if absence had not some alleviations.

I dare say he writes to no one unless to Portia oftner than to your Friend, because I know there is no one besides in whom he has an eaquel confidence. His Letters to me have been generally short, but he pleads in Excuse the critical state of affairs and the Multiplicity of avocations and says further that he has been very Busy, and writ near ten Sheets of paper, about some affairs which he does not chuse to Mention for fear of accident.

He is very sausy to me in return for a List of Female Grievances which I transmitted to him. I think I will get you to join me in a petition to Congress. I thought it was very probable our wise Statesmen would erect a New Government and form a new code of

Laws. I ventured to speak a word in behalf of our Sex, who are rather hardly dealt with by the Laws of England which gives such unlimitted power to the Husband to use his wife Ill.

I requested that our Legislators would consider our case and as all Men of Delicacy and Sentiment are averse to Exercising the power they possess, yet as there is a natural propensity in Humane Nature to domination, I thought the most generous plan was to put it out of the power of the arbitary and tyranick to injure us with impunity by Establishing some Laws in our favour upon just and Liberal principals.

I believe I even threatned fomenting a Rebellion in case we were not considered, and assured him we would not hold ourselves bound by any Laws in which we had neither a voice, nor representation.

In return he tells me he cannot but Laugh at My Extrodonary Code of Laws. That he had heard their Struggle had loosned the bands of Government, that children and apprentices were dissabedient, that Schools and Colledges were grown turbulant, that Indians slighted their Guardians, and Negroes grew insolent to their Masters. But my Letter was the first intimation that another Tribe more numerous and powerfull than all the rest were grown discontented. This is rather too coarse a complement, he adds, but that I am so sausy he wont blot it out.

So I have help'd the Sex abundantly, but I will tell him I have only been making trial of the Disintresstedness of his Virtue, and when weigh'd in the balance have found it wanting.

It would be bad policy to grant us greater power say they since under all the disadvantages we Labour we have the assendancy over their Hearts

And charm by accepting, by submitting sway.

I wonder Apollo and the Muses could not have indulged me with a poetical Genious. I have always been a votary to her charms but never could assend Parnassus myself.

I am very sorry to hear of the indisposition of your Friend. I am affraid it will hasten his return, and I do not think he can be spaired.

Though certain pains attend the cares of State
A Good Man owes his Country to be great

Should act abroad the high distinguished part
or shew at least the purpose of his heart.

Good Night my Friend. You will be so good as to remember me
to our worthy Friend Mrs. W———e when you see her and write
soon to your

Portia

To John Adams

B[raintre]e, May 7, 1776

How many are the solitary hours I spend, ruminating upon the
past, and anticipating the future, whilst you overwhelmd with the
cares of State, have but few moments you can devote to any
individual. All domestick pleasures and injoyments are absorbed in
the great and important duty you owe your Country "for our
Country is as it were a secondary God, and the First and greatest
parent. It is to be preferred to Parents, Wives, Children, Friends
and all things the Gods only excepted. For if our Country perishes it
is as imposible to save an individual, as to preserve one of the fingers
of a Mortified Hand." Thus do I supress every wish, and silence
every Murmer, acquiesceing in a painfull Seperation from the
companion of my youth, and the Friend of my Heart.

I believe 'tis near ten days since I wrote you a line. I have not felt
in a humour to entertain you. If I had taken up my pen perhaps
some unbecomeing invective might have fallen from it; the Eyes of
our Rulers have been closed and a Lethargy has seazd almost every
Member. I fear a fatal Security has taken possession of them. Whilst
the Building is on flame they tremble at the expence of water to
quench it, in short two months has elapsed since the evacuation of
Boston, and very little has been done in that time to secure it, or the
Harbour from future invasion 'till the people are all in a flame; and
no one among us that I have heard of even mentions expence, they
think universally that there has been an amaizing neglect some
where. Many have turned out as volunteers to work upon Nodles
Island, and many more would go upon Nantaskit if it was once set
on foot. " 'Tis a Maxim of state That power and Liberty are like

Heat and moisture; where they are well mixt every thing prospers, where they are single, they are destructive."

A Goverment of more Stability is much wanted in this colony, and they are ready to receive it from the Hands of the Congress, and since I have begun with Maxims of State I will add an other viz. that a people may let a king fall, yet sill remain a people, but if a king let his people slip from him, he is no longer a king. And as this is most certainly our case, why not proclaim to the World in decisive terms your own importance?

Shall we not be dispiced by foreign powers for hesitateing so long at a word?

I can not say that I think you very generous to the Ladies, for whilst you are proclaiming peace and good will to Men, Emancipating all Nations, you insist upon retaining an absolute power over Wives. But you must remember that Arbitary power is like most other things which are very hard, very liable to be broken—and notwithstanding all your wise Laws' and Maxims we have it in our power not only to free outselves but to subdue our Masters, and without violence throw both your natural and legal authority at our feet—

> Charm by accepting, by submitting sway
> Yet have our Humour most when we obey.

I thank you for several Letters which I have received since I wrote Last. They alleviate a tedious absence, and I long earnestly for a Saturday Evening, and experience a similar pleasure to that which I used to find in the return of my Friend upon that day after a weeks absence. The Idea of a year dissolves all my Phylosophy.

Our Little ones whom you so often recommend to my care and instruction shall not be deficient in virtue or probity if the precepts of a Mother have their desired Effect, but they would be doubly inforced could they be indulged with the example of a Father constantly before them; I often point them to their Sire

> engaged in a corrupted State
> Wrestling with vice and faction.

May 9

I designd to have finished the sheet, but an opportunity offering I close only just inform you that May the 7 our privateers took two prises in the Bay in fair sight of the Man of war, one a Brig from Irland the other from fyall [Fayal] loaded with wine Brandy and the other Beaf &c. The wind was East and a flood tide, so that the tenders could not get out tho they tried several times, the Light house fired Signal guns, but all would not do, they took them in triumph and carried them into Lyn.

Johnny and Charls have the Mumps, a bad disorder, but they are not very bad. Pray be kind enough to remember me at all times and write as often as you possibly can to your

Portia

BENJAMIN FRANKLIN ON WOMEN

Prominent among the colonial men most enlightened on the subject of women was Benjamin Franklin. However, Abigail Adams would have had no more luck petitioning Franklin than she did her husband, because even Franklin's attitudes were highly ambiguous and supported inferior roles for women. Although Franklin questioned the proposition that women were innately inferior, a view that seventeenth- and eighteenth-century men usually upheld by reference to scriptural authority, he did believe that women were less competent in society than men. He attributed their inferiority to inferior education and, accordingly, promoted the placing of women's education on a nonreligious basis. But he did not see improved education as equipping women to compete with men on an equal footing. Proper education, he proposed, should equip future wives to be more effective custodians of their husband's property, more learned educators of their children, and better-informed helpmates. (The practical character of Franklin's concept of the ideal wife, when united during the nineteenth century with a romantic-religious definition of the function of women, would yield the ideal of the Victorian woman and the educational system designed for her training.) The following letter suggests Franklin's notion of the ideal wife, including the obvious ambiguities of his view.

Although Franklin received practical support from his wife, Deborah, in managing his affairs, she did not grow intellectually and could not share in the development of his ideas. Franklin remained devoted to her, despite having illegitimate children and numerous extramarital escapades, some simply flirtations and others quite amorous. He praised and thanked Deborah often for her frugal qualities and her devotedness, but in his writing he stressed the desirability in marriage of qualities lacking in his own—frank sincerity and intellectual compatibility.

It should be noted that Victorian prudery and respect for the founding fathers resulted in the supression of Franklin's "A Letter on Marriage" until the 1920s. Previously, editors and biographers had refused to reproduce it, leaving its circulation to private printings.

"A Letter on Marriage"

June 25, 1745

My dear Friend

I know of no Medicine fit to diminish the violent natural Inclinations you mention; and if I did, I think I should not communicate it to you. Marriage is the proper Remedy. It is the most natural State of Man, and therefore the State in which you are most likely to find solid Happiness. Your Reasons against entering into it at present appear to me not well-founded. The circumstantial Advantages you have in View by postponing it, are not only uncertain, but they are small in comparison with that of the Thing itself, the being *married and settled*. It is the Man and Woman united that make the compleat human Being. Separate, she wants his Force of Body and Strength of Reason; he, her softness, Sensibility, and acute Discernment. Together they are more likely to succeed in the World. A single Man has not nearly the Value he would have in the State of Union. He is an incomplete Animal. He

From Leonard W. Labaree, ed., *The Papers of Benjamin Franklin*, vol. 3 (New Haven: Yale University Press, 1961), pp. 30–31.

resembles the odd Half of a Pair of Scissars. If you get a prudent, healthy Wife, your Industry in your Profession, with her good Economy, will be a Fortune sufficent.

But if you will not take this Counsel and persist in thinking a Commerce with the Sex inevitable, then I repeat my former Advice, that in all your Amours you should *prefer old Women to young ones*. You call this a Paradox and demand my reasons. They are these:

1. Because they have more Knowledge of the World, and their Minds are better stor'd with Observations, their Conversation is more improving, and more lastingly agreeable.

2. Because when Women cease to be handsome they study to be good. To maintain their Influence over Men, they supply the diminution of Beauty by an Augmentation of Utility. They learn to do 1,000 Services small and great, and are the most tender and useful of all Friends when you are sick. Thus they continue amiable. And hence there is hardly such a thing to be found as an Old Woman who is not a good Woman.

3. Because there is no Hazard of Children, which irregularly produc'd may be attended with much Inconvenience.

4. Because thro' more Experience, they are more prudent and discreet in conducting an Intrigue to prevent Suspicion. The Commerce with them is therefore safer with regard to your Reputation. And with regard to theirs, if the Affair should happen to be known, considerate People might be rather inclin'd to excuse an old Woman, who would kindly take care of a young Man, form his Manners by her good Counsels, and prevent his ruining his Health and Fortune among mercenary Prostitutes.

5. Because in every Animal that walks upright, the Deficiency of the Fluids that fill the Muscles appears first in the highest Part. The Face first grows lank and wrinkled; then the Neck; then the Breast and Arms; the lower Parts continuing to the Last as plump as ever: so that covering all above with a Basket, and regarding only what is below the Girdle, it is impossible of two Women to tell an old one from a young one. And as in the dark all Cats are grey, the Pleasure of corporal Enjoyment with an old Woman is at least equal, and frequently superior; every Knack being, by Practice, capable of Improvement.

6. Because the Sin is less. The debauching a Virgin may be her Ruin, and make her for Life unhappy.

7. Because the Compunction is less. The having made a young Girl *miserable* may give you frequent bitter Reflection; none of which can attend the making an old Woman *happy*.

8thly & lastly. They are *so grateful*!!

Thus much for my Paradox. But still I advise you to marry directly; being sincerely Your affectionate Friend.

                                                                Benjamin Franklin

II

Women on Farms

The economic development of the first half of the nineteenth century is most noted for the rise of the factory system. However, even as late as 1860, most of the American labor force was to be found on the nation's farms. If farm wives had been included in the labor-force counts, the proportion undoubtedly would have been higher. As had been the case during the colonial period, in the nineteenth century women did much of their work within households, rather than in the fields, and that work tended to be unspecialized in character, despite the premium attached to economic specialization by the social norm of economic growth. Consequently, there is a lack of firm data on the extent and character of economic participation, particularly for those farm women who were not working for wages. There are no reliable measures of the share of farm work performed by women in different parts of the nation, in different family situations, and in different periods. Nor is there a rigorous definition of the general character of women's farm work, particularly the extent to which it was distinguished from the work of men. We do have strong impressions, however.

For women on farms, work was more similar to that of men than was the case for urban women. Women's farm work was extremely diverse—indeed, as it ranged across the entire span of possible economic activity, it was more varied than the work of women removed from the countryside. And, as agriculture underwent an industrial revolution of its own (most marked in the late nineteenth century), women found themselves participating, for the most part, in lower-productivity activities—just as was their lot in urban society.

The lack of a sharp definition of women's agricultural work places an unusually high value on literary sources that reflect on the breadth of that work. The readings that follow will elucidate that breadth, providing examples of farm women living and working in a variety of situations, facing limited, but diverse, opportunities to develop skills and self-esteem; assessing their possibilities with a wide range of shadings; and often achieving awesome feats in the marketplace.

SLAVE WOMEN

Between 1936 and 1938, more than three hundred interviewers working with the New Deal Federal Writers Project (FWP) interviewed more than twenty-two hundred ex-slaves (over two per cent of the ex-slave population then alive) in seventeen states. Despite the massiveness of the sample, care must be exercised in using the interviews. Most of the interviewees were elderly persons recalling childhood experiences which, even if remembered accurately may not have reflected on the entirety of the slave system. Moreover, most of the interviewers were Southern whites who lacked adequate guidelines with respect to interviewing procedures. Nonetheless, those accounts that describe childhood and early maturity, focus attention on an important, but neglected, aspect of the social history of slavery; often the white interviewers did show sensitivity to the racism that clouded the interview process; and the large minority of black interviewers regularly elicited sharp-toned narratives. Thus, with respect to the implications of slavery for the work of black women, the data gathered by the FWP offers students considerable, largely unexploited evidence that helps to answer a variety of questions: How and to what extent were young girls conditioned for heavy field work? To what degree were maturing women offered incentives for childbearing? What were the extent and significance of physical oppression and punishment, including rape, in the conditioning of young slave women? How were certain young women selected for household service? To what extent were young women allowed to develop a home and family life of their own? Is it true that slavery included a deliberate and effective program to stifle the development of black family life? If so, were women more thoroughly involved in work similar to that of men than they were under a free-labor system? How did slave women respond to the conditioning practiced by slaveowners? What tactics did slave women use to advance their interests? To what extent were models of relatively strong, independent women available to young girls?

The following two selections from the FWP obviously cannot provide answers to very many of these questions.* But they can suggest answers to some and direct students to the FWP interviews as an invaluable source for exploring both the experience and consciousness of black women who spent their formative years in servitude.

MARTHA BRADLEY: MEMOIRS OF AN EX-SLAVE (1937)

Aunt Martha, as she is known to all her "white folks," claims to be 100 years old. She was a slave to Dr. Lucas of Mt. Meigs neighborhood long before the War between the States. Dr. Lucas is one of the well-known Lucas family, with whom General LaFayette spent some time while touring the United States in 1824.

"Our Marster wuz sho good to all his niggers," she said. "Us allus had plenty to eat and plenty to wear, but de days now is hard, if white folks gin you a nickel or dime to git you sumpin' t' eat you has to write everything down in a book before you can git it. I allus

---

* The most stimulating recent attempt to develop rigorous answers to some of these questions is Robert W. Fogel and Stanley L. Engerman, *Time on the Cross, The Economics of American Negro Slavery*, vol. 1 (Boston: Little, Brown, 1974), pp. 126–44. However, the authors admit that analysis of the critical relationships between slavery and demographic change is "still at a preliminary stage" (vol. 2, p. 114).

From Federal Writers Project. *Slave Narratives, A Folk History of Slavery in the U.S.*, vol. 1, Alabama Narratives, microfilmed by Library of Congress (Washington, D.C., 1941), pp. 46–47.

worked in the field, had to carry big logs, had strops on my arms and them logs was put in de strop and hauled to a pile where they all wuz. One morning hit was rainin' and I didn' wanna go to the field, but de oversee' he came and got me and started whooping me, I jumped on him and bit and kicked him 'til he lemme go, I didn't know no better then, I didn't know he was de one to do dat.

"But Marster Lucas gin us big times on Christmas and July. Us 'ud have big dinners and all the lemonade us could drink. The dinner'd be spread out on de ground an' all the niggers would stand roun' and eat all dey wanted. What was lef' us'd take it to our cabins. Nancy Lucas wuz de cook fer eber' body. Well, she'd sho cook good cake and had plenty of 'em but she wouldn't lak to cut dem cakes often. She keep 'em in a safe. One day I go to dat safe and I seed some and I wanted it so bad till I jes' had to have some. Nancy say to me, 'Martha, did you cut dat cake?' I say, 'No sir! dat knife just flew 'roun by itself and cut dat cake.'

"One day I wuz workin' in de field and de overseer he come 'roun and say sumpin' to me he had no bizness say. I took my hoe and knocked him plum down. I knowed I'se done sumpin' bad so I run to de bushes. Marster Lucas come and got me and started whoopin' me. I say to Marster Lucas whut dat overseer sez to me and Marster Lucas didn' hit me no more. Marse Lucas wuz allus good to us and he wouldn' let nobody run over his niggers.

"There wuz plenty white folks dat wuz sho bad to de niggers, and specially dem overseers. A nigger whut lived on the plantation jinin' ours shot and killed an overseer; den he run 'way. He come to de river and seed a white man on udder side and say, 'Come and git me.' Well, when dey got him dey found out whut he'd done, and wuz gwine to burn him 'live. Jedge Clements, the man dat keep law and order, say he wouldn't burn a dog 'live, so he lef'. But dey sho burn dat nigger 'live for I seed him atter he wuz burned up.

"Us'd go to meetin' to de Antioch Church some Sundays. Us'd go to de house and git a pass. When us'd pass by the *patterole*, us jes' hold up our pass and den us'd go on. Dar wuz a 'vidin' 'twixt de niggers and de white folks. De white preacher'd preach; den de colored man. Us'd stay at church most all day. When we didn' go to church, us'd git together in the quarters and have preachin' and singin' amongst ourselves.

"In cotton pickin' time us'd stay in de field till way atter dark and us'd pick by candle light and den carry hit and put hit on de scaffold. In de winter time us'd quilt; jes' go from one house to anudder in de quarter. Us'd weave all our ever' day clothes but Marster Lucas'd go to Mobile ever' July and Christmas and git our Sunday clothes, git us dresses and shoes and we'd sho be proud of 'em.

"In slavery time dey doctored de sick folks dif'funt frum what dey does now. I seed a man so sick dey had to put medicine down his throat lak he wuz a horse. Dat man got well and sho lived to turn a key in de jail. Ef it wuz in dese days dat man would be cay'd to de hospital and cut open lak a hawg.

"Dere wuz a slave whut lived in Macon county. He run 'way and when he wuz cetched dey dug a hole in de ground and put him crost it and beat him nigh to death."

Rose Williams

"What I say am the facts. If I's one day old, I's way over ninety, and I's born in Bell County, right here in Texas, and am owned by Massa William Black. He owns Mammy and Pappy, too. Massa Black has a big plantation, but he has more niggers than he need for work on that place, 'cause he am a nigger trader. He trade and buy and sell all the time.

"Massa Black am awful cruel, and he whip the colored folks and works 'em hard and feed 'em poorly. We-uns have for rations the corn meal and milk and 'lasses and some beans and peas and meat once a week. We-uns have to work in the field every day from daylight 'til dark, and on Sunday we-uns do us washing. Church? Shucks, we-uns don't know what that mean.

"I has the correct memorandum of when the war start. Massa Black sold we-uns right then. Mammy and Pappy powerful glad to git sold, and they and I is put on the block with 'bout ten other

From Federal Writers Project. *Slave Narratives, A Folk History of Slavery in the U.S.*, vol. 16, Texas Narratives, part IV, microfilmed by Library of Congress (Washington, D.C., 1941), pp. 174–78.

niggers. When we-uns gits to the trading block, there lots of white folks there what come to look us over. One man shows the interest in Pappy. Him named Hawkins. He talk to Pappy, and Pappy talk to him and say, 'Them my woman and childs. Please buy all of us and have mercy on we-uns.' Massa Hawkins say, 'That gal am a likely-looking nigger; she am portly and strong. But three am more than I wants, I guesses.'

"The sale start, and 'fore long Pappy am put on the block. Massa Hawkins wins the bid for Pappy, and when Mammy am put on the block, he wins the bid for her. Then there am three or four other niggers sold before my time comes. Then Massa Black calls me to the block, and the auction man say, 'What am I offer for this portly, strong young wench. She's never been 'bused and will make the good breeder.'

"I wants to hear Massa Hawkins bid, but him say nothing. Two other men am bidding 'gainst each other, and I sure has the worriment. There am tears coming down my cheeks 'cause I's being sold to some man that would make separation from my mammy. One man bids $500, and the auction man ask, 'Do I hear more? She am gwine at $500.' Then someone say, '$525,' and the auction man say, 'She am sold for $525 to Massa Hawkins.' Am I glad and 'cited! Why, I's quivering all over.

"Massa Hawkins takes we-uns to his place, and it am a nice plantation. Lots better than Massa Black's. There is 'bout fifty niggers what is growed and lots of children. The first thing Massa do when we-uns gits home am give we-uns rations and a cabin. You must believe this nigger when I says them rations a feast for us. There plenty meat and tea and coffee and white flour. I's never tasted white flour and coffee, and Mammy fix some biscuits and coffee. Well, the biscuits was yum, yum, yum to me, but the coffee I doesn't like.

"The quarters am pretty good. There am twelve cabins all made from logs and a table and some benches and bunks for sleeping and a fireplace for cooking and the heat. There am no floor, just the ground.

"Massa Hawkins am good to he niggers and not force 'em work too hard. There am as much difference 'tween him and Old Massa

Black in the way of treatment as 'twixt the Lord and the devil. Massa Hawkins 'lows he niggers have reasonable parties and go fishing, but we-uns am never tooken to church and has no books for larning. There am no education for the niggers.

"There am one thing Massa Hawkins does to me what I can't shunt from my mind. I knows he don't do it for meanness, but I always holds it 'gainst him. What he done am force me to live with that nigger, Rufus, 'gainst my wants.

"After I been at he place 'bout a year, the massa come to me and say, 'You gwine live with Rufus in that cabin over yonder. Go fix it for living.' I's 'bout sixteen year old and has no larning, and I's just ignomus child. I's thought that him mean for me to tend the cabin for Rufus and some other niggers. Well, that am start the pestigation for me.

"I's took charge of the cabin after work am done and fixes supper. Now, I don't like that Rufus, 'cause he a bully. He am big and 'cause he so, he think everybody do what him say. We-uns has supper, then I goes here and there talking, till I's ready for sleep, and then I gits in the bunk. After I's in, that nigger come and crawl in the bunk with me 'fore I knows it. I says, 'What you means, you fool nigger?' He say for me to hush the mouth. 'This am my bunk, too,' he say.

" 'You's teched in the head. Git out,' I's told him, and I puts the feet 'gainst him and give him a shove, and out he go on the floor 'fore he know what I's doing. That nigger jump up and he mad. He look like the wild bear. He starts for the bunk, and I jumps quick for the poker. It am 'bout three feet long, and when he comes at me I lets him have it over the head. Did that nigger stop in he tracks? I's say he did. He looks at me steady for a minute, and you could tell he thinking hard. Then he go and set on the bench and say, 'Just wait. You thinks it am smart, but you am foolish in the head. They's gwine larn you something.'

" 'Hush your big mouth and stay 'way from this nigger, that all I wants,' I say, and just sets and hold that poker in the hand. He just sets, looking like the bull. There we-uns sets and sets for 'bout an hour, and then he go out, and I bars the door.

"The next day I goes to the missy and tells her what Rufus wants, and Missy say that am the massa's wishes. She say, 'You am the portly gal, and Rufus am the portly man. The massa wants you-uns for to bring forth portly children.'

"I's thinking 'bout what the missy say, but say to myself, 'I's not gwine live with that Rufus.' That night when him come in the cabin, I grabs the poker and sits on the bench and says, 'Git 'way from me, nigger, 'fore I bust your brains out and stomp on them.' He say nothing and git out.

"The next day the massa call me and tell me, 'Woman, I's pay big money for you, and I's done that for the cause I wants you to raise me childrens. I's put you to live with Rufus for that purpose. Now, if you doesn't want whipping at the stake, you do what I wants.'

"I thinks 'bout Massa buying me offen the block and saving me from being separated from my folks and 'bout being whipped at the stake. There it am. What am I's to do? So I 'cides to do as the massa wish, and so I yields.

"When we-uns am given freedom, Massa Hawkins tells us we can stay and work for wages or sharecrop the land. Some stays and some goes. My folks and me stays. We works the land on share for three years, then moved to other land near by. I stays with my folks till they dies.

"If my memorandum am correct, it am 'bout thirty years since I come to Fort Worth. Here I cooks for white folks till I goes blind 'bout ten years ago.

"I never marries, 'cause one 'sperience am 'nough for this nigger. After what I does for the massa, I's never wants no truck with any man. The Lord forgive this colored woman, but he have to 'scuse me and look for some others for to 'plenish the earth."

A PLANTATION OWNER

Elizabeth Allston Pringle (1845–1921) not only owned, but successfully managed, a post–Civil War plantation. She was by no means unique: many Southern white women found themselves owner-managers of plantations after the death of their husbands. Their numbers were relatively greater, and growing more rapidly than those of independent woman farmers in Northern states. Part of the reason apparently was that Confederate landowners had experienced a higher rate of mortality than Union landowners and thus left relatively more widows in a position to take up land. The Southern caste system also made it easier for women to control labor in the South than in the North—a two-caste system creates unusually great opportunities for women in the dominant caste, for it allows them to direct the labor of men as well as women of the subordinate caste.

Certainly some of Elizabeth Pringle's acute expertise lay in the realm of labor policy, in which she proved highly adept at manipulating productivity incentives. But the death of a landed husband and the support of the caste system did not always yield success; even an acute individual needed an appropriate role model in order to prosper. Elizabeth Pringle could draw on the experience of generations of frugal, industrious planters in the South Carolina rice tidewater. She found particularly valuable the examples of her father, including his careful writings on rice culture, and her Great-Aunt Blyth, a single woman whose success in managing thousands of rice acres was a family and regional legend.

In 1870, Elizabeth had married a neighboring planter, John Pringle. His early death in 1876 sent her to her mother's household, but after securing title to her husband's property in 1880, Elizabeth assumed control of the plantation. In 1903 the diary in which she recorded her experiences as manager was published in the New York *Sun* under the pen name of Patience Pennington; in 1913, it was published for wider circulation. The following selections are from that diary, beginning with the letter in which Elizabeth introduced herself to readers of the *Sun*.

Elizabeth Pringle on Rice Planting

Cherokee, March 30, 1903

You have asked me to tell of my rice-planting experience, and I will do my best, though I hardly know where to begin.

From Patience Pennington, *A Woman Rice Planter* (New York: Macmillan Co., 1913), pp. 1–5, 38–41, 44, 66–67, 73–75, 286–87, and 445–46.

Some years ago the plantation where I had spent my very short married life, Casa Bianca, was for sale, and against the judgment of the men of my family I decided to put $10,000, every cent I had, in the purchase of it, to grow old in, I said, feeling it a refuge from the loneliness which crushed me. Though opposed to the step, one of my brothers undertook very kindly to manage it until paid for, then to turn it over to me. I had paid $5000 cash and spent $5000 in buying mules, supplies, ploughs, harrows, seed rice, etc., necessary to start and run the place. This left me with a debt of $5000, for which I gave a mortgage. After some years the debt was reduced to $3000, when I awoke to the fact that I had no right to burden and worry my brother any longer with this troublesome addition to his own large planting, and I told him the first of January of 18— that I had determined to relieve him and try it myself. He seemed much shocked and surprised and said it was impossible; how was it possible for me, with absolutely no knowledge of planting or experience, to do anything? It would be much wiser to rent. I said I would gladly do so, but who would rent it? He said he would give me $300 a year for it, just to assist me in this trouble, and I answered that that would just pay the taxes and the interest on the debt, and I would never have any prospect of paying off the mortgage, and, when I died, instead of leaving something to my nieces and nephews, I would leave only a debt. No; I had thought of it well; I would sell the five mules and put that money in bank, and as far as that went I would plant on wages, and the rest of the land I would rent to the negroes at ten bushels to the acre. He was perfectly dismayed; said I would have to advance heavily to them, and nothing but ruin awaited me in such an undertaking.

However, I assembled the hands and told them that all who could not support themselves for a year would have to leave the place. With one accord they declared they could do it; but I explained to them that I was going to take charge myself, that I was a woman, with no resources of money behind me, and, having only the land, I intended to rent to them for ten bushels of rice to the acre. I could advance nothing but the seed. I could give them a chance to work for themselves and prove themselves worthy to be free men. I intended to have no overseer; each man would be entirely responsible for the land he rented. "You know very well," I said, "that this land will bring my ten bushels rent if you just throw the seed in and leave it, so that every stroke of work that you do will go into your own pockets, and I hope you will prove men enough to work for that purpose."

Then I picked out the lazy, shiftless hands and told them they must leave, as I knew they would not work for themselves. All the planters around were eager for hands and worked entirely on wages, and I would only plant fifty acres on wages, which would not be enough to supply all with work. My old foreman, Washington, was most uneasy and miserable, and questioned me constantly as to the wisdom of what I was doing. At last I said to him: "Washington, you do not know whether I have the sense to succeed in this thing, Mass' Tom does not know, I don't know; but we shall know by this time next year, and in the meantime you must just trust me and do the best you can for me."

It proved a great success! I went through the burning suns all that summer, twice a week, five miles in a buggy and six in a boat! I, who had always been timorous, drove myself the five miles entirely alone, hired a strange negro and his boat and was rowed by him to Casa Bianca plantation. Then, with dear old Washington behind me, telling of all the trials and tribulations he had had in getting the work done, I walked around the 200 acres of rice in all stages of beauty and awfulness of smell.

But I was more than repaid. I paid off the debt on the place and lifted the mortgage. I had never hoped for that in one year. My renters also were jubilant; they made handsomely and bought horses and buggies and oxen for the coming year's work. When I had paid off everything, I had not a cent left in the bank to run on, however. Washington was amazed and very happy at the results, but when I said something to him about preparing the wages field for the coming crop, he said very solemnly: "Miss, ef yo' weak, en you wrastle wid a strong man, en de Lo'd gie you strenf fo' trow um down once, don't you try um 'gain." I laughed, but, remembering that I would have to borrow money to plant the field this year, I determined to take the old man's advice and not attempt it. This was most fortunate, for there was a terrible storm that autumn and I would have been ruined. My renters were most fortunate in getting their rice in before the storm, so that they did well again.

From that time I have continued to plant from 20 to 30 acres on wages and to rent from 100 to 150 acres. Of course I have had my ups and downs and many anxious moments. Sometimes I have been so unfortunate as to take as renters those who were unfit to stand alone, and then I have suffered serious loss; but, on the whole, I have been able to keep my head above water, and now and then have a little money to invest. In short, I have done better than most of my neighbors.

Five years ago the head of our family passed away, and the Cherokee plantation, which my father had inherited from his grandfather, had to be sold for a division of the estate. None of my family was able to buy it, and a syndicate seemed the only likely purchaser, and they wanted to get it for very little. So I determined the best thing I could do was to buy it in myself and devote the rest of my life to keeping it in the family, and perhaps at my death some of the younger generation would be able to take it. This would condemn me to a very isolated existence, with much hard work and anxiety; but, after all, work is the greatest blessing, as I have found. I have lived at Cherokee alone ever since, two miles from any white person! With my horses, my dogs, my books, and piano, my life has been a very full one. There are always sick people to be tended and old people to be helped, and I have excellent servants.

My renters here, nearly all own their farms and live on them, coming to their work every day in their ox-wagons or their buggies; for the first thing a negro does when he makes a good crop is to buy a pair of oxen, which he can do for $30, and the next good crop he buys a horse and buggy. . . .

————————

October 16, [1903]

I have threshed the May rice, and it has turned out very well, considering the hard time it had for two months after it was planted.

My wages field made twenty-five bushels to the acre and the hands nearly the same, only a little less, but it is good rice and weighs forty-six pounds to the bushel; and as I hear every one complaining of very light rice, I am thankful it is so good.

October 17, [1903]

I have had an offer of $1.05 for my rice in the rough, and I am going to take it, though I shall miss the cracked rice and the flour which we get when the rice is milled, and the rice will have to be bagged and sewed up, which is a great deal of work; but Mr. S. will pay for it at my mill, and that will relieve my anxiety about money.

October 18, [1903]

A hard day's work, but the sale has been most satisfactory, for as the standard weight per bushel for rice is forty-five, and my rice weighs forty-six or forty-seven, I have a good many more dollars than I had bushels, which is very cheering; and I have had grip and am greatly in need of cheering. Mr. S. weighed every sack and put down the weights and then added up the interminable lines of figures. I added them, too, but was thankful I did not have the responsibility, for they came out differently each time I went over them.

October 24, [1903]

The harvest of my June field (wages) began today. Though very weak and miserable from grip, I drove the twelve miles to Casa Bianca, and in a lovely white piqué suit went down on the bank. I timed myself to get there about 12 o'clock, and as I expected I met a procession of dusky young men and maidens coming out of the field. I greeted them with pleasant words and compliments on their nice appearance, as they all reserve their gayest, prettiest clothes for harvest, and I delight to see them in gay colors, and am careful to pay them the compliment of putting on something pretty myself, which they greatly appreciate. After "passing the time of day," as they call the ordinary polite greetings, I asked each: "How much have you cut?" "A quarter, Miss." "Well, turn right back and cut another quarter—why, surely, Tom, you are not content to leave the field with only a quarter cut! It is but a weakling who would do that!" And so on till I have turned them all back and so saved the day.

A field of twenty-six acres is hard to manage, and unless you can stir their pride and enthusiasm they may take a week over it. One tall, slender girl, a rich, dark brown, and graceful as a deer, whose name is Pallas, when I ask, "How much?" answers, "Three-quarters, Ma'am, an' I'm just goin' to get my break'us an' come back an' cut another quarter." That gives me something to praise, which is always such a pleasure. Then two more young girls have each cut a half acre, so I shame the men and urge them not to let themselves be outdone; and in a little while things are swimming. I break down some of the tops of the canes and make a seat on the bank, and as from time to time they come down to dip their tin buckets in the river to drink, I offer them a piece of candy and one or two biscuits, which I always carry in the very stout leather satchel in which I keep my time-books, etc.

Though the sun is fiery, I feel more cheerful than I have for a good while. The field of rice is fine, Marcus says,—"Miss, I put my flag on dat fiel',"—and insists it will make over forty bushels to the acre. I don't throw cold water on his enthusiasm, but I know it will not. However, the rice is tall, and the golden heads are long and thick. I count a few heads and find 200 grains on one or two, and am almost carried away with Marcus's hope, but will not allow myself to think how much it will make. One year this field put in the bank $1,080, but I know it will not do that this year. There is no use to think of it.

I stayed on the bank until sunset to encourage the slow workers to finish their task. All the work in this section is based on what was the "task" in slavery times. That it was very moderate is proved by the fact that the smart, brisk workers can do two or three tasks in a day, but the lazy ones can never be persuaded to do more than one task, though they may finish it by 11 o'clock. I feel placid tonight, for half the field is cut down and will dry on the stubble all day tomorrow.

November 6, [1903]

Threshed out the rice to-day. It made only twenty bushels to the acre, and I hear rice has gone down very much. The hands now are whipping out the seed rice, which is a tedious business, but no planter in this county will use mill-threshed rice for seed. Mr. S., who bought my rice and who travels all over the South buying rice for a mill in North Carolina, told me that everywhere else mill-threshed rice was used, simply putting a little more to the acre. Here it is thought the mill breaks the rice too much, so the seed rice is prepared by each hand taking a single sheaf at a time and whipping it over a log, or a smooth board set up, until all the rice comes off. Then the sheaves are laid on a clay floor and beaten with flails, until nearly every grain has left the straw. After all this trouble of course it brings a good price—$1.75, $1.50 per bushel, $1.25 being the very cheapest to be had.

March 12, 1904

At Cherokee I had to put down a new trunk, which is quite a business. It requires knowledge of a certain kind, but is very simple, like most things, to those who know. To me it seems a terrible undertaking, for if it is badly done, the trunk may blow out when the field is planted and ruin the crop. Knowing so little as I do, I thought it best to leave it to Bonaparte, so I did not go over to the place, which is about a mile away through winding creeks.

The tide suited the morning, January 12, and the weather was mild. I waited with great anxiety for the return of the hands in the evening. I rushed down to the barnyard when I heard the boat, and asked if the trunk was well down. Bonaparte smiled in his superior way.

"Well, no, ma'am; de fac' is we neber did git de ole trunk out."

"What," I said, "you have left it half done?"

"Oh, no, ma'am. We bruk up de ole trunk an' tuk out all but de bottom."

"Then the water is rushing through tonight, making the gulf wider and wider?"

"Yes, ma'am."

I was speechless. There was no use saying anything, but I decided to go over the next day and use my common sense, if I had no knowledge. Bonaparte told me he could not get the hands, any of them, to go down in the water, and no trunk can be buried with dry feet.

The next morning, January 13, I went, carrying lunch and a bottle of home-made wine, with a stick in it for those who were to get wet. It was a beautiful, bright day, with the thermometer at 50 at 9 o'clock, for which I was very thankful. The tide was not low enough for anything to be done until then. I had had three flatloads of mud cut and put on the bank, and everything was at hand. The getting up of the bottom planks was at last accomplished, and then the new trunk floated into place on the last of the ebb, so that it settled itself into its new bed on the low water, and then the filling up was a perfect race, so much mud to be put in before the tide began to rise, besides the inclination of the bank to cave in. I kept urging the two men down in the gulf to pack the fresh mud well as it was thrown in. The stringpiece and ground logs which Bonaparte had provided were, according to my ideas, entirely inadequate, and I sent four hands to an island near by to cut larger, heavier pieces. Altogether, the day was one of the most exciting and interesting I ever spent, though I stood six hours on the top of a pile of mud on a small piece of plank, where I had to balance myself with care to look into the gulf and not topple over. It was black dark when we left the trunk, but the mud was well packed, with every appearance of solidity and stability, and the next day I had two more flatloads of mud put on, and, though a freshet had come and gone since, "she" has not stirred, and the field drains beautifully.

The company which planted the places next to Cherokee has broken up. One of the principal investors told me that he had had his money in it for seven years, and never got a cent of interest, and he was thankful to get out of it. They have taken all my best hands, one by one, but they have not suceeded—did not make money for all that. And this year the price of rice has gone down, so that what has been made brings only half of what was hoped for.

I believe these lands would make a great deal if we understood the cutting and curing of hay, for the grass grows most luxuriantly if the land is ploughed and left, but the curing of hay is unknown to the rice-field darky. . . .

On Monday, April 18, I planted the wages field at Cherokee. Here we cannot so well use the machines, so I have the field sown by hand. I am planting mill-threshed rice in this field, which is an experiment on my part. In the autumn a buyer for a large rice mill in North Carolina came to make an offer for my rice; and he spoke of the "superstition," as he called it, of planters in this state that only hand-whipped rice could be planted to make good crops. He said the large crops made in Texas and Louisiana, which are practically ruining the rice industry in this section by keeping down the price, are the result of mill-threshed rice—none other is known or thought of. This made a great impression on me, for the whipping by hand is a very expensive process, more so than the actual cost of the work, because it gives such unlimited opportunity for stealing.

I had the habit formerly of planting twenty-five acres and dividing the rice; twelve and a half acres I sent to the threshing mill in a lighter, the other twelve and a half I had taken into the barnyard, stacked, and when thoroughly cured, had it whipped out for seed. The half sent to mill always turned out from twenty-five to thirty-five bushels to the acre; the part saved for seed turned out from fifteen to twenty bushels to the acre.

That happened several years in succession. I never have had a field hand-whipped turn out over twenty bushels to the acre, and I have seldom had one threshed in the mill until these last very bad years turn out under thirty.

All of this made me determine to try planting mill-threshed rice this year. I planted a small portion in a bowl of water on cotton, which is the approved way of trying seed, and nearly every single seed germinated and shot up a fine healthy leaf. So I felt no hesitation about it; and I began with my wages field, putting half a bushel more to the acre in case there should be some grains cracked in the mill. I went over early to the field and sat on the bank all day, while Bonaparte and Abram followed the sowers.

The women are very graceful as they sow the rice with a waving movement of the hands, at the same time bending low so that the wind may not scatter the grain; and a good sower gets it all straight in the furrow. Their skirts are tied up around their hips in a very picturesque style, and as they walk they swing in a wonderful way. This peculiar arrangement allows room for one or two narrow sacks (under the skirt), which can hold a peck of rice, and some of the sowers, if weighed on the homeward trip, would be found to have gained many pounds. They are all very gentle and considerate in their manner to-day, for a great sorrow has fallen on the family. Their tender, sympathetic manner is more to me than many bushels of rice, and I turn my back when they are dipping it out.

I have offered hand-whipped rice for sale at $1.30 a bushel, and mill-threshed at $1 per bushel, and have sold 159 bushels of the former and 225 bushels of the latter, which has been a great help. We have made a fine start on the upland crop, and the corn looks very well. The small acreage planted in cotton also looks well, and I hope it will be worked properly while I am gone.

January 9, 1905

Sewed nearly all day, which is a rare treat to me. The wood we are using burns out so fast, that I have been urging the men to cut enough logs from the live oaks (which I have at last got sawed down) to give each fireplace a back log; that makes such a difference in the permanence and heat of the fire. Joe Keit said the wood was too hard, might as well try to cut iron, and that it would take all day to cut one log, making it very dear wood. I was provoked, but never having sawed any wood at all, I did not know whether what he said was true or not—that always worries me—so I put down my sewing and got the big saw about $4\frac{1}{2}$ feet long with one handle, which is comfortable to grasp, and went out to the four splendid live oaks which were killed in the storm, whether by lightning or otherwise I don't know, but they have stood there in melancholy naked grandeur ever since, till this winter I bought a fine cross-cut saw, and had Jim and Joe Keit to saw them down. It was long and laborious, but they had become a menace to the cattle, as the limbs rotted and fell. I selected a limb of suitable height for me to work on and began very awkwardly to saw. The cattle seeing so unusual a sight gathered round me, and Equinox, the bull, feeling sure I must be fixing food for them, came nearer and nearer in his investigations, so that I was forced to an ignominious retreat, before I had made much progress on my "iron" limb. I was not going to give it up, however. I went into the next lot where there was an even more indestructible oak tree, which various men at various times had refused to tackle, and began afresh with the saw. I was pleased to find myself already a little handier and worked with great satisfaction. I remembered Dickens' " 'tis dogged does it" and my spirits rose as I got the knack of drawing back the big saw. Jim, who was engaged in cutting limbs from a green live oak, which is much less tough, and which I disapprove of entirely, some distance off, came and expressed great anxiety lest I overexert myself and said, "Let me finish it, Miss Patience, you'll be here till dark," but I proudly declined, and to his and my amazement I had the back log off in half an hour.

"Now," I said, "if I who have never handled a saw before in my life, can cut that log, seven inches in diameter, which has been here since the storm of '93, and rings like metal when you strike it, in half an hour, you and Joe Keit should be able to cut those logs of the same size from those oaks which are rotting a little, in ten minutes, and by giving a day to it, the house will be supplied with back logs for two months at least."

December 31, 1906

Spent this last day of the old year writing letters of thanks and affection, and after dark I made up a bright fire, Chloe and Patty Ann having gone away on their Sunday outing, and sat in the firelight without lighting the lamps and reviewed the mercies and blessings of the past year. God forgive me for my mistakes and sins therein, my blindnesses and lost opportunities.

I keep wondering if it is His will that I should give up this life. I do not want to be headstrong about it. I have so loved the freedom and simplicity of the life, in spite of its trials, and isolation. The living close to Nature—the trees, the birds, the clouds, and all the simple loving dumb things.

But it almost seems as though I was meant to give it up. The rice-planting, which for years gave me the exhilaration of making a good income myself, is a thing of the past now—the banks and trunks have been washed away, and there is no money to replace them. The experiment of planting cotton has not been a success with me. The cotton grew luxuriantly and bore well, but others gathered it, and I got but little. I cannot sit idle in the midst of all this fertile soil. But I must wait, and watch, and listen, in silence, for the still, small voice, which comes after the storm and the earthquake, and brings the message from above.

A NEW YORK FARM WIFE: AN IRONIC VIEW

The following selection is from a novel, *My Opinion and Betsy Bobbet's*, which appeared in 1873 and was written by Marietta Holley (1836–1926). Born the youngest of seven children to a farm family in Jefferson County, New York, she spent most of her life on or near the same farm where five generations of Holleys had lived. Despite her rural home, her career was fundamentally similar to that of many independent women throughout Victorian society. She rejected marriage, and the prosperity of her productive farm family allowed her to reject farm life as well. After a short attempt at giving piano lessons, Marietta Holley turned to literature and journalism— at first certainly more of a means of establishing an identity than as a way of contributing to the Holleys' income. With a childhood of writing sketches and verse for her local newspaper behind her, she found her essays and poems accepted by *The Independent, The Christian Union*, and *Peterson's Magazine*. Nationwide fame and a truly independent career began to come finally in 1873, with the publication of *My Opinion and Betsy Bobbet's*, written in the first person under the pen name of Josiah Allen's Wife (Samantha). For Holley's eminently practical Samantha, busy with her unending chores and distractions, accepting her lot was tolerable, but accepting the lofty idealism pressed on her by neighbors, friends, and preachers to elevate her farm work into an ethereal realm of redeeming virtue was impossible. In the midst of a life she felt powerless to change, Samantha drew satisfactions from an ironic posture of rigorous intellectual independence.

Samantha was a literary success and for the next forty years Marietta Holley continued the Samantha series. By World War I

Josiah Allen's wife had become familiar to most literate households; in fact, Holley's works circulated almost as widely as those of Mark Twain. Holley drew close to Susan B. Anthony and Frances E. Willard and used Samantha to speak on behalf of woman's suffrage and temperance and to make attacks on male corruption and stupidity in government. Holley's success in reaching middle-class women suggests not only that her ideas on women's issues may have persuaded, but also that Victorian women found something fundamentally appealing about Samantha: her effort to forge a unique identity in a smothering culture.

A FARMER'S WIFE

Prefais.

This is 2 be read, if it haint askin' 2 much of the kind hearted reader.

In the 1st days of our married life, I strained nearly every nerve to help my companion Josiah along and take care of his children by his former consort, the subject of black African slavery also wearin' on me, and a morgige of 200 and 50 dollars on the farm. But as we prospered and the morgige was cleared, and the children was off to school, the black African also bein' liberated about the same time of the morgige, then my mind bein' free from these cares—the grate subject of Wommen's Rites kept a goarin' me, and a voice kept a sayin' inside of me,

"Josiah Allen's wife, rite a book givin' ure views on the grate subject of Wimmen's Rites." But I hung back in spirit from the idee and says I, to myself, I never went to school much and don't know nothin' about grammer, and I never could spell worth a cent."

But still that deep voice kept a 'swaiden me—"Josiah Allen's wife, rite a book."

Says I, "I cant rite a book, I don't know no under ground dungeons, I haint acquainted with no haunted houses, I never see a hero suspended over a abyss by his galluses, I never beheld a heroine

From Marietta Holley, *My Opinion and Betsy Bobbet's* (Hartford, Conn.: American Publishing Co., 1873), vi–vii and 58–68.

swoon away, I never see a Injun tommy hawked, nor a gost; I never had any of these advantages; I cant rite a book."

But still it kep a sayin' inside of my mind, "Josiah Allen's wife, rite a book about your life, as it passes in front of you and Josiah, daily, and your views on Wimmen's Rite's. The grate publick wheel is a rollin' on slowly, drawin' the Femail Rase into liberty; Josiah Allen's wife, put your shoulder blades to the wheel."

And so that almost hauntin' voice inside of me kep' a 'swaidin me, and finally I spoke out in a loud clear voice and answered it—

"I will put my shoulder blades to the wheel!"

I well remember the time I said it, for it skairt Josiah almost 2 death. It was nite and we was both settin' by the fire relapsed into silense and he—not knowin' the konversation goin' on inside of my mind, thought I was krazy, and jumped up as if he was shot, and says he, in tremblin' tones,

"What is the matter Samantha?"

Says I, "Josiah I am goin' to rite a book."

This skairt him worse than ever—I could see, by his gastly countenance—and he started off on the run for the kamfire bottle.

Says I, in firm but gentle axents, "kamfire kant stop me Josiah, the book will be rote."

He see by my pale but calm countenance, that I was not delerious any, and (by experience) he knows that when my mind is made up, I have got a firm and almost cast iron resolution. He said no more, but he sot down and sithed hevily; finally he spoke out in a despairin' tone, he is pretty close (but honest),

"Who will read the book Samantha? Remember if you rite it you have got to stand the brunt of it yourself—I haint no money to hire folks with to read it." And agin he sithed 2 or 3 times. And he hadn't much more than got through sithein' when he asked me agin in a tone of almost agony—

"Who will read the book Samantha after you rite it?"

The same question was fillin' me with agonizin' aprehension, but I consealed it and answered with almost marble calm,

"I don't know Josiah, but I am determined to put my shoulder blades 2 the wheel and rite it."

Josiah didn't say no more then, but it wore on him—for that nite in the ded of nite he spoke out in his sleep in a kind of a wild way, "Who will read the book?"

I kinder hunched him with my elbo' to wake him up, and he muttered—"I wont pay out 1 cent of my money to hire any body to read it."

I pitied him, for I was afraid it would end in the Nite Mair, and I waked him up, and promised him then and there, that I never would ask him to pay out 1 cent to hire any body 2 read it. He has perfect konfidence in me and he brightened up and haint never said a word sense aginst the idee, and that is the way this book come to be rote. . . .

A Day of Trouble

Sugerin' time come pretty late this year, and I told Josiah that I didn't believe I should have a better time through the whole year to visit his folks, and mother Smith, than I should now before we begun to make sugar, for I knew no sooner had I got that out of the way, than it would be time to clean house, and make soap. And then when the dairy work come on, I knew I never should get off. So I went. But never shall I forget the day I got back. I had been gone a week, and the childern bein' both off to school, Josiah got along alone. I have always said, and I say still, that I had jest as lives have a roarin' lion do my housework, as a man. Every thing that could be bottom side up in the house, was.

I had a fortnights washin' to do, the house to clean up, churnin' to do, and bakin'; for Josiah had eat up everything slick and clean, the buttery shelves looked like the dessert of Sarah. Then I had a batch of maple sugar to do off, for the trees begun to run after I went away and Josiah had syruped off—and some preserves to make, for his folks had gin me some pound sweets, and they was a spilein'. So it seemed as if everything come that day, besides my common housework—and well doth the poet say—"That a woman never gets her work done up," for she don't.

Now when a man ploughs a field, or runs up a line of figgers, or writes a serming, or kills a beef critter, there it is done—no more to be done over. But sposen a woman washes up her dishes clean as a fiddle, no sooner does she wash 'em up once, than she has to, right over and over agin, three times three hundred and 65 times every year. And the same with the rest of her work, blackin' stoves, and fillin' lamps, and washin' and moppin' floors, and the same with cookin'. Why jest the idee of paradin' out the table and teakettle 3 times 3 hundred and 65 times every year is enough to make a woman sweat. And then to think of all the cookin' utensils and ingredients—why if it wuzzn't for principle, no woman could stand the idee, let alone the labor, for it haint so much the mussle she has to lay out, as the strain on her mind.

Now last Monday, no sooner did I get my hands into the suds holt of one of Josiah's dirty shirts, than the sugar would mount up in the kettle and sozzle over on the top of the furnace in the summer kitchen—or else the preserves would swell up and drizzle over the side of the pan on to the stove—or else the puddin' I was a bakin' for dinner would show signs of scorchin', and jest as I was in the heat of the warfare, as you may say, who should drive up but the Editor of the Agur. He was a goin' on further, to engage a hired girl he had hearn of, and on his way back, he was goin' to stop and read that poetry, and eat some maple sugar; and he wanted to leave the twins till he come back.

Says he, "They won't be any trouble to you, will they?" I thought of the martyrs, and with a appearance of outward composure, I answered him in a sort of blind way; but I won't deny that I had to keep a sayin', John Rogers! John Rogers' over to myself all the time I was on-doin' of 'em, or I should have said somethin' I was sorry for afterwards. The poetry woried me the most, I won't deny.

After the father drove off, the first dive the biggest twin made was at the clock, he crep' up to that, and broke off the pendulum, so it haint been since, while I was a hangin' thier cloaks in the bedroom. And while I was a puttin' thier little oversocks under the stove to dry, the littlest one clim' up and sot down in a pail of maple syrup, and while I was a wringin' him out, the biggest one dove under the bed, at Josiah's tin trunk where he keeps a lot of old papers, and come a creepin' out, drawin' it after him like a handsled. There was a gography in it, and a Fox'es book of martyrs, and a lot of other such light reading' and I let the twins have 'em to recreate themselves on, and it kep 'em still most a minute.

I hadn't much more'n got my eye offen that Fox'es book of Martyrs—when there appeared before 'em a still more mournful sight, it was Betsey Bobbet come to spend the day.

I murmured dreamily to myself "John Rogers"—But that didn't do, I had to say to myself with firmness—"Josiah Allen's wife, haint you ashamed of yourself, what are your sufferin's to John Roger'ses? Think of the agony of that man—think of his 9 children follerin' him, and the one at the breast, what are your sufferin's compared to his'en?" Then with a brow of calm I advanced to meet her. I see she had got over bein' mad about the surprise party, for she smiled on me once or twice, and as she looked at the twins, she smiled 2 times on each of 'em, which made 4 and says she in tender tones,

"You deah little motherless things." Then she tried to kiss 'em. But the biggest one gripped her by her false hair, which was flax, and I should think by a careless estimate, that he pulled out about enough to make half a knot of thread. The little one didn't do much harm, only I think he loosened her teeth a little, he hit her pretty near the mouth, and I thought as she arose she slipped 'em back in thier place. But she only said,

"Sweet! sweet little things, how ardent and impulsive they are, so like thier deah Pa."

She took out her work, and says she, "I have come to spend the day. I saw thier deah Pa bringin' the deah little twins in heah, aud I thought maybe I could comfort the precious little motherless things some, if I should come over heah. If there is any object upon the earth, Josiah Allen's wife, that appeals to a feelin' heart, it is the sweet little children of widowers. I cannot remember the time when I did not want to comfort them, and thier deah Pa's. I have always felt that it was woman's highest speah, her only mission to soothe, to cling, to smile, to coo. I have always felt it, and for yeah's back it has been a growin' on me. I feel that you do not feel as I do in this matter, you do not feel that it is woman's greatest privilege, her crowning blessing, to soothe lacerations, to be a sort of a poultice to the noble, manly breast when it is torn with the cares of life."

This was too much, in the agitated frame of mind I then was.

"Am I a poultice Betsey Bobbet, do I look like one?—am I in the condition to be one?" I cried turnin' my face, red and drippin' with prespiration towards her, and then attacked one of Josiah's shirt sleeves agin. "What has my sect done" says I, as I wildly rubbed his shirt sleeves, "That they have got to be lacerator soothers, when they have got everything else under the sun to do?" Here I stirred down the preserves that was a runnin' over, and turned a pail full of syrup into the sugar kettle. "Everybody says that men are stronger than women, and why should they be treated as if they was glass china, liable to break all to pieces if they haint handled careful. And if they have got to be soothed," says I in an agitated tone, caused by my emotions (and my pumpin' 6 pails of water to fill up the biler), "Why don't they get men to sooth'em? They have as much agin time as wimmen have; evenin's they don't have anything else to do, they might jest as well be a soothin' each other as to be a hangin' round grocery stores, or settin' by the fire whittlin'."

I see I was frightenin' her by my delerious tone and I continued more mildly, as I stirred down the strugglin' sugar with one hand—removed a cake from the oven with the other—watched my apple preserves with a eagle vision, and listened intently to the voice of the twins, who was playin' in the woodhouse.

"I had jest as soon soothe lacerations as not, Betsey, if I hadn't everything else to do. I had jest as lives set down and smile at Josiah by the hour, but who would fry him nut cakes? I could smoothe down his bald head affectionately, but who would do off this batch of sugar? I could coo at him day in and day out, but who would skim milk—wash pans—get vittles—wash and iron—and patch and scour—and darn and fry—and make and mend—and bake and bile while I was a cooin', tell me?" says I.

Betsey spoke not, but quailed, and I continued—

"Women haint any stronger than men, naturally; their backs and thier nerves haint made of any stouter timber; their hearts are jest as liable to ache as men's are; so with thier heads; and after doin' a hard day's work when she is jest ready to drop down, a little smilin' and cooin' would do a woman jest as much good as a man. Not what," I repeated in the firm tone of principle "Not but what I am willin' to coo, if I only had time."

A pause enshued durin' which I bent over the washtub and rubbed with all my might on Josiah's shirt sleeve. I had got one sleeve so I could see streaks of white in it (Josiah is awful hard on his shirt sleeves), and I lifted up my face and continued in still more reasonable tones, as I took out my rice puddin' and cleaned out the bottom of the oven, (the pudden had run over and was a scorchin' on), and scraped the oven bottom with a knife.

"Now Josiah Allen will go out into that lot," says I, glancein' out of the north window "and plough right straight along, furrow after furrow, no sweat of mind about it at all; his mind is in that free calm state that he could write poetry."

"Speaking of poetry, reminds me," said Betsey, and I see her hand go into her pocket; I knew what was a comin', and I went on hurriedly, wavin' off what I knew must be, as long as I could. "Now, I, a workin' jest as hard as he accordin' to my strength, and havin' to look 40 ways to once, and 40 different strains on my mind, now tell me candidly, Betsey Bobbet, which is in the best condition for cooin', Josiah Allen or me? but it haint expected of him," says I in agitated tones, "I am expected to do all the smilin' and cooin' there is done, though you know," says I sternly, "that I haint no time for it."

"In this poem, Josiah Allen's wife, is embodied my views, which are widely different from yours."

I see it was vain to struggle against fate, she had the poetry in her hand. I rescued the twins from beneath a half a bushel of beans they had pulled over onto themselves—took off my preserves which had burnt to the pan while I was a rescuin', and calmly listened to her, while I picked up the beans with one hand, and held off the twins with the other.

"There is one thing I want to ask your advice about, Josiah Allen's wife. This poem is for the Jonesville Augah. You know I used always to write for the opposition papah, the Jonesville Gimlet, but as I said the othah day, since the Editah of the Augah lost his wife I feel that duty is a drawing of me that way. Now do you think that it would be any more pleasing and comforting to that deah Editah to have me sign my name Bettie Bobbet—or Betsey, as I always have?" And loosin' herself in thought she murmured dreamily to the twins, who was a pullin' each other's hair on the floor at her feet—

"Sweet little mothahless things, you couldn't tell me, could you, deahs, how your deah Pa would feel about it?"

Here the twins laid holt of each other so I had to part 'em, and as I did so I said to Betsey, "If you haint a fool you will hang on to the Betsey. You can't find a woman nowadays that answers to her true name. I expect," says I in a tone of cold and almost witherin sarcasm, "that these old ears will yet hear some young minister preach abont Johnnie the Baptist, and Minnie Magdalen. Hang on to the Betsey; as for the Bobbet," says I, lookin' pityingly on her, "that will hang on for itself."

I was too well bread to interrupt her further, and I pared my potatoes, pounded my beefsteak, and ground my coffee for dinner, and listened. This commenced also as if she had been havin' a account with Love, and had come out in his debt. . . .

There was pretty near twenty verses of 'em, and as she finished she said to me—

"What think you of my poem, Josiah Allen's wife?"

"Says I, fixin' my sharp grey eyes upon her keenly, "I have had more experience with men than you have, Betsey;" I see a dark shadow settlin' on her eye-brow, and I hastened to apologise—"you haint to blame for it, Betsey—we all know you haint to blame."

She grew calm, and I proceeded, "How long do you suppose you could board a man on clear smiles, Betsey—you jest try it for a few meals and you'd find out. I have lived with Josiah Allen 14 years, and I ought to know somethin' of the natur of man, which is about alike in all of 'em, and I say, and I contend for it, that you might jest as well try to cling to a bear as to a hungry man. After dinner, sentiment would have a chance, and you might smile on him. But then," says I thoughtfully, "there is the dishes to wash."

Jest at that minute the Editor of the Augur stopped at the gate, and Betsey, catchin' up a twin on each arm, stood up to the winder, smilin'.

He jumped out, and took a great roll of poetry out from under the buggy seat—I sithed as I see it. But fate was better to me than I deserved. For Josiah was jest leadin' the horse into the horse barn, when the Editor happened to look up and see Betsey. Josiah says he swore—says he "the d————!" I won't say what it was, for I belong to the meetin' house, but it wasn't the Deity though it begun with a D. He jumped into the buggy agin, and says Josiah,

"You had better stay to dinner, my wife is gettin' a awful good one—and the sugar is most done."

Josiah says he groaned, but he only said—

"Fetch out the twins."

Says Josiah, "You had better stay to dinner—you haint got no women folks to your house—and I know what it is to live on pancakes," and wantin' to have a little fun with him, says he, "Betsey Bobbet is here."

Josiah says he swore agin, and agin says he, "fetch out the twins." And he looked so kind o' wild and fearful towards the door, that Josiah started off on the run.

Betsey was determined to carry one of the twins out, but jest at the door he tore every mite of hair offen her head, and she, bein' bald naturally, dropped him. And Josiah carried 'em out, one on each arm, and he drove off with 'em fast. Betsey wouldn't stay to dinner all I could do and say, she acted mad. But one sweet thought filled me with such joyful emotion that I smiled as I thought of it—I shouldn't have to listen to any more poetry that day.

FARM LIFE: A ROMANTIC PERSPECTIVE

This selection is taken from *Life in Prairie Land*, written in 1846 by Elizabeth Farnham (1815–64) to promote western settlement. Since she was a pioneer wife herself, her romantic images of the pure and ennobling western environment suggest that not all farm women who turned to literature found their material circumstances depressing. However, it should be pointed out that she returned to New York after only six years in the West and never resumed her idyllic career as farm wife. Following a period of work in New York prison reform and the death of her husband in California, she sailed west, taking along a group of young women with the intent of heightening the moral tone of the Gold Rush frontier. There followed a stormy, unsuccessful second marriage, embarkation on a lecturing career, and, after her return East, a stint as a Civil War nurse, during which she contracted a fatal disease. Through her California life, Farnham became an increasingly intense believer in the spiritual and even biological superiority of women—a useful notion, perhaps, to many Victorian women who were pursuing independence. However, it was an idea that ultimately reinforced the dominant view that woman's uniqueness called for confinement in the home, where she might practice her superiority undistracted by the marketplace.

LIFE IN PRAIRIE LAND

The following work was commenced with the intention of writing one or two brief sketches descriptive of Life at the West. And until some hundred and fifty pages were written, I never contemplated the possibility of extending them to a volume. At that point, I was so far from having said all I felt, that I very willingly resigned myself to the current of my feelings and wrote on.

To those who read the volume first, and afterward, in some idle moment, turn back to the preface, I need not say that I have been impelled in every step by love of my theme. That will have been apparent enough to them, without any such declaration. I have loved the West, and it still claims my preference over all other portions of the earth. Its magnitude, its fertility, the kindliness of its climate, the variety and excellence of its productions are unrivaled in our own country, if not on the globe.

In these characteristics, it presents itself to my mind in the light of a strong and generous parent, whose arms are spread to extend protection, happiness, and life to throngs who seek them from other and less friendly climes. Setting a high value upon these resources, I rejoice to hear of emigration to the country possessing them—not

From Eliza Farnham, *Life in Prairie Land* (New York: Harper & Brothers, 1846), pp. iii–viii and 235–43.

alone because those who go will find there abundance for the supply of their natural wants, but because the influences with which it will address their spiritual natures are purifying, ennobling, and elevating. If nature ever taught a lesson which the endwarfed, debased mind of man could study with profit, it is in these regions of her benignest dispensations. The burden of her teaching here, is too palpable to be wholly rejected by any. Even vulgar minds do not altogether escape its influence. Their perceptions become more vivid, their desires more exalted, their feelings purer, and all their intellectual action more expanded.

The magnificence, freedom, and beauty of the country form, as it were, a common element, in which all varieties of character, education, and prejudice are resolved into simple and harmonious relation. Living near to nature, artificial distinctions lose much of their force. Humanity is valued mainly for its intrinsic worth—not for its appurtenances or outward belongings.

It must not be forgotten, however, that a large class of minds have no adaptation to the conditions of life in the West. This is more especially true of my own sex. Very many ladies are so unfortunate as to have had their minds thoroughly distorted from all true and natural modes of action by an artificial and pernicious course of education, or the influence of a false social position. They cannot endure the sudden and complete transition which is forced upon them by emigration to the West. Hence a class may always be found who dislike the country; who see and feel only its disadvantages; who endure the self-denial it imposes without enjoying any of the freedom it confers; who suffer the loss of artificial luxuries, but never appreciate what is offered in exchange for them. Persons so constituted ought never to entertain for a moment the project of emigration. They destroy their own happiness, and materially diminish that of others. Their discontent and pining are tolerated with much impatience, because those who do not sympathize with them, see so much to enjoy and so little to endure, that their griefs command little or no respect.

I had no such experience, for I loved the country, and when compelled to return to the crowded and dusty marts of the East, I did so with many and deep regrets; and these still linger and mingle largely with the emotions of my life. The writing of these sketches has, therefore, been a labor of love. While engaged upon them, I have lived again in the land of my heart. I have seen the grasses wave, and felt the winds, and listened to the birds, and watched the springing flowers, and exulted in something of the old sense of freedom which these conferred upon me. Visions, prophetic of the glory and greatness which are to be developed here, have dwelt in my mind and exalted it above the narrow personal cares of life.

It is the enjoyment afforded by this kind of emancipation which so endears the western country to those who have resided in it. It steals upon the heart like what it is, the very witchery of nature; so that those who are susceptible to it, feel the charm but not the inconvenience through which it is invoked. Such persons delight in the perfection and beauty of the natural, and these suffice them.

After what has been said, it would be superfluous to add that of this latter class I am an humble member; that no deprivation or suffering incident to the country could sever my attachment to it, and that any portraiture of its life which I should draw would, therefore, abound in gay and cheerful colors. The sombre tints would not dwell in my heart, and I cannot reproduce them. This may make my picture appear to be a partial one, but to me and those who are of like spirit it will be honest.

Conscious of the intent to make it so, I shall dismiss it without care in that regard, and leave it to tell its own story of the great and generous land whose name it bears. . . .

I have sometimes, when looking over our past lives, compared ourselves to two helmless, rudderless ships, floating on the storm-wrought ocean. For a moment they approach each other, and seem as if they would journey on together, but the next, they are parted and driven about on the waste for years; perhaps never to meet again 'til they decay and sink into a common sepulchre. It has been almost so with us. We parted; you to seek the education and mental culture which should have been the work of earlier years; I to make such preparation as I might, for the great event before me. The next spring I was married. You know my husband had meantime visited this country, and returned a few weeks previous to our union, with such glowing descriptions of its beauty and advantages, that his father gathered the little means he had, and proposed that we should all start west together after our marriage. We did so, and it will be eight years in a few weeks (I may live to see the day), since we bade adieu to our friends and commenced our journey. This state at that time was thought, among the stable population of our mountain region, to be almost beyond the knowledge of civilized man. Our friends bade us farewell as if we were about to plunge into the deserts of the old world, instead of the richest and most beautiful region of the new.

I rejoiced in that journey. It was the season of life fullest of hope and trust, and all nature seemed like me, to be exulting in the future that was opening before it. We journeyed several weeks through the blooming orchards and fields of the cultivated country, and at last plunged into the heavy forests of Ohio and Indiana. Here we sometimes slept in our waggon or on the ground, and took our meals in the woods. At last we emerged upon the great prairie which extends from the Wabash, west and north, nearly three hundred miles. Here the magnificence of the country to which we were bound began to appear. I remember, as we journeyed day after day across its heaving, verdant bosom, that I seemed to be living in a new world. All the noise, all the selfish hurry and turmoil in which my past years had been spent, faded away. They seemed as remote as if the barrier of eternity had been placed between me and them. A new creation was around me. The great, silent plain, with its still streams, its tender verdure, its lovely flowers, its timid birds and quadrupeds, shrinking away from our sight; its soft winds, its majestic storms—was a sublime spectacle! Occasionally a herd of deer bounded across our path, or a solitary pair of grouse, startled from their parental cares, rose and cleft the air like the arrows of their old pursuers; but save these we were alone, in silence broken only by our own voices. I thought how many ages that plain had been spread out beneath those soft skies and that genial sun; how its flowers had bloomed and faded, its grasses grown and decayed; how storms had swept over all its wide expanse, and the thunder echoed from its bosom; how the solemn winds of autumn had sighed over it, and the raging fires marched in unrestrained fury from one border to the other; how long all this power and magnificence had displayed itself unseen of any eye, save His who made it! How long all these mighty and beautiful phenomena had followed each other, and awoke no human emotion, appealed to no enlightened soul. Nature disporting with herself, frolicking in merriment, fading in sadness or raging in anger; the sole witness of her own acts! . . .

But we left the prairie at last; I was not sorry; neither could I rejoice, except for those who suffered more than I. But the long journey, the excitement attendant upon the strange features of the country, and the broken rest, were too much for me. When we reached the crossings of the Mackinaw, about thirteen miles from here, you know where it is, I was in a raging fever. We traveled on, however, for there was then no house where we could stop. Our people heard in some way that this "claim" was for sale. They wished to buy an improved one—that is, one with a cabin in which we could live till a house was built, and with grain enough on the ground for the season's use. I have pointed out to you the very small, low cabin which we found here. There were also several acres of grain growing. We all liked the situation, and so a bargain was soon made with the owner, or the "squatter," as he termed himself, for his place. But there was one circumstance which was very awkward for us. He could not leave the larger cabin till autumn, and we were therefore obliged all to live in that little pen until our people could build another. I scarcely know how things went on those few weeks. I was sick and wretched in person; but at last the other cabin was finished, and we felt ourselves very comfortable in it. When the family of the "squatter" left us, John and I moved into the old one, and lived there until the framed house was built. That was our first introduction to cabin life. The summer was considerably advanced when we arrived, and our people were soon engaged in the harvest. The grain was stacked in the cow-yard, for there were then no barns or outbuildings of any description. When the harvest was over, they began their preparations for carrying on farming more systematically the next year. They made fences, ploughed and sowed, and built a small log stable for their horses.

I remember the whole land seemed to me a paradise that summer and autumn. The profusion of late flowers and wild fruits, the abundance of game, the richness of vegetation, the mildness of the climate, the sublime storms, and the soft musical winds delighted me. Our men worked much in the woods, and I used at noon to take a small basket of dinner to them. The sound of their distant axes, and, as I drew nearer, of their cheerful voices, contrasted delightfully with the silence of the sleeping grove.

We all had good health so far, and appetites that led to many jokes between ourselves about famine, et cet. You have now learned by experience how this climate acts on the appetite, and you may judge of the amount of food which nine persons, in this stage of acclimation, would consume. But we had plenty of grain stacked, and meats more delicious than the dantiest markets of the east afford, were abundant everywhere, so we only exulted in our fine health, and pursued our labors joyfully.

The prairie below us where there are now so many pleasant farms, was then unsettled. There was no house on the south between us and the Mackinaw, and at the crossings of that stream was the only family whom I visited for the first two years. You ask if those were not lonely years. I answer that there were many, many hours when John and I talked of the friends we had left, when the cheerful social circles where we had sometimes met were named with moistened eyes, and yet there was no day of them all when we would have returned and forsaken the land of our adoption. Much as we wished for the society of our absent friends, we could not have consented to exchange for it, the joys we had won in the new country. We loved everything in the new land too much for that. . . .

By the next summer the unnatural appetite which had beset us all, disappeared, and the succeeding stage of acclimation came on. Part of our number were prostrated with bilious fever, which in almost every case was followed by ague, and the others were visited with that cutaneous disease which you know sometimes takes the place of prostrating fevers. It is the safer process, but scarcely the more agreeable. Some of our people suffered extremely with it. Their arms and hands were perfectly denuded of skin, and in such a state, that, for two or three weeks, those who were not so afflicted had to feed them as if they were infants. My husband and I both underwent the severe ordeal of a long fever, succeeded by ague, but we came through, apparently with unimpaired constitutions. All recovered in time, and there has been little sickness among us since, except the poor invalid sister, who seems to have been born to suffer.

Still we have had many seasons of trial. There has been more or less sickness in the country every summer, and we cannot sit down in our own homes in peace when our neighbors are afflicted. I have sometimes rode one, two, or three miles every day, or every alternate day, to visit a sick neighbor; and here our visits are not calls. We go to perform the duties of nurse for a day or night, and having no servants at home, are obliged to return as soon as possible, and, notwithstanding our weariness, proceed at once to the cares of the family. We had beside, as I have already informed you, many strangers in our homes, some of whom were long and dangerously ill while there; and these circumstances increased our burthens: nevertheless we were happy. . . .

A WISCONSIN FARM GIRL

These selections are from a simple diary that was begun in January 1865, during a bleak Wisconsin winter, by a 19-year-old farm girl, Sarah E. Beaulieu. With her father and two brothers at war, she and the other women in the family had been left to manage a farm that even in good years was only marginally successful. For additional support, Sarah undertook school teaching, with its very minimal returns, and her mother made hats that she sold in De Pere and Green Bay. Although the war created unique economic pressures, the family's financial situation was not changed dramatically by it. Sarah's father had never been able to support his family and had volunteered for the army as a substitute to gain the bonus that would ease the family's financial distress. For Sarah, as for her sisters, there was little attraction in remaining at home. One month after her last entry in the diary, Sarah married a returning veteran who offered the prosperity and security that had eluded her family.

A Farm Girl's Diary

Morrison, Wisconsin, Wednesday, March 1, 1865

Went to Mrs. Snider's quilting, stayed until three o'clock, came home. In a few minutes Ma came saying Mrs. Cain required my services the next day.

Thursday, March 2

Went to Cain's. Daniel seems better. Did some washing in the afternoon, baked. Took a very bad cold and it has given me a bad head ache.

Friday, March 3

Arose very early, did our washing which was a very big one. At six Ma came home but has gone back with Millard [Sarah's brother, Millard Fillmore Beaulieu]. He took the team and carried her there as the walking was bad.

Saturday, March 4

Scrubbed and did my ironing. In the evening Millard went to the P.O. but got no mail. I think our friends are getting rather negligent about writing.

Sunday, March 5

Spent the day reading some of Byron's writing together with Mrs. Southworth's and am greatly taken up with the latter. Ma came home and I must go back with her, so goodbye.

Monday, March 6

Sat up at Mrs. Cain's all last night. I lay down towards morning but did not sleep more than an hour or so. Went home after breakfast. The sick are some better. Passed the day very reluctantly.

From the unpublished diary of Sarah E. Beaulieu, Morrison, Wisconsin, 1865, by permission of Helen Brenna.

Tuesday, March 7

Went up to Cain's last night late. Daniel was not expected to live and found him almost choked. Quinn [the Justice of the Peace] came after Ma about six and I went up too. Today I feel as if I needed sleep. In the evening went to sit up at Clark's. . . .

Saturday, March 25

This day was passed thinking of the responsibility I had taken upon myself to teach the school in our town this summer. I always had an antipathy to school teaching. Mrs. Dyer and Ellen made us a call.

Sunday, March 26

Passed this day very pleasantly with Mrs. Dyer and daughter. Had a good visit and enjoyed myself as far as could be expected. Millard has the measles and feels pretty sick this evening.

Monday, March 27

Did our usual work. In the afternoon yoked up the oxen and drawed logs for firewood then went to sugar bush with Mother and brought down some sap on the little sleigh and had a queer time driving oxen.

Tuesday, March 28

Did the washing and in the afternoon had a sugaring off. Ate all the warm sugar I wanted for once this year.

Wednesday, March 29

Went in the bush and helped tap trees. In the evening I took the oxen and went and gathered the sap and brought it home. Spent the evening reading Hart's class book of poetry.

Thursday, March 30

Ironed the clothes and gathered sap in the evening. Millard got a letter from Huldah [Sarah's older sister]. She seems very indignant about not receiving our letters that we addressed to Chicago.

Friday, March 31

Moved about twenty bushels of potatoes with Ma's help and put them in the cellar. Mr. Wagner is tapping trees for us today. He will tap about two hundred. . . .

Monday, April 3

Emma and myself carried in fifty bushels of turnips out of the pit. We did not think it was so hard a job until after we got at it. . . .

Tuesday, April 4

Did not feel very well. Sugared off about fourteen lbs. of the nicest sugar. In the afternoon went to the woods where they were boiling down sugar water. Stayed two hours.

Wednesday, April 5

Passed this day in the bush boiling sap. Did not do anything of importance. In the afternoon I went home and felt very bad. Went to bed early. . . .

Thursday, April 13

Prepared to go to the Bay and pass examination. If there is anything I dislike it is to have a man ask questions and be obliged to answer them in order to get that little paper licensing one to teach school.

Friday, April 14

Feel very tired having walked fourteen miles and at last arrived at my place of destination [Green Bay]. Found Delphin suffering very much, having had another sick spell as she is subject to in the Spring.

Saturday, April 15

Rained all the forenoon. Took the cars at De Pere went to Fort Howard. After I got to the Bay I had one difficulty in getting my certificate. O, the bad news our President is killed. . . .

Monday, April 24

Went to the sugar bush and carried sap together and helped boil it away. With all together there were about one hundred and fifty pails. Retired very early thinking of my duties for the morrow.

Tuesday, April 25

Arose very early and prepared to go to commence school. Went to the district clerk and got the key of the school house. Commenced school. Had only eight scholars. Passed the day in teaching those little minds in the right direction of their books.

Wednesday, April 26

Taught school one half day, cleaned the school house. In the afternoon received two letters. Went down to Mrs. Wagner's in the evening. Stayed all night, dressed that sick girl's hand which was so badly burned trying to save her mother.

Thursday, April 27

Felt very indisposed and would have like to have stayed at home if I could have been allowed. Took a bad cold and a very sore throat. . . .

Friday, April 28

Taught school all day as usual. In the evening ironed and sewed a little for Little Loolie Paige which I had promised to do. . . .

Saturday, April 29

Taught school, went home in the evening very lonesome and weary. I think I am getting very much like the old maid that sat down on Monday morning and cried because Saturday did not come twice a week. Her house was dirty and she was waiting 'til Saturday. . . .

Wednesday, June 28

Taught school. At noon went to the district clerk's and drew an order for eighteen dollars. Stopped at the store to get it cashed but no money in the treasury.

FROM FARM TO MEDICAL SCHOOL

These reminiscences of Bethinia Angelina Owens-Adair (1840–1926) describe a critical portion of her decidedly exceptional career where she transformed herself from a lightly-schooled teen-age farm wife into a prominent medical practitioner. One of nine children of a pioneer Oregon family, Owens-Adair married a neighboring farmer and appeared to embark on a perfectly routine life pattern. However, within four years she had broken with her husband, returned to her parents' farm, launched divorce proceedings, and begun a lifelong commitment to self-improvement. Divorce was extremely rare among farm women before the Civil War, and Owens-Adair's reminiscences offer no full explanation of her deviance. Clearly, its cause is contained in some combination of her marriage at 14 years of age (young even for a girl from a family of modest means); her unusual economy, determination, resourcefulness, and ambition; the fundamental incompetence of her husband, expressed in part in the physical abuse of their small child; and the presence of parents who supported her desire for well-being and independence. The following reading begins at the point of her return to her parents' household. Analysis of the events that follow, up to her embarkation upon a medical career, is left to the reader. An understanding of the factors that contributed to the unusual success of Owens-Adair may clarify one's conception not only of the potential of Victorian women, but also of the general conditions under which they lived, particularly those with rural or small-town backgrounds.

It should be added that, following a year of study at a Philadelphia medical college, Owens-Adair began treating women and children in Portland, Oregon. At age 38, she enrolled in a regular medical course at the University of Michigan, obtaining her M.D. in 1880, and followed that with clinical work in Chicago and Europe. In 1881, she returned to Oregon, where she specialized in the treatment of ear and eye diseases, became a promoter of eugenic sterilization, took a position of leadership in the Women's Christian

Temperance Union, and became an active advocate of women's suffrage.

MOBILITY IN THE NORTHWEST

And now, at eighteen years of age, I found myself, broken in spirit and health, again in my father's house, from which, only four short years before, I had gone with such a happy heart, and such bright hopes for the future.

It seemed to me now that I should never be happy or strong again. I was, indeed, surrounded with difficulties seemingly insurmountable,—a husband for whom I had lost all love and respect, a divorce, the stigma of which would cling to me all my future life, and a sickly babe of two years in my arms, all rose darkly before me.

At this time, I could scarcely read or write, and four years of trials, and hardships and privations sufficient to crush a mature woman, had wrought a painful change in the fresh, blooming child who had so buoyantly taken the duties and burdens of wifehood and motherhood on her young shoulders. I realized my position fully, and resolved to meet it bravely, and do my very best.

Surrounded with an atmosphere of affection and cheerfulness, with an abundance of nourishing food, my health rapidly returned, and with it came an increasing desire for education, that I might fit myself for the duties of a mother, and for the life yet before me.

At this time, there was as good a school as the country then afforded in Roseburg, distant not more than half a mile.

My little George, too, felt the beneficial change, fully as much as I did, for my mother's idea of raising children could not be improved upon—simply to give them sufficient wholesome food, keep them clean and happy, and let them live out of door as much as possible.

George was such a tiny creature, and so active in his movements that my young brothers and sisters felt him no burden, and always had him with them out of doors; so after pondering the matter for some time, I said one day:

From B. A. Owens-Adair, *Dr. Owens-Adair, Some of Her Life Experiences* (privately published, Portland, Oreg., 1906), pp. 51–52, 56–69, and 72–80.

"Mother, do you think I might manage to go to school?"

"Why, yes," she answered; "go right along. George is no trouble. The children will take care of him."

I joyfully accepted this opportunity, and from that day on, I was up early and out to the barn, assisting with the milking, and doing all the work possible in the house, until 8:30, when I went to school with the children, my younger brothers and sisters. Saturdays, with the aid of the children, I did the washing and ironing of the family, and kept up with my studies.

At the end of my first four months' term I had finished the third reader, and made good progress with my other studies of spelling, writing, geography and arithmetic. . . .

Before going to Clatsop [her parents' Oregon home], in the fall of 1859, with my sister, I applied for a divorce, and the custody of my child and petitioned for the restoration of my maiden name of Owens.

In the spring of 1859, my brother Flem met me in Salem with a team, and together we returned to Roseburg in time for the session of court before which my case was to appear.

The suit was strongly contested on account of the child, which Mr. Hill's widowed mother was anxious to have, thinking her son would be thus induced to make his home with her, so that she might remain in her own home, all her other children now having homes of their own.

My father employed Hon. Stephen F. Chadwick on my behalf, and he won my suit, including the custody of my child, and the permission to resume my maiden name. . . .

After the decree of the court was rendered giving me custody of my child, and my father's name, which I have never since discarded, and never will, I felt like a free woman.

The world began to look bright once more, as with renewed vigor and reviving hope, I sought work in all honorable directions, even accepting washing, which was one of the most profitable occupations among the few considered "proper" for women in those days.

(I am here reminded of a characteristic, courageous, and, at the time, iconoclastic, declaration by Mrs. Duniway in the New Northwest, at the time of the bitter uprising against Chinese labor, and the summary expulsion of all Chinese from many localities on the Pacific Coast, to-wit: "White men will not wash. White women have no business to wash, and we must have Chinamen for that purpose!")

My father objected to my doing washing for a living, and said:

"Why can't you be contented to stay at home with us; I am able to support you and your child?"

But no. No amount of argument would shake my determination to earn my own livelihood, and that of my child, so father brought me a sewing machine, the first that ever came into that town, and so, with sewing and nursing, a year passed very profitably.

My sister, Mrs. Hobson, now urged me to return to her on Clatsop, as she greatly needed my help. I went, but soon became restless, because of my intense thirst for learning. An education I must have, at whatever cost. Late in the fall of 1860, sister and I went over to Oysterville, Wash., to visit my old and much-beloved girl-friend, Mrs. S. S. Munson. The few days which my sister had arranged to stay, passed all too quickly, so Captain and Mrs. Munson assured Mrs. Hobson that they would see that I reached home safely if I might stay till we "got our visit out."

I told Mrs. Munson of my great anxiety for an education, and she immediately said:

"Why not, then, stay with me, and go to school? We have a good school here, and I should like so much to have you with me, especially farther on."

To this generous offer I replied that I would gladly accept it if I could only find some way of earning my necessary expenses while attending school. Mrs. Munson replied:

"There are my brother and his hired man; I can get you their washing, which will bring you in from $1.00 to $1.50 per week, which will be all you will need."

To this I gratefully assented; and I did their washing evenings. Work to me then, was scarcely more than play, and, as "change in work brings rest," I assisted in the other domestic work with pleasure, especially as Mrs. Munson was a methodical and excellent housekeeper, and I loved and enjoyed order and neatness in the home above all things.

Thus passed one of the pleasantest, and most profitable winters of my life, while, "whetted by what it fed on," my desire for knowledge grew daily stronger.

My sister, Mrs. Hobson, now urged me to come back to her, and I said to her:

"I am determined to get at least a common school education. I now know that I can support and educate myself and my boy, and I am resolved to do it; furthermore, I do not intend to do it over the washtub, either. Nor will I any longer work for my board and clothes, alone. You need me, and I am willing to stay with you the next six months, if you will arrange for me to go to school in Astoria next winter."

She agreed to this. Some time later, I said to her: "Diana, don't you think I could teach a little summer school here on the plains? I can rise at four, and help with the milking, and get all the other work done by 8 A.M., and I can do the washing mornings and evenings, and on Saturdays."

She said: "You can try," so the following day I asked Mr. Hobson if he would not get up a little school for me. He replied:

"Take the horse and go around among the neighbors and work it up yourself."

I lost no time in carrying out his suggestion, and succeeded in getting the promise of sixteen pupils, for which I was to receive $2 each for three months.

This was my first attempt to instruct others.

I taught my school in the old Presbyterian church—the first Presbyterian church-building ever erected in Oregon. Of my sixteen pupils, there were three who were more advanced than myself, but I took their books home with me nights, and, with the help of my brother-in-law, I managed to prepare the lessons beforehand, and they never suspected my incompetency.

From this school I received my first little fortune of $25; and I added to this by picking wild blackberries at odd times, which found a ready sale at fifty cents a gallon.

Fall found me settled at the old Boelling hotel in Astoria, with my nephew, Frank Hobson, and my little son George. Our board was paid, I taking care of our small room, and our clothes, with the privilege of doing our washing and ironing on Saturdays. And now I encountered one of my sharpest trials, for, on entering school, and being examined in mental arithmetic, I was placed in the primary class!

Mr. Deardorff, the principal, kindly offered to assist me in that study after school, and, later, permitted me to enter both classes. Words can never express my humiliation at having to recite with children of from eight to fourteen years of age. This, however, was of brief duration, for in a few weeks I had advanced to the next class above, and was soon allowed to enter the third (and highest) class in mental arithmetic.

At the end of the term of nine months, I had passed into most of the advanced classes;—not that I was an apt scholar, for my knowledge has always been acquired by the hardest labor,—but by sheer determination, industry and perseverance. At 4 A.M. my lamp was always burning, and I was poring over my books,—never allowing myself more than eight hours for sleep.

Nothing was permitted to come between me and this, the greatest opportunity of my life. . . .

Judge Cyrus Olney was then county school superintendent, and it was with fear and trembling that I applied to him for examination and a certificate. But he said to me:

"I know you are competent to teach that school. I have had my eye on you for over a year, and I know you will do your duty. I will send you a certificate." And he did.

This was a great encouragement to me, and increased my determination to do my best.

I accepted the school, and with my boy, I was away the very next day after my Astoria term closed, to Bruceport, where I began teaching at once. After I had taught here two weeks, a subscription was raised among the few families, and more numerous oystermen, for another three months' school, (making a six months' term, in all).

Before this was completed, I received and accepted an offer of the Oysterville school (the same school I first attended), where I "boarded around," as was then the prevailing custom. . . .

I had, in this way, so far, managed to save up all my school money, and at the end of this term of four months, at $40 per month, I would have $400. My ambition now was to have a home of my own, and, with this brilliant prospect in view, I bought a half lot in Astoria, and contracted with a carpenter to build me a small, three-roomed cottage, with a cosy little porch.

To this, my last school, I can look back with pleasure and satisfaction. The neighboring farmers and their families were kindness itself to me. They never forgot the teacher, and her little boy, but continually brought us good things to eat, and invitations to visit them over Sunday.

I was invariably up by five o'clock, looking over all the lessons for the day. Then came breakfast, and at 8:30 we were off for the pleasant mile walk to the school-house.

Thus the four months sped pleasantly away, and when my school closed, my little home in Astoria was ready for me. It stood on the back end of that beautiful and sightly lot on which I. W. Case, the banker, later built his handsome residence. I was as proud as a queen of my pretty little home, which was the first I had ever really owned; and the fact that I had earned it all myself made it doubly prized.

I had won the respect of all, and now work came to me from all directions. As I could "turn my hand" to almost anything, and was anxious to accumulate, I was never idle. . . .

In the fall I rented my little home, and went to visit my people in Roseburg. My brother and two of my sisters had married, and they all urged me to spend the winter among them. . . .

Mr. Abraham, my new brother-in-law, was a merchant, and, among them all, I was persuaded to go into the business of dressmaking and millinery. Consequently, when spring opened, I established myself in a house just across the street from Mr. Abraham's store, he buying me a nice little stock of goods. Here for two years I plodded along, working early and late, and getting ahead pecuniarily much faster than I had ever yet done. I had saved my earnings, with which I had bought my home there, and had a good start, and a growing business, with plenty to eat, drink, and wear.

My front yard, 12 x 20, was a gorgeous glory of color, and my beautiful flowers were the admiration of all the passersby, while my back yard supplied an abundance of vegetables.

My boy was in school, and with the respect of the community, added, why was I not happy? I was. Work brought its own pleasure, and sweet rewards. Five A.M. never found me in bed, though often did I awake at two A.M. in my chair, with my work still in my hand. But the young are soon rested, and as a change of work gives rest and health, I was blest with both. I had a time and place for everything, and I have found adherence to this rule throughout my life to be one of the greatest aids to succees in any pursuit.

It was also then, as it still is, my habit to plan today for tomorrow. And now I am going over my past life, step by step, gleaning here and there what I hope may be of service to those who come after me, knowing full well how undesirable and seemingly impossible such a life will seem to the youth of today, yet believing its lessons ought to be of use to them in this age of teeming wealth, and lavish expenditure, surrounded and protected as they are from all the hardships of frontier life, with the fountains of knowledge flowing free for them to drink, "without money, and without price."

As I have already said, I had had two years of uninterrupted success in my millinery and dressmaking business in Roseburg. The town had steadily grown, and now a new milliner made her advent. She moved in next door to me, and came right in, and looked me over, stock and all, also getting all the information I could give her. She told me incidentally that she had been a milliner for years; that she had learned the trade, and understood it thoroughly, and had come there to begin business, and intended to remain.

I was soon made to feel her power. She laughed at, and ridiculed my pretensions, saying that mine was only a "picked-up" business, and that I did not know the first principles of the trade.

"She knew how to bleach and whiten all kinds of leghorn and white straws; she could renew and make over all shapes and kinds of hats; she could also make hat-blocks, on which to press and shape hats, and make new frames," all of which was Greek to me, practically speaking. She came late in the fall, and her husband went, with his team, throughout the country, gathering up all the old hats, and advertising his wife's superior work as a milliner.

All this was not only humiliating to me personally, but was a severe blow to my business. I was at my wits' end to know what to do, and how to do it. One beautiful day I sat thinking the matter over while eating my dinner at the table in front of a window which overlooked my new neighbor's kitchen door. I had seen her husband drive past the evening before, and unload several open boxes filled with old hats, and that day they were getting ready for cleaning, bleaching, and pressing.

They set a table out in the sun, and placed upon it two new plaster of paris hat-blocks. Then the work began, not twenty feet from me. My house was above them, so that they could not see me, but I could not only see them, but could hear every word they said.

For more than an hour I sat there, and in that brief time I learned the art of cleaning, stiffening, fitting, bleaching, and pressing hats.

Oh, what a revelation it was to me! My heart was beating fast, and I felt that I had never learned so much in any one hour of my life before. I saw how easily it was all done, and how much profit there was in it.

The new hats that year were very, very small ("pancakes"), and some of those old-fashioned hats would make three of them. Certainly two new ones could be made from each of most of the old ones. Of course, the remnants would be considered useless by the owners, and were turned to profit by the expert milliner.

I now knew that if I could get the blocks I could do the work, so I stepped down to the new milliner's shop, and asked her how much she would charge to make me two blocks.

She said: "Thirty dollars."

I said: "I will think it over. I did not expect them to be so high."

"You don't expect me to give away my business, do you?" she asked. Then, smiling, she added, "Can you press hats?"

I passed out, and as the door closed, I heard them laughing at my expense. This roused me almost to desperation, and I said to myself, "The day will come when I will show you that I can not only press hats, but do several other things; and first of all, I will find out how to make hat-blocks."

I now remembered a book I possessed, entitled, "Inquire Within." From this I learned how to mix plaster of paris for molds, and this gave me a foundation on which to experiment. I had the buckram frame, like those two new blocks of Mrs. ———, and I knew they must have made and shaped their blocks by the use of those frames, so I bought 50 cents' worth of plaster of paris at the drug-store, and set to work. My first attempt was a failure, but it proved to me that I was on the right road. I was in such a state of anxiety and excitement that I slept little that night.

As soon as the stores were open in the morning, I purchased a dollar's worth of plaster of paris. During that anxious, wakeful night, I had gone over the ground thoroughly in my mind, and was confident of success; and succeed I did.

Words failed to express my triumphant joy that in less than twenty-four hours, I had obtained, and now held, the key to that mysterious knowledge whose wonderful results had charmed away my customers.

I began at once to put my freshly acquired knowledge into practice, resolving not to let a soul know how it was obtained. . . .

As has been said, I set about putting my newly acquired knowledge into practical use. Going about among the stores, I bought up all their old, out-of-date, unsalable millinery, for almost nothing, and began at once to prepare it for future use, knowing that the fall styles in straws would be in demand in the spring, and that, in this way, with a small stock from San Francisco, I could make a good showing; which I did. But, though my goods were in every way equal to those of my rival, the customers passed me by, and bought of her. She managed to checkmate me at every turn.

Thus the summer and autumn wore away, and left me stranded, but not conquered. My time had not all been lost, however, and I knew that I had gained much that would be of service to me in the future.

I had surmounted other formidable difficulties, and I would yet wring a victory out of this defeat. For one thing, I had learned more of average human nature during that year than I had in all my previous life, and I saw that I must convince that community that I was not a pretender, but was, in reality, mistress of my business; and that could not be accomplished alone by the skillful making over of old hats and bonnets.

Therefore, in November, 1867, leaving my boy in charge of a

minister and his wife, who occupied my little home; and borrowing $250, I left for San Francisco.

I had previously announced in both the Roseburg papers that I should spend the winter in the best millinery establishment in San Francisco, with the purpose of perfecting myself in the business, and would return in the spring, bringing with me all the latest and most attractive millinery. This I carried out to the letter.

Bearing letters of recommendation from two of the principal merchants of Roseburg who dealt with Madame Fouts, I was kindly received by her, and given every advantage. For three months I sat beside her head-trimmer, where I could see and hear everything. Those three months in San Francisco were worth more to me than ten years of such opportunities as I had hitherto had. Madame took me to the wholesale houses, and showed me how to purchase goods, and especially how to select odd lots of nice, but out of date materials, and how to convert these into new and attractive styles. I saw her daily selling hats which had not cost her over fifty cents, for from four to six dollars. Meantime, I worked only on my own goods, and when spring came, I had a lovely stock secured with very little expense. I wrote home ordering a show-window put into the front of my little store—almost the first show-window in that town. I also had printed announcements stuck off, and sent on ahead to all of my patrons, and to be posted, stating the day I had fixed for my grand opening.

I reached home a week or ten days beforehand, and had everything in complete and elegant readiness at the appointed time.

I now felt equal to the situation, and was mistress of my art, a fact which I used to the best possible advantage.

The profits from the sales of that year amounted to $1,500, and the business continued to increase as long as I conducted it.

In 1870, I placed my son in the University of California, at Berkeley. I had always had a fondness for nursing, and had developed such a special capacity in that direction by assisting my neighbors in illness, that I was more and more besieged by the entreaties of my friends and doctors, which were hard to refuse, to come to their aid in sickness, oftentimes to the detriment of business, and now that money came easily, a desire began to grow within me for a medical education. One evening I was sent for by a friend with a very sick child. The old physician in my presence attempted to use an instrument for the relief of the little sufferer, and, in his long, bungling, and unsuccessful attempt he severely lacerated the tender flesh of the poor little girl. At last, he laid down the instrument to wipe his glasses. I picked it up, saying, "Let me try, Doctor," and passed it instantly, with perfect ease, bringing immediate relief to the tortured child. The mother, who was standing by in agony at the sight of her child's mutilation, threw her arms around my neck, and sobbed out her thanks. Not so the doctor! He did not appreciate or approve of my interference, and he showed his displeasure at the time most emphatically. This apparently unimportant incident really decided my future course.

A few days later, I called on my friend, Dr. Hamilton, and confiding to him my plans and ambitions, I asked for the loan of medical books. He gave me Gray's *Anatomy*. I came out of his private office into the drug-store, where I saw Hon. S. F. Chadwick, who had heard the conversation, and who came promptly forward and shook my hand warmly, saying: "Go ahead. It is in you; let it come out. You will win."

The Hon. Jesse Applegate, my dear and revered friend, who had fondled me as a babe, was the one other person who ever gave me a single word of encouragement to study medicine.

Realizing that I should meet opposition, especially from my own family, I kept my own counsel.

I now began in good earnest to arrange my business affairs so that I could leave for the East in one year from that time, meantime studying diligently to familiarize myself with the science of anatomy, the groundwork of my chosen profession. Later, I took Mrs. Duniway, of Portland, editor and proprietor of *The New Northwest*, into my confidence, and arranged with her to take my boy into her family, and give him work on her paper.

I also wrote to my old friend, Mrs. W. L. Adams, of Portland, and asked her to take a motherly interest in my boy. She responded promptly, saying:

"My husband, Dr. Adams, is in Philadelphia, partly for study, and partly for his health. Why not go there? He could be of great help to you, and it would be a relief to me to know that you were near in case of sickness. You can trust me to look after the welfare of your boy."

This letter was a genuine comfort to me, and I decided to accept her advice. In due time, I announced that in two weeks I would leave for Philadelphia, to enter a medical school. As I have said, I expected disapproval from my friends and relatives, but I was not prepared for the storm of opposition that followed. My family felt that they were disgraced, and even my own child was influenced and encouraged to think that I was doing him an irreparable injury, by my course. People sneered and laughed derisively.. Most of my friends seemed to consider it their Christian duty to advise against, and endeavor to prevent me taking this "fatal" step. That crucial fortnight was a period in my life never to be forgotten. I was literally kept on the rack. But as all things must have an end, the day of my departure was at last at hand.

III

Women in Factories:
The Industrial Revolution, 1820–70

In this section are presented reflections on the role of women in the initial phases of the industrial revolution. It should be kept in mind that during the critical 1820s and 1830s the mobilization of women who played a central role in the new factories was by no means the mustering of "underemployed" labor. Those women were highly productive individuals who were enjoying wide opportunities for useful, rewarding work, particularly in the expanding agricultural sector. Indeed, more women turned to such opportunities than entered factories. The immigrant women who, along with immigrant men, replaced these native women during the 1840s and 1850s tended to be of peasant stock and were more willing to accept low wages and oppressive working conditions. They found that factory work provided significant material advances over their previous situations and was a useful vehicle for entry into a more secure future. However, the degeneration of factory conditions for women that accompanied massive immigration was unsettling to much of American society, and even during this early period there developed a movement to ameliorate them. Some of the sources of the movement that climaxed after 1870 with the high tide of immigration and the cresting of enthusiasm for Victorian culture are suggested here.

THE FIRST INVESTIGATION

Despite the fact that an industrial revolution occurred in the United States during the first half of the nineteenth century, the transformation of the economy during that period was by no means either swift or complete. One example of the gradual character of the transformation is the extent to which women engaged in manufacturing outside the factory system even after the onset of the industrial revolution. During the 1820s, the rapid expansion of the economy and the swiftly increasing pace of urbanization created a sharp increase in the demand for ready-made clothing. This demand, interacting with protection afforded by the tariffs of 1816 and 1828 and the presence of large numbers of women either requiring employment for support or desiring employment to escape a household, led to the development of a large class of women workers employed not only in households but, more importantly, in small shops outside their homes. Concentrated in the large cities of Boston, New York, and Philadelphia, these women, largely unskilled, sewed by hand the garments that had been cut by skilled tailors; these garments, primarily cheap work clothing, reached national markets. Indeed, the structure of the garment industry remained unmodified until the 1840s, when the introduction of the sewing machine permitted some increase in scale of production and increased the competition between unskilled seamstresses and the skilled tailors who dominated the custom-garment trade.

The following selection indicates that the problems associated with the rise of the large-scale factory were present considerably earlier—in the small garment shops of Philadelphia during the 1820s. Mathew Carey, an early promoter of American manufacturing, an enterprising printer and publisher, and a philanthropist, launched a campaign to support those unskilled women who seemed unable to support themselves on their earnings in the garment industry. Carey did not indicate how many of the workingwomen were incapable of supporting themselves and did not attempt a thorough explanation of their plight, but he did make the first suggestion of a "day-care" center to enable women, or at least widows, to work effectively. Moreover, his appeal to middle- and upper-class consciences helped to launch the systematic scrutiny of women's work that would thrive during the Victorian era.

REPORT ON FEMALE WAGES

Philadelphia, March 25, 1829

. . . a committee appointed by the Town Meeting of the citizens of the city and county of Philadelphia, on the 21st ult. "to ascertain whether those who are able and willing to work, can in general procure employment—what is the effect upon the comfort, happiness and morals of the females who depend on their work for a support, of the low rate of wages paid to that class of society—to what extent the sufferings of the poor are attributable to those low wages—and what is the effect of benevolent or assistance societies on the industry of the labouring poor,"—beg leave to report . . . .

That they are convinced, from a careful examination of the subject, that the wages paid to seamstresses who work in their own apartments—to spoolers—to spinners—to folders of printed books —and in many cases to those who take in washing, are utterly inadequate to their support, even if fully employed, particularly if they have children unable to aid them in their industry, as is often the case; whereas, the work is so precarious that they are often unemployed—sometimes for a whole week together, and very frequently one or two days in each week. In many cases no small portion of their time is spent in seeking and waiting for work, and in taking it home when done:

That in the different branches above specified, industrious and expert women, unencumbered with families, and with steady employment, cannot average more than a dollar and a quarter per week; that their room rent is generally fifty cents, sometimes sixty-two and a half; and fuel probably costs about a quarter of a dollar per week, on an average through the year. Thus, in the case of constant unceasing employment, (a case that rarely occurs,) there remains but about half a dollar per week, or twenty-six dollars per annum, for meat, drink, and clothing; and supposing only eight weeks in the year unemployed through sickness, want of work, or attention to children, (and this is but a moderate calculation), the

From Mathew Carey, *Miscellaneous Essays* (Philadelphia: Carey and Hart; 1830), pp. 267–71 and 309–12.

amount for food and clothing would be reduced to the most miserable pittance of sixteen dollars per annum! Can we wonder at the harrowing misery and distress that prevail among this class, under such a deplorable state of things?

That it is a most lamentable fact, that among the women thus "ground to the earth" by such inadequate wages, are to be found numbers of widows, with small children, who, by the untimely death of their husbands, and those reverses of fortune to which human affairs are liable have been gradually reduced from a state of comfort and affluence to penury, and thrown upon the world, with no other dependence than their needles to support themselves and their offspring:

That although it is freely admitted that great distress and poverty arise from habits of dissipation and intemperance of husbands, and their shameful neglect to make that provision for their wives and children which they are bound to do by the laws of God and man, (and which, it is to be deeply regretted, the laws do not duly enforce,) yet we feel satisfied that those deplorable and pernicious habits do not produce half the wretchedness to which meritorious females are subjected in this city, of which the greater portion arises from the other source which we have stated, and which places before this class the alternatives of begging—applying to the overseers of the poor—stealing—or starving. We might add another—but we forbear.

That the scenes of distress and suffering which we have witnessed in our various visits to the dwellings of women who depend on their labour for support, resulting from inadequate wages, are of the most afflicting kind, and can scarcely be believed but by those whom they have been beheld. We have found cases of women, whose husbands have been for weeks disabled by accidents, or by sickness produced by working on canals, surrounded by pestiferous miasmata—who have had to support their husbands and three or four children, by spooling at 20 cents per hundred skeins—by spinning at as low a rate of compensation—by washing and rough drying at 20 or 25 cents per dozen—or by making shirts and pantaloons at 12½ cents each:

That it is a great error to suppose, as is too frequently supposed, that every person in this community, able and willing to work, can procure employment; as there are many persons of both sexes, more particularly females, who are at all times partially, and frequently wholly unemployed, although anxious to procure employment. There is almost always a great deficiency of employment for females, which is the chief reason why their wages are so disproportioned to those of males:

That there are few errors more pernicious, or more destitute of foundation, than the idea which has of late years been industriously propagated, that the benevolent societies of this city produce idleness and dissipation, by inducing the poor to depend on them, instead of depending on industry. The whole of the *annual subscriptions* for last year, to seven of the most prominent of these societies, embracing, it is believed, nearly all of any importance, was only 1,068 dollars—and the whole of their disbursements, only 3,740 dollars, a sum which obviously could not materially affect the industry of the many thousands, male and female, who have to work for their living. And it is of the last importance, in the consideration of this question, to take notice, that most part of these disbursements, was for *work done by aged women, and for food and clothing furnished to superannuated men and women, and destitute children:*

That those societies, far from increasing idleness and pauperism, have a directly contrary tendency; as, by the timely aid they afford, in seasons of distress and pressure, they very frequently produce the important effect of rescuing deserving persons from sinking into hopeless poverty, and thus becoming chargeable as paupers. Cases of this kind are of frequent occurrence. And it is not improbable that the consequent annual diminution of the poor tax exceeds the whole amount contributed to those societies by our citizens:

That numerous proofs of the industry of the classes which depend for support upon their labour, and of the injustice of the denunciations levelled against them, might be produced; but we shall confine ourselves to two, one as regards males, the other as regards females. The first is, the thousands of men, who eagerly seek for labour on canals, often in pestilential situations, with death staring them in the face—the second, the fact that from 1000 to 1100 women have weekly travelled three, four, six, eight or ten squares, and anxiously waited for hours at the Provident Society's rooms for work, although it was known that they could not procure more than enough to employ themselves two, three or four days in the week. These two facts alone, ought to settle this question beyond the power of cavil or appeal.[1]

For evils of the magnitude and inveteracy of those under which the women suffer, who depend on their labour for support, it is difficult to devise a remedy. A complete remedy is perhaps impracticable. They may, however, and we hope will, be mitigated. The mitigation must wholly depend on the humanity and the sense of justice of those by whom they are employed, who, . . . ought to, increase those wages. Although the great and increasing competition in trade, renders it necessary to use rigid economy in the expense of producing articles for market, it can never palliate, far less justify the oppression of the ill-fated people engaged in the production, by whose labours large fortunes are made, and their employers enabled to live in ease and opulence.

It is peculiarly incumbent on those wealthy ladies, who employ for the sufferings of their sex, to give them such wages as will not only yield them a present support, but enable them to make provision for times of sickness or scarcity of employment. . . .

It is to recommend to the most serious consideration of the benevolent of their fellow citizens, the establishment of "a society for bettering the condition of the poor," [2] by encouraging habits of order, regularity and cleanliness in their persons and apartments; by instructing them in the most economical modes of cooking their food; by inducing them to send their children to school, and, when arrived at a proper age, to bind them apprentices to useful trades,

1. Subsequent inquiries have established the fact that numbers of those women came from Kensington, a distance of two miles from the society's rooms, and of course had to travel four miles for four shirts, which would require three days labour, and for which they received but half a dollar.

2. [July 8, 1830] Two societies on this plan have been since formed in this city—one for bettering the condition of the poor, generally—and the other for bettering the condition of indigent Roman Catholics.

and to lodge the little surplus of their earnings, when they have any surplus, in the saving fund; by enabling them to purchase fuel and other necessaries at reasonable rates; in a word, by inculcating on them those principles and that kind of conduct, which are calculated to elevate them in their own estimation, and in that of society at large. Societies of this description have produced the most salutary effects on the comfort and morals of the poor in various parts of Great Britain.

And while the Committee press on the humane and wealthy part of the community, the propriety of aiding in a greater degree than heretofore, (by their own exertions and through the various benevolent societies that exist among us, and whose funds are at present greatly reduced,) to alleviate the distresses of the numerous widows and orphans, and the really deserving poor and helpless of very description; they would likewise suggest to housekeepers and heads of families the propriety of seeking out and employing in the situation of domestics in their several families, destitute females, who, by the frowns of fortune, have been reduced to distress. Hundreds of this description are to be found within the precincts of the city and liberties, who, if properly encouraged, would be grateful for the means of employment thus afforded them, and who might profit by precept and example set before them in the houses of respectable citizens. . . .

THOUGHTS ON "INFANT SCHOOLS"

Philadelphia, June 18, 1827

A large portion of the poorer classes of society, male and female, particularly the former, are obliged to leave their homes daily, to labour for support in the houses of those by whom they are employed. When thus absent, their children, as soon as able to walk, spend the chief part of their time prowling about the streets—a seminary, where it would be almost miraculous if they did not imbibe of every species of vice and wickedness of which human nature is capable. These, as they progressively advance in life, germinate luxuriantly—produce copious harvests of crime, from petty larceny to highway robbery, and murder—and furnish our criminal courts and penitentiaries with the crowds which they unfortunately exhibit. This seminary, alas! does not afford the smallest chance of the acquisition of a single countervailing virtue.

The case of the children of the poor whose employments do not require them to leave their homes, though not quite so deplorable as that of those above referred to, is not very materially better. For however attentive the parents may be to their duty, however, watchful over their offspring, it is impossible to restrain them from spending a large portion of their time in the streets, exposed to the same contamination as the children of the other class.

The object of the proposed plan is to lay the axe to the root of this evil, by the establishment of a school or schools, for the reception and tuition of children below six years of age, in which they will be habituated to order and regularity—taught whatever may be suitable to their capacities—inspired with correct principles —and rescued from the perilous situation in which they are placed at present. Those who have attended to the development of the faculties of children, must have observed that their susceptibility of impressions, good or evil, calculated to produce lasting effects, commences at a far earlier period, than is usually supposed. Most of the benevolent and malevolent propensities—of the virtues which adorn, of the crimes which disgrace human nature—flow from circumstances, apparently of little importance, which take place at two, three, four, or five years of age. . . .

The rescue of the offspring, although the chief object, is by no means the only advantage of the proposed plan. It will greatly relieve the parents from the waste of time and the anxiety attendant on the care of their children—it will thus increase happiness, of a very useful, and, let me add, in general, a very deserving class of our inhabitants. Attention to their children, although necessarily but very imperfectly afforded, must occupy important portions of the time which ought to be devoted to that labour whereon they depend for the support of themselves and families—and which, it is to be regretted, even when fully and skillfully employed, is at best but scantily remunerated! It is an appalling fact, that there are probably six or seven thousand females in this city, some brought up in affluent circumstances, whose utmost industry cannot earn more than a dollar and a quarter, or at most a dollar and a half per week, out of which many of these unfortunates have to support not only two, three, four, or five children, but dissolute, idle husbands some of whom not only contribute little or nothing to the support of wives or offspring, but squander the earnings of their wives. The attempt to alleviate the distresses of fellow beings thus unhappily circumstanced cannot fail to meet the cordial approbation and zealous support of the friends of humanity.

It is too much the fashion to regard the mass of the poor as dissipated and idle—and their sufferings as the result of their vices. It is too true, that society, under whatever aspect it may be viewed, exhibits enough of vice and guilt, to humble pride, and commiseration. But that there is a great mass of honesty and virtue among the poor, there cannot be a doubt in the minds of those who have had a fair opportunity to decide on the subject. And whatever superiority of virtue may exist in the middle and upper classes of society, is no more than might reasonably be expected, when we consider the advantages they possess—the good examples and the moral and intellectual cultivation most of them have had—and the restraints, which the sphere wherein they move imposes on them. "Unto whomsoever much is given, of him shall much be required." On the other hand, if we weigh in an even balance the disadvantages under which the poor labour—the pressure of poverty—the want of good examples—the fascination of bad examples to which they are so much exposed—the destitution of cultivation, either moral or intellectual—instead of wondering that there is so much depravity among them, the wonder is, that there is not far more.

To sum up all. The success of this plan will diminish the sufferings of poor parents, by enabling them to employ their time to advantage—elevate the character of the rising generation of that class—save our property from depredation by larcenies and burglaries—diminish the business of our criminal courts—and in a great degree depopulate our penitentiaries. And are not these glorious objects amply sufficient to excite the benevolent to the exertions necessary to carry this grand plan into execution? What person of liberal mind, can be indifferent to the success of such a beneficent undertaking?

The smallness of the subscription, only two dollars per annum, a sum not beyond the means of a day labourer, together with the importance and benevolence of the object in view, will, it is hoped, insure an unusually large list of subscribers.

P.S. It is highly probable, if this plan be carried into immediate operation, and prove as beneficial as we have reason to expect, that the legislature at its next session, will incorporate it into the system of public schools, and thus render it, as it ought to be, a public charge.

EARLY DAYS AT LOWELL

The following selection by Lucy Larcom (1824–93) is from her book, *A New England Girlhood*, in which she describes her ten years as one of the young girls in the mills of Lowell, Massachusetts. She was active in the factory Improvement Society and the *Lowell Offering*, a magazine edited by two former mill operatives that attempted to prove there was a "mind among the spindles." Lucy was a daughter of a sea captain from Beverly, Massachusetts, who died when she was a child. She then moved to Lowell with her mother, who took a position as supervisor of a textile-mill dormitory. Workingwomen were more the rule than the exception in Lucy's large family of nine children and, led on by the marriage of example and economic necessity, Lucy began work when she was eleven and remained in the mill for ten years. In 1846 she moved westward to Illinois with her sister and a great tide of other New Englanders. There she taught school and acquired a college education (1849–52), but did not marry. Aspiring to a literary career, she soon returned to Beverly to be closer to New England's cultural circuits. She subsequently taught English literature at a girl's seminary, edited a children's magazine, *Our Young Folks*, and wrote verse for other children's magazines and the *Atlantic Monthly*.

Although her sensitivities were greater and her education more substantial than those of hundreds of other New England mill girls, her career was not significantly different. Often the girls found adjustment to mill life easy and attractive but then, after a few years, usually when mill owners began to speed up work to increase the return on their capital, turned to what appeared to be even more promising opportunities. Also, she and most of the other mill girls saw their personal future as far greater than that available within the factory system. They tended to consider employment at Lowell a means of passage to a brighter day. They rarely worked to improve conditions in the mills but believed instead in the power of an individual approach to an end that was self-improvement. But the tantalizing question remains: Even if this was a sound course for Lucy Larcom—and many other factory girls—to follow, for how many others, then and later, did it serve to limit what the future might provide?

GIRLHOOD IN THE MILL

. . . I heard it said one day, in a distressed tone, "The children will have to leave school and go into the mill."

There were many pros and cons between my mother and sisters before this was positively decided. The mill-agent did not want to take us two little girls, but consented on condition we should be sure to attend school the full number of months prescribed each year. I, the younger one, was then between eleven and twelve years old.

I listened to all that was said about it, very much fearing that I should not be permitted to do the coveted work. For the feeling had already frequently come to me, that I was the one too many in the overcrowded family nest. Once, before we left our old home, I had heard a neighbor consoling with my mother because there were so many of us, and her emphatic reply had been a great relief to my mind:—

"There isn't one more than I want. I could not spare a single one of my children."

But her difficulties were increasing, and I thought it would be a pleasure to feel that I was not a trouble or burden or expense to anybody. So I went to my first day's work in the mill with a light heart. The novelty of it made it seem easy, and it really was not

From Lucy Larcom, *A New England Girlhood* (Boston: Houghton Mifflin Co., 1889), pp. 153–55, 181–83, and 196–200.

hard, just to change the bobbins on the spinning-frames every three quarters of an hour or so, with half a dozen other little girls who were doing the same thing. When I came back at night, the family began to pity me for my long, tiresome day's work, but I laughed and said,—

"Why, it is nothing but fun. It is just like play."

And for a little while it was only a new amusement; I liked it better than going to school and "making believe" I was learning when I was not. And there was a great deal of play mixed with it. We were not occupied more than half the time. The intervals were spent frolicking around among the spinning-frames, teasing and talking to the older girls, or entertaining ourselves with games and stories in a corner, or exploring, with the overseer's permission, the mysteries of the carding-room, the dressing-room, and the weaving-room.

I never cared much for machinery. The buzzing and hissing and whizzing of pulleys and rollers and spindles and flyers around me often grew tiresome. I could not see into their complications, or feel interested in them. But in a room below us we were sometimes allowed to peer in through a sort of blind door at the great waterwheel that carried the works of the whole mill. It was so huge that we could only watch a few of its spokes at a time, and part of its dripping rim, moving with a slow, measured strength through the darkness that shut it in. It impressed me with something of the awe which comes to us in thinking of the great Power which keeps the mechanism of the universe in motion. Even now, the remembrance of its large, mysterious movement, in which every little motion of every noisy little wheel was involved, brings back to me a verse from one of my favorite hymns:—

> Our lives through various scenes are drawn,
>   And vexed by trifling cares
> While Thine eternal thought moves on
>   Thy undisturbed affairs.

There were compensations for being shut in to daily toil so early. The mill itself had its lessons for us. But it was not, and could not be, the right sort of life for a child, and we were happy in the knowledge that, at the longest, our employment was only to be temporary.

When I took my next three months at the grammar school, everything there was changed, and I too was changed. The teachers were kind, and thorough in their instruction; and my mind seemed to have been ploughed up during that year of work, so that knowledge took root in it easily. It was a great delight to me to study, and at the end of the three months the master told me that I was prepared for the high school.

But alas! I could not go. The little money I could earn—one dollar a week, besides the price of my board—was needed in the family, and I must return to the mill. It was a severe disappointment to me, though I did not say so at home. . . .

Some of the girls could not believe that the Bible was meant to be counted among forbidden books. We all thought that the Scriptures had a right to go wherever we went, and that if we needed them anywhere, it was at our work. I evaded the law by carrying some leaves from a torn Testament in my pocket.

The overseer, caring more for law than gospel, confiscated all he found. He had his desk full of Bibles. It sounded oddly to hear him say to the most religious girl in the room, when he took hers away, "I did think you had more conscience than to bring that book here." But we had some close ethical questions to settle in those days. It was a rigid code of morality under which we lived. Nobody complained of it, however, and we were doubtless better off for its strictness, in the end.

The last window in the row behind me was filled with flourishing house-plants—fragrant-leaved geraniums, the overseer's pets. They gave that corner a bowery look; the perfume and freshness tempted me there often. Standing before that window, I could look across the room and see girls moving backwards and forwards among the spinning-frames, sometimes stooping, sometimes reaching up their arms, as their work required, with easy and not ungraceful movements. On the whole, it was far from being a disagreeable place to stay in. The girls were bright-looking and neat, and everything was kept clean and shining. The effect of the whole was rather attractive to strangers.

. . . Still, we did not call ourselves ladies. We did not forget that we were working-girls, wearing coarse aprons suitable to our work, and that there was some danger of our becoming drudges. I know that sometimes the confinement of the mill became very wearisome to me. In the sweet June weather I would lean far out of the window, and try not to hear the unceasing clash of sound inside. Looking away to the hills, my whole stifled being would cry out

Oh, that I had wings!

Still I was there from choice, and

The prison unto which we doom ourselves,
No prison is.

And I was every day making discoveries about life, and about myself. I had naturally some elements of the recluse, and would never, of my own choice, have lived in a crowd. I loved quietness. The noise of machinery was particularly distasteful to me. But I found that the crowd was made up of single human lives, not one of them wholly uninteresting, when separately known. I learned also that there are many things which belong to the whole world of us together, that no one of us, nor any few of us, can claim or enjoy for ourselves alone. I discovered, too, that I could so accustom myself to the noise that it became like a silence to me. And I defied the machinery to make me its slave. Its incessant discords could not drown the music of my thoughts if I would let them fly high enough. Even the long hours, the early rising, and the regularity enforced by the clangor of the bell were good discipline for one who was naturally inclined to dally and to dream, and who loved her own personal liberty with a willful rebellion against control. Perhaps I could have brought myself into the limitations of order and method in no other way.

Like a plant that starts up in showers and sunshine and does not know which has best helped it to grow, it is difficult to say whether the hard things or the pleasant things did me most good. But when I was sincerest with myself, as also when I thought least about it, I know that I was glad to be alive, and to be just where I was. . . .

The girls who toiled together at Lowell were clearing away a few weeds from the overgrown track of independent labor for other women. They practically said, by numbering themselves among factory girls, that in our country no real odium could be attached to any honest toil that any self-respecting woman might undertake.

I regard it as one of the privileges of my youth that I was permitted to grow up among those active, interesting girls, whose lives were not mere echoes of other lives, but had principle and purpose distinctly their own. Their vigor of character was a natural development. The New Hampshire girls who came to Lowell were descendants of the sturdy backwoodsmen who settled that State scarcely a hundred years before. Their grandmothers had suffered the hardships of frontier life, had known the horrors of savage warfare when the beautiful valleys of the Connecticut and the Merrimack were threaded with Indian trails from Canada to the white settlements. Those young women did justice to their inheritance. They were earnest and capable; ready to undertake anything that was worth doing. My dreamy, indolent nature was shamed into activity among them. They gave me a larger, firmer ideal of womanhood. . . .

We used sometimes to see it claimed, in public prints that it would be better for all of us mill girls to be working in families, at domestic service, than to be where we were.

Perhaps the difficulties of modern housekeepers did begin with the opening of the Lowell factories. Country girls were naturally independent, and the feeling that at this new work the few hours they had of every-day leisure were entirely their own was a satisfaction to them. They preferred it to going out as "hired help." It was like a young man's pleasure in entering upon business for himself. Girls had never tried that experiment before, and they liked it. It brought out in them a dormant strength of character which the world did not previously see, but now fully acknowledges. Of course they had a right to continue at that freer kind of work as long as they chose, although their doing so increased the perplexities of the housekeeping problem for themselves even, since many of them were to become, and did become, American house-mistresses. . . .

THE LABOR MOVEMENT AT LOWELL

By the 1840s, the promise of New England factory life for young women had acquired at least a few blemishes. Dissatisfaction focused in particular on the increasing speed of spindle and loom operation designed to increase the productivity of capital. During the 1830s women operatives had occasionally participated in limited strikes but had not formed anything resembling a formal organization. However, in 1845, a group of Lowell workers, under the leadership of Sarah G. Bagley, a skilled weaver, formed the Lowell Female Labor Reform Association (LFLRA), created an association magazine *(The Voice of Industry)*, and linked their organization to the New England Workingmen's Association, whose formation had inspired the women to action. Despite widespread dissatisfaction among the operatives over the sustained speed-up, the LFLRA mobilized its only successful work stoppage among the skilled weavers. Instead of urging more strikes, it resorted to joining with other labor associations in agitating for legislative enactment of a ten-hour maximum to the working day.

The petitions of the LFLRA and other workers' associations that came to the Massachusetts legislature between 1842 and 1845 produced the appointment of its first special committee to investigate labor conditions and suggest legislation. The selection that follows is the report of that committee. The arguments of the textile manufacturers prevailed. Certainly contributing to that victory was the fact that the chairman of the special committee was William Schouler, a Lowell editor who had purchased the *Lowell Offering* in 1843 and turned it into a company organ that opposed the ten-hour day and stressed individual mental and spiritual development as the most appropriate concerns for working women. The results were similar elsewhere in New England. New Hampshire, in 1847, became the first state to enact a ten-hour day law (applying to both men and women), but the law proved very ineffective as it allowed longer working days by specific contract. Rhode Island's 1853 legislation contained an identical loophole. Only where large-scale factories were less significant did more effective hours legislation pass (in Pennsylvania and Maine in 1848, in Ohio in 1852, and in California and Georgia in 1853) and this legislation also tended to have severe limitations.

The Lowell women did not forget Schouler's role and they contributed to his defeat in campaigning for reelection. But, despite that electoral victory, the LFLRA probably never had the active support of a majority of the Lowell workers, particularly the unskilled spindle operators, and after the legislative rebuff it turned to promoting insurance among skilled workers until its disappearance in 1847. In general, during the 1840s, the labor movement tended to be dominated by skilled workers, most often members of the artisan classes who were losing both status and economic position in the face of industrial revolution. It was propelled by an "antimonopolist" ideology that sought to re-create a community of farmers, small manufacturers, and tradesmen rather than civilize the new industrial order. A labor movement among skilled factory workers that embraced the realities of industrialization would not emerge until the 1850s; a similar movement among the unskilled had to await the 1890s.

For the Lowell girls who had protested changing industrial conditions the most common solution turned out to be exodus from the mills rather than collective action. The older textile manufacturers of interior towns such as Lowell met increased competition from manufacturers along the coast who could tap immigrant labor more easily and who, beginning in the 1840s, could utilize inexpensive steam power. In the face of increasing competition, all manufacturers became even more relentless in their efforts to use their capital efficiently. They found in the new Irish and French-Canadian immigrants a labor pool more willing than the native American girls to accept factory conditions. Furthermore, the experienced women operatives found that the increasing organization of skilled men into unions meant greater barriers to advancement. Thus, by the 1850s, for those women with ambition, the factory generally had become a place to avoid or, at some point, to abandon.

THE FIRST GOVERNMENTAL INVESTIGATION OF
LABOR CONDITIONS, 1845

The Special Committee to which was referred sundry petitions relating to the hours of labor, have considered the same and submit the following Report:

The first petition which was referred to your committee, came from the city of Lowell, and was signed by Mr. John Quincy Adams Thayer, and eight hundred and fifty others, "peaceable, industrious, hard working men and women of Lowell." The petitioners declare that they are confined "from thirteen to fourteen hours per day in unhealthy apartments," and are thereby "hastening through pain, disease and privation, down to a premature grave." They therefore ask the Legislature "to pass a law providing that ten hours shall constitute a day's work," and that no corporation or private citizen "shall be allowed, except in cases of emergency, to employ one set of hands more than ten hours per day." . . .

On the 13th of February, the Committee held a session to hear the petitioners from the city of Lowell. Six of the female and three of the male petitioners were present, and gave in their testimony.

The first petitioner who testified was Eliza R. Hemmingway. She had worked 2 years and 9 months in the Lowell Factories; 2 years in the Middlesex, and 9 months in the Hamilton Corporations. Her employment is weaving—works by the piece. The Hamilton Mill manufactures cotton fabrics. The Middlesex, woollen fabrics. She is now at work in the Middlesex Mills, and attends one loom. Her wages average from $16 to $23 a month exclusive of board. She complained of the hours for labor being too many, and the time for meals too limited. In the summer season, the work is commenced at 5 o'clock, A.M., and continued till 7 o'clock, P.M., with half an hour for breakfast and three quarters of an hour for dinner. During eight months of the year, but half an hour is allowed for dinner. The air in the room she considered not to be wholesome. There were 293 small lamps and 61 large lamps lighted in the room in which she

From Massachusetts *House Document*, no. 50 (March 1845).

worked, when evening work is required. These lamps are also lighted sometimes in the morning. About 130 females, 11 men, and 12 children (between the ages of 11 and 14) work in the room with her. She thought the children enjoyed about as good health as children generally do. The children work but 9 months out of 12. The other 3 months they must attend school. Thinks that there is no day when there are less than six of the females out of the mill from sickness. There was more sickness in the Summer than in the Winter months; though in the Summer, lamps are not lighted. She thought there was a general desire among the females to work but ten hours, regardless of pay. Most of the girls are from the country, who work in the Lowell Mills. The average time which they remain there is about three years. She knew one girl who had worked there 14 years. Her health was poor when she left. Miss Hemmingway said her health was better where she now worked, than it was when she worked on the Hamilton Corporation. She knew of one girl who last winter went into the mill at half past 4 o'clock, A.M., and worked till half past 7 o'clock, P.M. She did so to make more money. She earned from $25 to $30 per month. There is always a large number of girls at the gate wishing to get in before the bell rings. . . . One fourth part of the females [of the Middlesex Corporation] go into the mill before they are obliged to. They do this to make more wages. A large number come to Lowell to make money to aid their parents who are poor. She knew of many cases where married women came to Lowell and worked in the mills to assist their husbands to pay for their farms. The moral character of the operatives is good. There was only one American female in the room with her who could not write her name.

Miss Sarah G. Bagley said she had worked in the Lowell Mills eight years and a half, six years and a half on the Hamilton Corporation, and two years on the Middlesex. She is a weaver, and works by the piece. She worked in the mills three years before her health began to fail. She is a native of New Hampshire, and went home six weeks during the summer. Last year she was out of the mill a third of the time. She thinks the health of the operatives is not so good as the health of females who do house-work or millinery business. The chief evil, so far as health is concerned, is the shortness of time allowed for meals. The next evil is the length of time employed—not giving them time to cultivate their minds. She spoke of the high moral and intellectual character of the girls. That many were engaged as teachers in the Sunday schools. That many attended the lectures of the Lowell Institute; and she thought, if more time was allowed, that more lectures would be given and more girls attend. She thought that the girls generally were favorable to the ten hour system. She had presented a petition, same as the one before the Committee, to 132 girls, most of whom said that they would prefer to work but ten hours. In a pecuniary point of view, it would be better, as their health would be improved. They would have more time for sewing. The intellectual, moral and religious habits would also be benefited by the change. Miss Bagley said, in addition to her labor in the mills, she had kept evening school during the winter months, for four years, and thought that this extra labor must have injured her health.

Miss Judith Payne testified that she came to Lowell 16 years ago, and worked a year and a half in the Merrimack Cotton Mills, left there on account of ill health, and remained out over seven years. She was sick most of the time she was out. Seven years ago she went to work in the Boott Mills, and has remained there ever since; works by the piece. She has lost, during the last seven years, about one year from ill health. She is a weaver, and attends three looms. Last pay-day she drew $14.66 for five weeks work; this was exclusive of board. She was absent during the five weeks but half a day. She says there is a very general feeling in favor of the ten hour system among the operatives. She attributes her ill health to the long hours of labor, the shortness of time for meals, and the bad air of the mills. She had never spoken to Mr. French, the agent, or to the overseer of her room, in relation to these matters. She could not say that more operatives died in Lowell than other people. . . .

On Saturday the 1st of March, a portion of the Committee went to Lowell to examine the mills, and to observe the general appearance of the operatives therein employed. They arrived at Lowell after an hour's ride upon the railroad. They first proceeded to the Merrimack Cotton Mills, in which are employed usually 1,200 females and 300 males. They were permitted to visit every part of the works and to make whatever inquiries they pleased of the persons employed. They found every apartment neat and clean, and the girls, so far as personal appearance went, healthy and robust, as girls are in our country towns.

The Committee also visited the Massachusetts and Boott Mills, both of which manufacture cotton goods. The same spirit of thrift and cleanliness, of personal comfort and contentment, prevailed there. The rooms are large and well lighted, the temperature comfortable, and in most of the window sills were numerous shrubs and plants, such as geraniums, roses, and numerous varieties of the cactus. These were the pets of the factory girls, and they were to the Committee convincing evidence of the elevated moral tone and refined taste of the operatives.

The Committee also visited the Lowell and the Middlesex mills; in the first of which carpets are manufactured, and in the second, broadcloths, cassimeres, &c. These being woolen mills, the Committee did not expect to find that perfect cleanliness which can be and has been attained in cotton mills. It would, however, be difficult to institute a comparison between the mills on this point, or to suggest an improvement. Not only is the interior of the mills kept in the best order, but great regard has been paid by many of the agents to the arrangement of the enclosed grounds. Grass plots have been laid out, trees have been planted, and fine varieties of flowers in their season, are cultivated within the factory grounds. In short, everything in and about the mills, and the boarding houses appeared, to have for its end, health and comfort. The same remark would apply to the city generally. Your committee returned fully satisfied, that the order, decorum, and general appearance of things in and about the mills, could not be improved by any suggestion of theirs, or by any act of the Legislature.

During our short stay in Lowell, we gathered many facts, which we deem of sufficient importance to state in this report, and first, in relation to the Hours of Labor.

The following table shows the average hours of work per day, throughout the year, in the Lowell Mills:

	Hours	Min.			Hours	Min.
January	11	24		July	12	45
February	12			August	12	45
March	11	52		September	12	23
April	13	31		October	12	10
May	12	45		November	11	56
June	12	45		December	11	24

The General Health of the Operatives

In regard to the health of the operatives employed in the mills, your Committee believe it to be good. The testimony of the female petitioners does not controvert this position, in general, though it does in particular instances. The population of the city of Lowell is now rising 26,000, of which number, about 7,000 are females employed in the mills. It is the opinion of Dr. Kimball, an eminent physician of Lowell, with whom the Committee had an interview, that there is less sickness among the persons at work in the mills, than there is among those who do not work in the mills; and that there is less sickness now than there was several years ago, when the number was much less than at present. This we understood to be also the opinion of the city physician, Dr. Wells, from whose published report for the present year, we learn that the whole number of deaths in Lowell, during the year 1844, was 362, of which number, 200 were children under ten years of age.

In order to give the House a full statement of the facts connected with the factory system in Lowell, and in other towns in the Commonwealth, it would be necessary to answer interrogatories like these:

1st. The kind of work of the girls—is it proportioned to their age and intelligence?

2d. The amount of their wages, and how the girls dispose of them?

3d. Are the girls separated from the men?—what surveillance is exercised over them?—what police is used?

4th. What is their religious, moral or literary instruction?

5th. Where do they pass the time not occupied in work?

Diseases	1840	1841	1842	1843	1844
Consumption	40	54	70	73	77
Inflammation of Lungs	17	20	38	16	24
Cholera Infantum	12	30	34	27	31
Scarlet Fever	7	43	32	6	3
Measles	0	4	12	0	10
Dysentery	47	18	17	11	2
Inflammation of Brain	7	11	6	8	4
Croup	7	10	12	6	11
Other [Ed.]	289	266	261	216	200
Total mortality each year	426	456	473	363	362

6th. What are their general habits and character? What is the common age of entering the mill, and how long does a girl remain there?

In addition to which we have been permitted to copy the following memoranda from a book kept by John Clark, Esq., agent of the Merrimack Mills:

May 6th, 1841. I have ascertained, by inquiries this day, that 124 of the females now at work in the Merrimack Mills have heretofore taught school; and that in addition 25 or 30 have left within the last 30 days to engage their schools for the summer, making in all 150 or more. I also find, by inquiries at our boarding houses, that 290 of our girls attended school during the evenings of the last winter.

January 1st, 1842. We have this day in our five mills 40 females including sweepers and other day hands, who cannot write their names; of this number, 30 are Irish. The average wages of 20 job hands of the above, as compared with the same number of the best writers in the same rooms, is over 18 per cent below them. All our weavers sign their names except four, in No. 4, upper room.

February 26, 1842. We have this day in our five mills, 50 foreigners, 37 are Irish, (including 15 sweepers) 10 English and 3

Scotch, and not one hand in all our works, under 15 years of age either male or female. Usual number of hands employed by the Merrimack Company in their five mills is about 1,200 females and 300 males.

There are many interesting facts connected with this inquiry which your Committee have not included in the foregoing remarks, and which we could not include without making our report of too voluminous a character.

We will state, however, in this connection, that the evidence which we obtained from gentlemen connected with the Lowell Mills all goes to prove that the more intelligent and moral the operatives are, the more valuable they are to the employers, and the greater will be the amount of their earnings.

Your Committee have not been able to give the petitions from the other towns in this State a hearing. We believed that the whole case was covered by the petition from Lowell, and to the consideration of that petition we have given our undivided attention, and we have come to the conclusion unanimously, that legislation is not necessary at the present time, and for the following reasons:

1st. That a law limiting the hours of labor, if enacted at all, should be of a general nature. That it should apply to individuals or copartnerships as well as to corporations. Because, if it is wrong to labor more than ten hours in a corporation, it is also wrong when applied to individual employers, and your Committee are not aware that more complaint can justly be made against incorporated companies in regard to the hours of labor, than can be against individuals or copartnerships. But it will be said in reply to this, that corporations are the creatures of the Legislature, and therefore the Legislature can control them in this, as in other matters. This to a certain extent is true, but your Committee go farther than this, and say, that not only are corporations subject to the control of the Legislature but individuals are also, and if it should ever appear that the public morals, the physical condition, or the social well-being of society were endangered, from this cause or from any cause, then it would be in the power and it would be the duty of the Legislature to interpose its prerogative to avert the evil.

2d. Your Committee believe that the factory system, as it is called, is not more injurious to health than other kinds of indoor labor. That a law which would compel all of the factories in Massachusetts to run their machinery but ten hours out of the 24, while those in Maine, New Hampshire, Rhode Island and other States in the Union, were not restricted at all, the effect would be to close the gate of every mill in the State. It would be the same as closing our mills one day in every week, and although Massachusetts capital, enterprise and industry are willing to compete on fair terms with the same of other States, and, if needs be, with European nations, yet it is easy to perceive that we could not compete with our sister States, much less with foreign countries, if a restriction of this nature was put upon our manufactories.

3d. It would be impossible to legislate to restrict the hours of labor, without affecting very materially the question of wages; and that is a matter which experience has taught us can be much better regulated by the parties themselves than by the Legislature. Labor in Massachusetts is a very different commodity from what it is in foreign countries. Here labor is on an equality with capital, and indeed controls it, and so it ever will be while free education and free constitutions exist. And although we may find fault, and say, that labor works too many hours, and labor is too severely tasked, yet if we attempt by legislation to enter within its orbit and interfere with its plans, we will be told to keep clear and to mind our own business. Labor is intelligent enough to make its own bargains, and look out for its own interests without any interference from us; and your Committee want no better proof to convince them that Massachusetts men and Massachusetts women, are equal to this, and will take care of themselves better than we can take care of them, then we had from the intelligent and virtuous men and women who appeared in support of this petition, before the Committee.

4th. The Committee do not wish to be understood as conveying the impression, that there are no abuses in the present system of labor; we think there are abuses; we think that many improvements may be made, and we believe will be made, by which labor will not be so severely tasked as it now is. We think that it would be better if the hours for labor were less, if more time was allowed for meals, if more attention was paid to ventilation and pure air in our manufactories, and work-shops, and many other matters. We acknowledge all this, but we say, the remedy is not with us. We look for it in the progressive improvement in art and science, in a higher appreciation of man's destiny, in a less love for money, and a more ardent love for social happiness and intellectual superiority. Your Committee, therefore, while they agree with the petitioners in their desire to lessen the burthens imposed upon labor, differ only as to the means by which these burthens are sought to be removed. . . .

William Schouler, Chairman

FACTORY CONDITIONS AND REFORM

The interest in maximum-hours legislation that the woman of Lowell had done so much to initiate during the 1840s continued long afterward in Massachusetts, even though the labor movement among women fell on lean times. During the 1850s and 1860s, laboring men in Massachusetts gained in strength, pushing their hour and wage interests through union action and, when union action proved inadequate, through political action. Indeed, political action was central to labor activity and was particularly attractive to the union supporters in the textile industry because that industry had proved highly resistant to labor's demands.

The textile trade unionists were uninterested in organizing women workers and apathetic about the conditions of workingwomen, but they did press for legislation to set maximum hours on the work of women and children. Their strategy was simple: reduce the hours of women and children and, given the dominance of women and children in the textile mills, manufacturers will have to reduce the hours of work of men as well. The political strength of the unionists grew. The movement for hours legislation found increasing support from middle-class reformers, who gradually became aware of the fact that the unskilled women workers in the mills were no longer hardy, independent Yankee farm girls. Responding to this growing political force, the Massachusetts state government continued to undertake studies, increasingly systematic, of the environment of workingwomen. In the following selections some of the results of such inquiry are presented. They portray not only accurate impressions of the conditions under which women worked—in the textile mills and elsewhere—but reveal the incipient forms of middle-class attitudes toward women working in factories. These attitudes developed and hardened in the face of the great wave of immigration from Southern and Eastern Europe that would begin subsequently, during the 1880s.

The investigations of the Massachusetts Bureau of Statistics of Labor focused the combined efforts of labor, middle-class reformers, and a few manufacturers who believed that a reduced working day would increase productivity. Endorsed by the governor, a ten-hour maximum day won the support of the legislature in 1874 and was enacted into law. Although weak by comparison with twentieth-century legislation, the law was by far the strongest yet enacted. By 1887, agents of various interests in Massachusetts induced Rhode Island, Maine, Connecticut, and New Hampshire to revise their hours laws up to the standard set by Massachusetts. Whether the legislation was critical in reducing the working day and week remains moot, however. The conditions of the marketplace, particularly manufacturers' desire to increase productivity and workers' desire to take more time as leisure, were also working to reduce the hours of work, and throughout the 1880s and 1890s the working week of women remained below the legal maximum.

TESTIMONY OF TWO WORKINGWOMEN, 1871

We append two cases which are samples of hundreds, and represent an average—neither the most successful nor the most unfortunate. We were able to investigate them thoroughly, and give assurance of their perfect reliability.

Miss A——— B———. . . . [I work] in a large wholesale clothing establishment; came to Boston in April, 1868, a stranger in

From Massachusetts Bureau of Statistics of Labor, 1871 (Boston: Wright and Potter, 1871), pp. 222–24 and 419–22.

the city; obtained board on Harrison Avenue at $5 per week; could not find a respectable boarding-place for less money; was not willing to live in a dirty or disreputable place; worked three months, earning on an average from $8 to $7 per week; worked fifteen hours every day; constant application on heavy work resulted in slow fever; was sent (July 7th) to the Massachusetts General Hospital, through the influence of my attending physician; was unable to leave the ward 'til August 9th, when I walked out a little way; expected to be obliged to leave the hospital at once, as I was able to walk; but my savings were exhausted, I had nowhere to go; in my weak state I was almost in despair. On my return met Dr. Shaw and asked him if I might stay until morning. He questioned me, and upon hearing that I had no friends, and that it was the dull season, and that I should have no work 'til September, said that I would not be able to work 'til then, and that I yet needed medical treatment and had best remain until well. I staid until September 15th, but little improved in strength; but work had begun to come in, and to secure my place I was obliged to begin at once. My former boarding-mistress refused me admittance to my own room (where my trunk was), unless I could pay a week's board in advance; I went out penniless, not knowing which way to turn; stayed with one of the shop-girls that night. Worked eight days before receiving any pay; slept with one of my shopmates, borrowed fifty cents and bought bread; that was all I had to eat through the week except as my shopmates gave me a cup of tea or shared their lunch with me; was not very strong and earned only $5.75 during the eight days. Saw that I must live more economically; hired an attic room with three other girls, paying $1 per week each; furniture of the room consisted of two beds, three chairs and a broken washstand; there was no fireplace and was obliged to sew in a cold room during the winter evenings, with a cloak, shawl or blanket over my shoulders; there is no room in the home where I am allowed the privilege of a fire; saw no prospect of ever being any better off; work only half the year that I can depend upon; am forced to remain idle so much that it exhausts all that I am able to save. Am obliged to be idle more than I should had I a trade by which I could command better wages during the season, which would afford me means of obtaining more comfortable living, and dressing suitably for church and better society; with my present means I prefer none to associating with the coarse people about me.

Miss B——— C———. Am a New Hampshire girl; came to Boston March, 1865, to live with Mrs. ——— on Beacon Street, in capacity of seamstress, and to take some care of the children three and five years old; lived there until October, 1869, receiving $3 per week. Was allowed Thursday evening of each week, and one Sabbath per month. Became tired of the service, for as the children grew older they became restive oftentimes, using their small violence against me. The mother said she should not correct them for it unless they confessed it to her. As the boys grew older and heavier, found it impossible to carry them up and down stairs from kitchen to attic, as had to be done several times during the day. Finding my health failing, I resolved to seek employment in some shop, not thinking I should find any difficulty in obtaining work which would afford me a living. In this I was sorrowfully disappointed; procured board in Tyler Street at $4 per week, sharing a room with three others. This was unlike the living and accommodations I had been having, but I preferred to submit to it rather than to return to service. Indeed I could not easily procure another situation, for my former mistress had notified all the respectable intelligence offices that I was unworthy, having left her without just cause. This influence I felt would prevent my obtaining a situation in a good family, as I should be required to give recommendations from my former mistress, and she had warned the intelligence offices to beware of me. With these obstacles I resolved not to attempt a return to service until I had given something else a trial. I obtained work in a clothing shop at finishing pants; earned $3.85 the first week, the next a little more, and so on for thirteen weeks, paying $4 per week for board. I was then again taken sick and unable to work for two weeks; drew some of the money I had earned while in service from the savings bank; cold weather came on and I was obliged to draw more to procure clothing for the winter; dull times coming, was discharged, or rather told there would be no more work for two months. Day after day I went in pursuit of work, but having no trade was refused many times where I might have obtained it had I been qualified to make a garment entire, or to do nice embroidery. My inability was the bar to my obtaining work in dull times, so I was refused at every place. I went to my lodgings discouraged and sick: had no home to flee to, no work and was using my little savings faster than I had earned them. Was taken sick, stayed in my boarding-place until I had drawn my last dollar from the bank; growing still worse my physician advised me to go to the hospital; this I had great dread of doing, but was growing worse so fast I went, and stayed four weeks; was then able to work a little; returned to my boarding-house and was refused board without payment in advance; was obliged to accept the hospitality of two former shopmates and sleep three in one bed; next day obtained work, finishing pants; soon we were cut down ten and fifteen cents every payment. Workwomen are constantly discharged and new girls hired so often that I am now in constant dread of a discharge.

Homework

It is well known that women, whether in town or country, who work at their houses, receive, as a rule, less pay for the same work than the girls who work in shops. A great deal of Boston work, clothing and other, is sent out to different parts of New England, because it can be done more cheaply at country homes than in town. For instance, eight or ten years ago, the country storekeepers, experiencing the difficulty of getting ready cash for their sales, and being overburdened with agricultural products, introduced, through the direction of the Boston clothing trade, the making of clothing among their female customers, as a means of earning funds to meet the necessary store purchases. From very small beginnings, this has grown to gigantic proportions. The goods, cut and boxed, are sent to regular agents who distribute them among the farmers' and mechanics' wives and daughters. They make the garments and receive from the agent the ready cash. The goods thus made are re-shipped to Boston. This system has been found to work much more successfully than the employment of regular hands in large cities. About $2,000,000 were paid out for labor in Maine and New Hampshire by the clothing trade during 1870. The money thus

A Table of Average Earnings in Principal Employments

Occupation	Length of Seasons in Months	Hours of Labor per Day	Average Daily Wages				Average Yearly Earnings			
			Men	Women	Young Persons	Children	Men	Women	Young Persons	Children
Farm Laborers	12	10–14	$1.58	$1.00	$1.02	$0.50	$ 328.00	$200.00	$204.00	$100.00
Fishermen	3	Irregular			2.50		300.00		200.00	
Coach Drivers	12	10–15	1.75		1.75		525.00		525.00	
Hostlers	12	10–15	2.75		1.50		525.00		450.00	
Expressmen	12	10–12	2.50				750.00			
Teamsters	12	10–12	2.00		1.50		600.00		450.00	
Horse-car Conductors	12	10–15	1.75		1.75		525.00		525.00	
Horse-car Drivers	12	10–15	1.75		1.75		525.00		525.00	
Watchmen	12	10–12	2.00				600.00			
Blacksmiths	12	10	3.00				900.00			
Horse-shoers	12	10	2.50				750.00			
Harness-makers	12	10	2.50				750.00			
Railroad Engineers	12	10–12	3.50				1,050.00			
Railroad Brakemen	12	10–12	2.00				600.00			
Railroad Firemen	12	10–12	2.00				600.00			
Railroad Mechanics	12	10	2.50				750.00			
Railroad Laborers	12	10	1.75				525.00			
Seamen	12	12	1.45		1.65		435.00		315.00	
Steamboat-hands	12	12	1.82				546.00			
Stevedores	12	10	1.67				500.00			
House-workers	12	12–14		1.00	.50			300.00	150.00	
Shop-work	10	10		1.00	.50	.25		250.00	125.00	62.50

Store-work	12	7–12	$2.00	$1.25	$0.75	$0.20	$ 600.00	$375.00	$225.00	$ 60.00
Boots and Shoes	10	10	3.50	1.50	1.25	.75	625.00	375.00	250.00	187.50
Button-makers	12	10	2.37	.92	.80		711.00	276.00	240.00	
Hatters	8	9–10	2.35	1.00	.85		476.00	200.00	170.00	
Hosiery-workers	10	10	1.83	1.00	.75	.50	457.50	250.00	187.50	125.00
Rubber and Elastic Goods	10	10	2.12	1.25	1.00	.65	530.00	312.50	250.00	162.50
Straw-workers	7	10	2.50	1.25	.85		462.50	281.25	212.50	
Cotton-workers	12	11–12	1.67	1.05	.90	.55	501.00	315.00	270.00	165.00
Print Works	12	10	1.50	.87	.87		450.00	261.00	261.00	
Corset-makers	7½	10	2.50	1.17	.87		450.00	210.60	156.60	
Hoop Skirts	7½	10		1.00	.55			180.00	99.00	
Woollen-workers	12	11–12	1.57	1.04	.83	.58	471.00	312.00	249.00	174.00
Candle-makers	12	11	2.00				600.00			
Soap-makers	12	10	1.75				525.00			
Chemical-makers	12	10	1.87		.75		561.00		225.00	
Gas-work Laborers	10	10	1.75				437.50			
Butchers	12	10–12	2.00				600.00			
Millers	12	10–11	2.50				750.00			
Sugar Refiners	12	10	2.00		1.00		600.00		300.00	
Cigar-makers	12	10	3.00	1.25	0.50		900.00	375.00	150.00	
Brick-makers	7	11	1.50		1.00		262.50		175.00	
Pottery-workers	12	10	2.50	.92	.55		750.00	276.00	165.00	
Glass-makers	12	10	2.00	.75	.87	.67	600.00	225.00	261.00	201.00
Lime-makers	10	10	1.87				467.50			
Quarry Labor	10	10	2.00		.75		500.00		187.50	
Stone-cutters	11	9–10	3.00		0.90		825.00		270.00	
Bookbinders	10	10	3.00	1.00	.75		750.00	250.00	187.50	
Wood Engraving	12	8	4.00		1.25		1,200.00		375.00	

A Table of Average Earnings in Principal Employments

Occupation	Length of Seasons in Months	Hours of Labor per Day	Average Daily Wages				Average Yearly Earnings			
			Men	Women	Young Persons	Children	Men	Women	Young Persons	Children
Lithographers	12	8	$3.50		$1.00		$1,050.00	$336.00	$300.00	
Paper-makers	12	10	1.87	$1.87	.87	$0.70	551.00	300.00	261.00	$210.00
Paper-collar Makers	10	10	2.50	1.00	.75		750.00	285.00	225.00	
Paper Ruling	12	9	2.12	.95	.58		636.00	300.00	174.00	
Printers	12	10	2.50	1.00	.87		750.00	300.00	261.00	
Type-founders	12	10	3.00	1.00	.75		900.00	300.00	225.00	
Bleacheries	12	11	2.25	1.00	1.00	.80	675.00	300.00	300.00	240.00
Broom-making	12	10	1.75				525.00			
Brush-making	12	10	1.87	1.00	.75		561.00	300.00	225.00	
Comb-making	12	11	2.30	1.12	.90		690.00	336.00	270.00	
Felting-making	12	11	2.00	.83	.78	.70	600.00	249.00	234.00	210.00
Jewelry-making	12	10	2.50	1.25	.87		750.00	375.00	261.00	
Watchmakers	12	10	3.00	1.50	1.16	.72	900.00	450.00	348.00	216.00
Tanners and Curriers	12	10	2.00				600.00			
Pocket-book Makers	12	10	2.62	1.15	.89		786.00	375.00	267.00	
Sewing Silk	12	10	2.50	1.15	1.00	.75	750.00	336.00	300.00	225.00
Cordage	12	10	1.67	.80	.33		501.00	240.00	99.00	
Flax	12	10	2.00	1.00	1.00	.55	600.00	300.00	300.00	165.00
Whips	12	10	2.75	1.25	1.10	.58	825.00	375.00	330.00	174.00
Carriage-making	12	10	2.00		1.17		600.00		351.00	
Carpenters	10	10	2.75				687.50			
Masons	8	10	3.75		1.50		750.00		300.00	
Painters	8	9-10	2.50		1.50		500.00		300.00	

176

Occupation	Hours								
Plasterers	8	$4.00		$1.50		$800.00			$300.00
Sash and Blinds	12	2.50				750.00			
Sawing and Planing	12	1.75				600.00			
Machinists	12	2.50				755.00			
Cabinet-makers	12	2.50				750.00			
Chair-makers	12	2.25	$ .87	.67	$ .37	675.00	$261.00	201.00	$111.00
Upholstering	12	3.00	1.17	.83		900.00	351.00	249.00	
Plane-makers	12	2.50				750.00			
Boiler-makers	12	2.50				750.00			
Brass and Copper workers	12	2.50				750.00			
Moulders	12	2.50		1.00		750.00	300.00		
Iron Founders	12	2.25				675.00			
Sewing-machine Makers	12	2.82		1.77	.78	846.00	531.00		
Nail-makers	12	2.87		.96		861.00	288.00		
Tool-makers	12	2.62		1.37		786.00	411.00		
Tinsmiths	12	3.00				900.00			
Tin-ware Men	12	2.17	1.00	.62		651.00	300.00	186.00	
Cutlery-makers	12	2.25	1.00	1.25	.75	675.00	300.00	375.00	225.00
Bakers	10–12	2.00	1.00	.75		600.00	300.00	225.00	
Shipwrights	9	3.00				675.00			
Tailors and Tailoresses	10	3.50	1.25	.87		875.00	312.50	217.50	

Total number of occupations tabulated   94

Average yearly earnings of men $635.80
        of women   259.69
        of young persons   269.04
        of children   167.41

earned is less for absolute support, than for aid to gratify some desire, and to make some addition to the comfort or refinement of the household, or to aid in education of self, child, or relative. Were wage or earnings on such a basis of justice, that instead of getting the least amount of money for the greatest amount of work, the husband and father could earn all that is needed to meet the proper and justifiable demands of his family, not only of food and raiment, but of reasonable refinement, this outside work would not come in to keep down wages. The contrast is between women working at their own comfortable country homes, at such hours as they please, and women working in a town attic, at many and forced hours, without comfort of heat, or even of proper food or light, each at hand work and at wages depressed to 4 cents a shirt, and 3 shirts a day, wages that must be accepted by the city worker, as her only protection, if even that, from starvation or infamy.

The variety of work taken home is very great, embracing almost every article manufactured by the needle. Embroiderers of flannel and cambric are among those who earn the most, making from $3 to $7 per week. But work is precarious, as it is in every other department, some having regular seasons, others depending upon the state of trade and the orders received by contractors. We found women making bed-comfortables for 20 cents a piece, a smart woman making one a day. Linen coats are made for 8 cents a piece; pants for 10 cents a pair, and the list might be indefinitely extended, but it would be merely repetition. This work is universally done upon a machine, and this only renders it possible to live at it, if the word live may be used at all.

We found persons who had no machines, making woollen shirts at 4 cents a piece, being mostly girls out of employment at their regular business. Should they attempt to obtain a machine in response to the advertisements "sewing machines for sale and paid for in work," they are liable to such imposition as came under our own observation in the following cases. A girl bought a machine, paying part in money, and the agent agreeing to furnish her with work to the amount of $5 per month till the whole was paid for. He failed to furnish the work, and after $40 had been paid, the machine was taken away in default of the remaining $25. The girl appealed to a lawyer, and found that what she supposed to be the bill of sale of the machine, was merely waste paper, giving her no claim whatever, and law being too expensive a resort, the matter was dropped. Another girl took one from an employment office, paying $15 down. After three weeks the machine was taken away without refunding the money, and the girl was unable to obtain any satisfaction. These matters are mentioned to show some of the obstacles in the way of those who have their living to seek, and to record the fact that there are such fraudulent practices.

Women who take washing at home, especially fine washing, do better than many others, earning more money in the same time. If they are skilful and obtain plenty of work, they earn a comfortable living.

Shop and Manufacturing Work

The work-rooms of this division are almost always up three or four flights of stairs, and are filled with women as closely as they can sit at their work. They have no means of ventilation except by the windows, which are frequently on but one side of the room, and in many cases incapable of being opened excepting at the lower sash. Fully one-half of these rooms are without water-closets or water for drinking. In many instances where they have water, the women supply their own ice. The hours of labor in the shops are almost invariably 10, but in those shops where work is done by the piece, nearly all the women take work home to do in the evening. Many thus work from 12 to 14 hours a day to earn the sums with which they are credited on the books of the firm.

The wages differ widely, according to the employment and skill of the employés, ranging from $15 to $1.50 per week. It is fully ascertained that there are some who do not earn more than $1.50 per week. The fact that so very large a proportion of the employment in which women are engaged, last but half, or less than half the year, is one of the first to which our attention has been called. It is the cause of very much of the suffering and crime that prevail. When we are told that girls earn $6, $10, or even $15 a week, it has a comfortable sound, if unconnected with its accompanying fact that it is from sixteen to thirty-four weeks of the year only that they earn these wages, very few earning $15. There is a great disproportion between the yearly earnings and the weekly wages. For instance, milliners earn from $20 to $30 per week, but the season lasts only sixteen weeks. After that time a few are retained, but the majority are immediately discharged. In other trades the seasons are twenty, twenty-four, and thirty-four weeks per year. But from all the dress-making, cap-making, cloak and papercollar establishments in the city, a large portion of the employés are turned away, unable, for nearly or quite half the year, to obtain any employment, and the circumstances specially distressing are, that the dull season occurs in nearly all these trades at about the same time, destroying all chance of obtaining employment at any price at some other occupation, even were they fit for that other. The fancy-goods stores are a partial exception to this rule, they taking on a few extra hands for the holidays, but after New Year's day reducing the number of employés. A few fortunate ones only, they, of course, the best work-women, are occasionally retained. If paid by the week their wages are reduced; if by the piece, the scanty amount of work furnished effects the same results of hardship. A few women who have parents to whose homes they can flee, without paying board, when work fails are able to save money. A few more, who are able to obtain work all through the dull season at the highest wages above named, can do the same. But it is readily perceived that a woman commanding $15 a week earns in twenty-four weeks but $360, which sum does not leave much margin for savings. This is supposing all these women to be of robust health, and capable of working from 12 to 14 hours every day while the season lasts. How far this supposition is from the fact, it needs but a glance into any large manufacturing establishment to perceive. If these prices commanded by the few leave small margin for the "rainy day," to which all are liable, it is a fearful inquiry what becomes of the vast number discharged from employment twice a year, whose earnings have amounted to but $6, $5, $4, $3, and $1.50 a week!

Not a few cases have come under our personal observation, where insufficient food and the want of proper clothing have ended in a death that could be called nothing but starvation; and, alas, many more have confessed to us, some with shame and remorse, others with the defiant question, "What else could I do?" that they had sold their womanhood for bread to sustain life. Think of this ye women who sit safely near firesides, delicately clothed and fed, and with every want satisfied! Realize, if you can, what it is to sit for hours far into the night, thinly clad, in a fireless room, toiling for the food that in proper supply has not passed your lips for days! Who that has not been tried, can be sure their virtue would have stood the test of hunger? The wonder is not that so many, but that so few fall!

Of one thing these researches have convinced us, that no matter how zealously missionaries may labor, or how reformatories or Magdalen asylums may be multiplied, the root of the evil will not be reached until women's wages will supply them with the necessities and some of the comforts of life, elevating them above the clutch of sin, and freeing them from the necessity of making merchandise of body and soul. What we have seen and heard lessens our wonder that an evil of so appalling a nature continues, for hunger and craving want are relentless foes to virtue. We execrate the hideous sin, while grieving and mourning for the sinner.

Many of these women, who earn what is called good wages, by employment as tenders in stores and saloons, seek also for sewing to take home, thus entering into competition with another class and helping to reduce their small wages. There are instances among the girls also, earning good wages in the season of work in the shop, who, when regular work stops, make woollen shirts for four cents apiece. The majority of these live in cheap boarding or lodging houses, many occupying attics with three, four, and even six in one room. As a rule, there are no conveniences for a fire, unless furnished by themselves. But few can afford this, and as no privileges are given lodgers outside of their own rooms, the industrious ones who are mistresses of their evenings, and devote them to necessary sewing, or in reading, are obliged to sit in their rooms without fire, with a shawl or blanket over their shoulders while at work or study. They are oftentimes forced during the dull times to lessen their living expenses by taking their meals cold in their rooms. Under this diet instances are numerous where they become so debilitated in health, as to require medical treatment for two and three weeks at different times during the year. A case came to our notice of a sickness of nineteen weeks, and another of two weeks, with no means.

Others younger, and without needful education to a thorough keeping of their own clothing in proper order, find little in these dismal, comfortless lodging-rooms to induce them to spend their evenings in them. As a consequence, they rush heedlessly into the streets and into questionable society for recreation—a recreation too often ending in sin.

When long out of work, and their means run low, they take lodging only, and live upon bakers' bread, with occasionally a meal at a restaurant. It is not unusual for them to come to charity or the kindness of their sister-workers. With them they live for weeks, by crowding into one bed, because unable to pay for lodging.

We append a table giving the wages of cap and hat makers, with number of employés, number of establishments visited and number of weeks of work per year.

Wages of Cap and Hat Makers

No. of Employés	Wages of Cap-Makers	No. of Employés	Wages of Hat-Sewers	No. of Employés	Wages of Machine Operators
35	$15.00*	24	$12.00*	3	$14.00*
27	12.00*	12	9.50*	5	12.00*
30	9.50	17	8.00	35	10.00
40	7.50	27	7.00	24	8.00
74	6.00	12	6.00	9	7.25
79	5.00			4	6.00
29	4.50			12	5.00
64	3.25			20	4.50
62	2.50				

Number of establishments visited	23
of employés	644
of weeks of work per year	24
of hours of labor per day	10

*Custom work.

In this trade there is a great difference between the wages in custom and in manufacturing establishments, the former averaging from $15 to $9 per week, the latter from $8 to $2.50 per week; the season of work averages 24 weeks. Most of the workrooms are up three or four flights of stairs, with ventilation from windows only. The hours of labor per day are 10. With few exceptions, all work by the piece and carry their work home evenings, working from two to three hours additional. The majority carry their dinners in preference to going for them, owing to the long distance of boarding places and many stairs to climb.

Wages of Cloak Makers

No. of Employés	Wages		No. of Employés	Wages	
	Highest	Lowest		Highest	Lowest
28	$15.00	$14.00	169	$7.50	$6.00
137	13.00	12.00	130	6.00	5.00
12	12.00	10.00	40	5.00	4.00
111	11.00	10.00	7	5.65	2.30
176	10.00	9.00	97	4.50	3.00
141	9.00	8.00	42	3.00	2.75
10	9.00	7.00	24	2.00	
180	8.00	7.00	9	1.50	

Number of establishments visited	12
of employés	1313
of weeks of work per year	20–24
of hours per day	10

IV

Women in Factories: Continuing Industrialization, 1870–1929

The pace of industrial revolution quickened in the late nineteenth century and created expansive employment opportunities for women in all categories of work, even in manufacturing, where women faced increasingly impervious barriers to advancement. Thus, even though the relative significance of women employees in manufacturing declined sharply between the Civil War and the onset of the Great Depression in 1929, their absolute numbers continued to grow rapidly. This growth of the ranks of women factory workers was profoundly disturbing to Americans of widely divergent social perspectives. To those who became absorbed, for a variety of reasons, with the enforcement of Victorian cultural standards, the ideal solution was simply to remove women from the factories. To others, the ideal was an industrial system that would allow women to participate on terms that would open opportunities for self-advancement equal to those available to men. The variety of viewpoints held by the critics of the terms under which women undertook factory labor are presented in this section.

The solutions favored most enthusiastically by those seeking equal opportunity involved various programs of unionization. Such programs are the focus of attention for this section. However, it should be remembered that during this period the unionization of women made little headway, for the various reasons to be discussed here, except in the garment industry. Even during the peak of union success during World War I, fewer than 10 per cent of the women working in manufacturing were members of labor unions of any type. (The comparable percentage for men was more than twice as great.) Also unsuccessful was the removal of women from factories; the relative number of women workers in factories declined consistently, but the continuing necessity of lower-class women to pursue marketplace employment prevented that trend from becoming swift. These two trends lay, in a sense, on opposite ends of a spectrum of social choices. More rapid in pace than either was a trend that amounted to a liberal compromise between the extremes. That trend was the development of governmental arrangements to provide special protection for women factory workers.

The special protection of workingwomen by statute included, most significantly, restriction of the hours women could work. In the economic up-turn of the late 1890s, almost all states embarked on a vigorous program of enacting such legislation. Although in 1896 only thirteen states had any kind of legislation regulating the hours of women's work, by 1933 all but six states had in force comprehensive laws limiting women's hours in manufacturing. The most feverish period of activity was between 1909 (after the Supreme Court upheld such legislation in *Muller* v. *Oregon* in 1908) and the American entry into World War I. During those eight years, nineteen states and the District of Columbia passed hours laws and twenty others either expanded or tightened their existing laws. The interest in protection also extended to setting minimum wages for the work of women; such protection was embodied in legislation in fifteen states and the District of Columbia from 1912 until 1923, when the Supreme Court (in *Adkins* v. *Children's Hospital*) ruled such regulation unconstitutional.

These legal arrangements represented compromise solutions to the dilemma of workingwomen; the groups and people holding sharply divergent views as to the nature of the dilemma often reached agreement as to the desirability of special consideration for women. Those, like Theodore Roosevelt, who believed in the physical delicacy of women and feared the effects of women's work on the future of the white race and nation, could approve protective legislation as promising to protect the health of mothers and future mothers. In the *Muller* case the Court, holding that "sex is a valid basis for classification," used that argument to establish a rationale for future discrimination. (Even in *Bunting* v. *Oregon* [1917], which upheld hours laws applying to *both* sexes, it held to the constitutionality of discrimination by sex.) Perhaps regulators also hoped that employers, finding women workers too expensive, or unable to work sufficiently long hours, would have to let them go. Although support for adopting protective legislation was forthcoming from opponents of women's work, leadership came from a coalition of laboring women and middle-class women reformers, working through such organizations as the Women's Trade Union League, the National Consumers' League, the American Association for Labor Legislation, federations of Women's Clubs, and the Young Women's Christian Association. The sincere intent of this leadership was to provide for women the benefits of increased wages and increased leisure that they would have received had unionization been a more effective force among women workers. Only unions tended to abstain from the consensus supporting protection of women workers. This was understandable. Organized labor was less than enthusiastic about an implied indication of its failure. Consequently, unions either lent only the most nominal support of such legislation or actually engaged in active opposition, particularly in the campaigns for minimum-wage legislation, which appeared to be a serious potential threat to the union organizing appeal.

Currently, the movement to create conditions of equality for workingwomen has led to criticism of protective labor legislation for the way in which it has functioned to narrow employment opportunities for women. The criticism may well be justified, although the historical evidence as to the impact of the legislation on employment and wages of women is ambiguous. But sympathy for, or agreement with, the critique should not lead us to misread the past. The leading edge of the reforms that lent women protection in the marketplace was highly idealistic and conceived in a spirit of expanding, rather than constricting, opportunities for women. However, an examination of the motivation behind the legislation does lend support for the current feminist interpretation of present-day protective legislation in that some proponents of protection believed that independent women immersed in Victorian culture could not compete with men on equal terms. If those proponents were alive today, in an era in which both the collective and individual situation of factory women are dramatically different, most might well be found among the critics of sex-based protection.

AN INVESTIGATION IN THE 1880S

During the 1880s, the federal government, frightened by the prospect of class warfare between labor and capital, launched extended investigations of working conditions prevailing in American industry. Among the topics studied was the condition of the life of women factory workers. A part of one of the resulting reports is reprinted here.

From the work of the commissioner of labor one can derive reasonably balanced impressions of the diversity of circumstances under which urban women worked. But the report was distinctly in error in suggesting that women were tending to replace men in industrial employments: by the 1880s the trend was just the reverse, as Edith Abbott argued persuasively in her *Women in Industry* (New York: D. Appleton, 1909). However, for all occupations, the trend identified by the commissioner did prevail in the sense that the relative contribution of women to the labor force had been growing since the 1860s and that men and women had come into competition for certain jobs—particularly those of a clerical nature. Most of those jobs assumed by women were new ones, created by the striking expansiveness of the economy after the Civil War. The emphasis on competition between men and women competing for scarce jobs that was given credence by the commissioner only encouraged interest in restricting the roles of women within the marketplace.

Despite the commissioner's concern over competition between the sexes, he did reject one argument that was often advanced to cast doubt on the rectitude of young women working in factories: that factory work, as a result of its supposed low wage level and the disruption of family life, had a potent tendency to force young women into prostitution. Neither the commission nor numerous others who studied the potential connection between factory labor and prostitution was able to find confirmation of the linkage. Nonetheless, the fear of moral corruption continued to be compelling in fueling middle-class attacks on factory work for women.

CONDITIONS OF WORKING WOMEN IN LARGE CITIES

Boston

The most striking feature of the home life of working women in Boston is the great number who live in lodging houses. This is especially noticeable because of the large number of girls coming from the surrounding country places and from the British provinces. These, having usually few or no kindred in the great city, are forced into the lodging houses which abound, for comparatively few private families will receive boarders, and the working girls' homes, though becoming more numerous than formerly, are still entirely inadequate to provide for all these homeless strangers. Such conditions necessarily weaken the hold of the home life upon the memory and the affections; they do away with the sense of proprietorship which even the poorest tenant feels in the house which shelters him; and they also do away with that privacy which is one of the best features of the separate home.

Space being valuable, there is sometimes no parlor or reception room attached to the lodging house of the working girl, and she is forced to receive her friends in her chamber or not to receive them at all. Such a condition tends either in the direction of crushing out social intercourse, especially between the sexes, or of carrying it beyond the limit of prudence. Yet there are some compensations for this cheerless home life, if home life it may be called, and these are found in the proprietorship which the working women may have in the intellectual life of the city, in its educational privileges, in its libraries, museums, and exhibitions. Music, literature, art, lectures, are all within easy reach, and the working girls of Boston avail

From U.S. Commissioner of Labor, Fourth Annual Report, 1888, *Working Women in Large Cities* (Washington, D.C.: Government Printing Office, 1889), pp. 13–76.

themselves of such privileges to a great extent. A button-hole maker gave as her reason for not living in the suburbs, where living was cheaper, that she would then be debarred from lectures, concerts, and oratorios. A necktie maker contributes excellent verses to a first-rate magazine. Suspender makers, who have taught school, belong to Browning clubs, and discuss the tariff and similar vital issues. Work is regarded as honorable, and the barriers which exist between people of leisure and wage earners may in some cases be overcome.

The shops and factories are in fair sanitary condition in a majority of cases, and in very many the employers seem anxious to add to the comfort of their employes. The factory laws are more generally posted, and as regards the employment of children under age, more generally observed here than elsewhere. The work is, generally speaking, quite regular during the entire year. Many rumors were heard of improper proposals being made to girls when applying for work, or entering thereon, but such rumors were generally found to be groundless, only one authenticated case of the kind having been discovered in the investigation.

Brooklyn

Though not so crowded as New York, the life conditions in Brooklyn are almost as hard. Whole streets and districts of tenement houses are given over to poverty, filth, and vice, the sanitary and moral unwholesomeness of which is manifest. Better homes distinguish the districts remote from business centres, but the great distance of these homes is a tax as to hours and car fare. Model tenements and improved apartment houses are to be found, and ownership of the house is frequent. Rent is cheaper than in New York and the commodities of life a shade less dear.

The moral conditions, in general, vary from the best to the worst, but respectability and education are greatly in the ascendant.

A large number of Brooklyn girls work in New York, pay being higher than in Brooklyn and the industries more diversified. The making at home of clothing for the New York shops is universal in the suburbs of Brooklyn, though at prices on which no woman could live were there not other workers in her family.

Some occupations in Brooklyn involve great risks to girls, the loss of joints of fingers, the hand, or sometimes the whole arm. There is a growing public demand for shorter hours, half holidays, and equal pay to women with men for equal work.

Chicago

The tenement house system is largely engrafted on the life of Chicago. The houses, however, are rarely in long blocks, often have light and air on four sides, and seldom contain more than six families. Two or three families living in a separate house is the general rule, and often each family has a single home. The sanitary condition of houses and streets is bad, but these evils are being remedied by the vigorous action of the health department. Rents are high, the markets inconvenient, and the cost of living greater than in any other western city. There is a large foreign element in Chicago, which furnishes a rough class of girls, sometimes unfamiliar with the English language, and again speaking it fairly. Habits of economy do not prevail among the working classes, and there are cases of poverty as extreme as in New York.

Wages are higher than in the East, and expert workers scarcer. Even employments requiring no skill command pay enough to render girls independent; if displeased they leave on the slightest pretexts, and the employer must fall behind his orders or hire whom he can get. Workwomen are always in demand, and as a rule employers make no requirements as to good character. Notwithstanding the indifference of proprietors the general morality in most callings is surprisingly good.

In order to prevent absenteeism and to insure prompt attendance, the employers have adopted an oppressive system of fines. Bad work also occurs so often that fines are imposed for this cause. As a result the workingwomen are inclined to be antagonistic to employers, and discontent is more outspoken than in the East, where work is scant and competition strong.

The sanitary condition of one or two large shops is worse than any visited elsewhere during this inquiry. In the new establishments the ordinary provisions are made and gross neglect is rare.

Cincinnati

The percentage of working girls living at home is higher in Cincinnati than in any other city visited in the course of the investigation, but the homes are unusually uninviting, even in the newer quarters. The streets are dirty and closely built up with ill-constructed houses, holding from two to six families. Many poorer parts of Cincinnati are as wretched as the worst European cities, and the population looks as degraded. Rents are disproportionately high and commodities dear. German food and drinks are largely consumed, and continental customs prevail. Sunday concerts and dance halls are more popular than the churches. Too many young children are employed in the workshops, and illiteracy is not infrequent even among the native-born.

Labor organizations are a striking feature of Cincinnati, especially in two of the larger industries—boot and shoe making and cigar making. The Hannah Powderly Assembly, K. of L., numbered over 1,100 women at the time of this inquiry, and practically controlled the shoe trade, but since then its power and influence have declined. The workers at this branch are intelligent and respectable. Some shoe factories are commodious and handsome, but in these, as well as in the cigar factories, the sanitation is defective.

The system of fining works great hardship among the shop girls, and petty regulations hamper their freedom. Wages and the moral tone of the shops are not high. Diversity of occupation is considerable, but the skilled worker is rare.

Much is heard at the present time of the very low wages paid workingwomen. It must be clear that they do not rise, on the average, above $5 per week, or $5.24 as indicated by this report. The summary by cities would seem to indicate that the majority are in receipt of fair wages, when the whole body of workingwomen is considered; but 373 earn less than $100 a year, and quite a large number (1,212) earn from $100 to $150 a year, that is, the earnings of these women, distributed by weeks over the whole year, do not amount to more than $2 or $3 per week. These are the great exceptions, but the figures tell a sad story, and one is forced to ask how women can live on such earnings.

Average Weekly Earnings, by Cities

Cities	Average Weekly Earnings	Cities	Average Weekly Earnings
Atlanta	$4.05	New Orleans	$4.31
Baltimore	4.18	New York	5.85
Boston	5.64	Philadelphia	5.34
Brooklyn	5.76	Providence	5.51
Buffalo	4.27	Richmond	3.93
Charleston	4.22	Saint Louis	5.19
Chicago	5.74	Saint Paul	6.02
Cincinnati	4.59	San Francisco	6.91
Cleveland	4.63	San Jose	6.11
Indianapolis	4.67	Savannah	4.99
Louisville	4.51		
Newark	5.10	All cities	5.24

. . . What are the influences which keep earnings at so low a point? Are they really low earnings, or is it simply an appearance? It is quite clear, from the various investigations that have been made, that there is little, if any, improvement in the amount of earnings which a woman can secure by working in the industries open to her; her earnings seem not only ridiculously low, but dangerously so. While it is not possible to determine an economic law which regulates her earnings, it is possible to consider a few elements which enter into the case. A generation ago women were allowed to enter but few occupations. Now there are hundreds of vocations in which they can find employment. The present report names three hundred and forty-three industries in which women have been found actively engaged. The result of this vast extension of opportunity is the same as under like conditions in other directions. Whenever any industrial operations are simplified to such an extent that the weaker person can perform what was done of old by the stronger one, the cheaper labor comes in, and wages must of necessity be lowered temporarily, whether to the one formerly performing the labor or to the new-comer who undertakes to occupy his place. So, as the adult man in light occupations has given place to the woman or to the young person, wages in specific employments have decreased, as compared with the former wages of the man, but they have vastly increased, as compared with the former wages of the woman or young person. In other words, by the progress or change in industrial conditions the limit to the employment of women has been removed, or at least greatly extended, and their opportunities for earning wages correspondingly increased and the wages themselves greatly enhanced. In so far as women have displaced men, they have taken advantage of opportunities which were not open to them before such displacement. They could only displace men because they were willing to work for less wages. Now the workingwomen find themselves in the condition of new elements of labor, and no action can be taken which will increase abnormally their earnings, for they are now earning something where formerly they could earn little or nothing. For an increase in wages, certainly a most desirable result to be gained, women must depend upon industrial and economic conditions, and not upon legislative enactment, or even upon concerted actions of persons charitably and benevolently disposed. They contribute largely now to the support of the family. Formerly they were the subjects of expense to a considerable degree. As we have seen, so far as the women involved in this investigation are concerned, there were 2.78 persons classified as earners in each family. Not all this number of earners were women, to be sure, because the earners comprehend the head of the family and all others, but the woman has come in as a factor, and a new economic factor, and as such must take her place at the bottom of the ladder. She will gain step by step as she becomes more valuable as such factor, but the gain will be slow.

A few statistics of a negative character have been collected, relating to prostitution. This partial investigation has been made as to how far the ranks of prostitution are recruited from girls belonging to the industrial classes. It should be distinctly borne in mind that this partial investigation was applied only to what may be called professional prostitutes; for no statistical investigation can disclose the amount of immoral conduct of any class of people. So that quiet, unobtrusive, and unobserved prostitution, which exists in all communities, has no place in the present consideration.

Original investigation was made in the following cities: Brooklyn,

Buffalo, Chicago, Cincinnati, Cleveland, Indianapolis, Louisville, Newark, New Orleans, New York, Philadelphia, Richmond, Saint Louis, and San Francisco.

In 1884 the Massachusetts Bureau of Statistics of Labor made a report as to the previous occupations of one hundred and seventy professional prostitutes in the city of Boston, and the facts then given have been incorporated in this report.

The number of prostitutes as stated in the following table, for any one of the cities named, falls far below the total number of prostitutes in that city, but the number and variety of those from whom information has been received are sufficient to insure representative results. Thus in Chicago, for example, there are, or were at the time of the investigation of the Department, 302 houses of ill-fame, assignation houses, and "rooming" houses, known to the police, containing 1,097 inmates. This investigation involved 557 of this number. In some of the other cities, Philadelphia and Brooklyn notably, the proportion of prostitutes interviewed was not so large as in Chicago, but a sufficient number of reports were obtained to afford a basis for a fair conclusion as to the part played, if any, by the workingwomen in swelling the ranks of these unfortunates.

In certain of the cities in which this subject was investigated return was made of the number of women who had been married before entering on a life of shame. Some of these women were married before engaging in industrial work, some between periods of industrial employment; some after working at various employments were married, and then entered upon a life of prostitution, and some of the married prostitutes had never been industrially employed.

The facts as to marriage are shown by the following brief table, which gives the number of prostitutes furnishing information in the cities referred to, the number reporting themselves as having been married, and the per cent of the total number who were married.

The number of prostitutes giving information was 3,866, and the following summary exhibits the occupations of this number preceding their entry upon their present life. For this purpose, occupations similar in character have been grouped, and no occupation or group containing less than ten persons has been included in the classifica-

City	Number of Prostitutes Furnishing Information	Number of Prostitutes Reported Having Been Married	Percent Married of Total Number
Boston	170	13	7.65
Chicago	557	143	25.67
Cincinnati	382	77	20.16
Louisville	263	70	26.62
New Orleans	167	4	2.40
Philadelphia	100	3	3.00
San Francisco	323	81	25.08

tion—those numbering under ten being put into the general classification of "various occupations":

Actresses, ballet girls, circus performers, singers, etc.	52
Bead-trimming makers, embroiderers, lace workers	21
Bookbinderies	18
Bookkeepers, clerks, copyists, stenographers, typewriters, etc.	31
Candy factories	10
Cigarette, cigar, and tobacco factories	78
Corset factories	16
Dressmakers, seamstresses, employés of cloak and shirt factories, button-hole makers, etc.	505
Hairdressers and hair workers	15
House work, hotel work, table work, and cooking	1,155
Laundry work	70
Milliners and hat trimmers	71
No previous occupation (home)	1,236
Nurses (hospital and house), and nurse girls	22
Paper box factories	32
Rope and cordage factories	12
Saleswomen and cashiers	126
Shoe factories	43
Students (at schools or convents)	14
Teachers, governesses, etc.	23
Telegraph and telephone operators	11
Textile factories	94
Various occupations	211

The preceding figures are exceedingly instructive. By them it will be seen that the largest number coming from any occupation has been taken from those doing house work, hotel work, and cooking; this number, 1,155, being 29.88 per cent of the whole number comprehended in the statement.

The next largest number, so far as occupation is concerned, ranks with the seamstresses, including the dressmakers, employes of cloak and shirt factories, etc., this number being 505.

A fact which strikes one sadly is the large number who enter prostitution directly from their homes. This number is 1,236, being 31.97 per cent of the whole number comprehended.

It can not be said, therefore, so far as this investigation shows, that the employes in workshops are to be burdened with the charge of furnishing the chief source whence the ranks of prostitution are recruited.

The experience of the writer in making an examination in many cities, both in the United States and in Europe, sustains the statement, but more strongly than the figures here given, that workingwomen do not recruit the houses of prostitution.

Nor does the investigation show that employers of labor are guilty of reducing their employes to a condition of prostitution, as is often alleged. Only in the rarest cases can one meet with a whisper that this is the case. And these whispers, followed to their source, have rarely disclosed any facts which would lead to the conclusion that employers make bargains based on the loss of character of their employes.

From all that can be learned one need not hesitate in asserting that the workingwomen of the country are as honest and as virtuous as any class of our citizens.

All the facts are against the idea that they are not virtuous women. The statistics given show that a very large percentage of them are living at home. They are living in whatever moral atmosphere there is in their homes.

FACTORY WORK: A MIDDLE-CLASS PERSPECTIVE

Conditions of women's work in a Pittsburgh pickle factory are described in the following selection from Bessie van Vorst's *The Woman Who Toils.* An upper middle-class woman looking for excitement and possessing some empathy with lower-class women, van Vorst spent about nine months working in various factories and then described her experience to generate sympathy for workingwomen. Her narrative yields impressions of the motivations of workingwomen, speculations on the obstacles to the development of class consciousness among them, and images of the character of working conditions. However, van Vorst had little sensitivity to the social forces that caused women to seek factory employment; she tended to view those who worked for independent income as frivolous and looked for a way to return them to their homes. One prominent reader at least found that van Vorst reinforced his own views. Theodore Roosevelt, writing a preface to her book from the White House, declared that "the man or woman who deliberately avoids marriage, and has a heart so cold as to dislike having children, is in effect a criminal against the race, and should be an object of contemptuous abhorrence by all healthy people." He concluded that "if the women do not recognize that the greatest thing for any woman is to be a good wife and mother, why, that nation has cause to be alarmed about its future."

In a Pittsburgh Factory

. . . I feel a fresh excitement at going back to my job; the factory draws me toward it magnetically. I long to be in the hum and whir of the busy workroom. Two days of leisure without resources or amusement make clear to me how the sociability of factory life, the freedom from personal demands, the escape from self can prove a distraction to those who have no mental occupation, no money to spend on diversion. It is easier to submit to factory

From Maria van Vorst, *The Woman Who Toils* (New York: Doubleday Co., 1903), pp. 31–37 and 52–58.

government which commands five hundred girls with one law valid for all, than to undergo the arbitrary discipline of parental authority. I speed across the snow-covered courtyard. In a moment my cap and apron are on and I am sent to report to the head forewoman.

"We thought you'd quit," she says. "Lots of girls come in here and quit after one day, especially Saturday. To-day is scrubbing day," she smiles at me. "Now we'll do right by you if you do right by us. What did the timekeeper say he'd give you?"

"Sixty or seventy a day."

"We'll give you seventy," she says. "Of course, we can judge girls a good deal by their looks, and we can see that you're above the average."

She wears her cap close against her head. Her front hair is rolled up in crimping-pins. She has false teeth and is a widow. Her pale, parched face shows what a great share of life has been taken by daily over-effort repeated during years. As she talks she touches my arm in a kindly fashion and looks at me with blue eyes that float about under weary lids. "You are only at the beginning," they seem to say. "Your youth and vigour are at full tide, but drop by drop they will be sapped from you, to swell the great flood of human effort that supplies the world's material needs. You will gain in experience," the weary lids flutter at me, "but you will pay with your life the living you make."

There is no variety in my morning's work. Next to me is a bright, pretty girl jamming chopped pickles into bottles.

"How long have you been here?" I ask, attracted by her capable appearance. She does her work easily and well.

"About five months."

"How much do you make?"

"From 90 cents to $1.05. I'm doing piece-work," she explains. "I get seven-eighths of a cent for every dozen bottles I fill. I have to fill eight dozen to make seven cents. Downstairs in the corking-room you can make as high as $1.15 to $1.20. They won't let you make any more than that. Me and them two girls over there are the only ones in this room doing piece-work. I was here three weeks as a day-worker."

"Do you live at home?" I ask.

"Yes; I don't have to work. I don't pay no board. My father and my brothers supports me and my mother. But," and her eyes twinkle, "I couldn't have the clothes I do if I didn't work."

"Do you spend your money all on yourself?"

"Yes."

I am amazed at the cheerfulness of my companions. They complain of fatigue, of cold, but never at any time is there a suggestion of ill-humour. Their suppressed animal spirits reassert themselves when the forewoman's back is turned. Companionship is the great stimulus. I am confident that without the social entrain, the encouragement of example, it would be impossible to obtain as much from each individual girl as is obtained from them in groups of tens, fifties, hundreds working together.

When lunch is over we are set to scrubbing. Every table and stand, every inch of the factory floor must be scrubbed in the next four hours. The whistle on Saturday blows an hour earlier. Any girl who has not finished her work when the day is done, so that she can leave things in perfect order, is kept overtime, for which she is paid at the rate of six or seven cents an hour. A pail of hot water, a dirty rag and a scrubbing-brush are thrust into my hands. I touch them gingerly. I get a broom and for some time make sweeping a necessity, but the forewoman is watching me. I am afraid of her. There is no escape. I begin to scrub. My hands go into the brown, slimy water and come out brown and slimy. I slop the soap-suds around and move on to a fresh place. It appears there are a right and a wrong way of scrubbing. The forewoman is at my side.

"Have you ever scrubbed before?" she asks sharply. This is humiliating.

"Yes," I answer; "I have scrubbed . . . oilcloth."

The forewoman knows how to do everything. She drops down on her knees and, with her strong arms and short-thumbed, brutal hands, she shows me how to scrub.

The grumbling is general. There is but one opinion among the girls: it is not right that they should be made to do this work. They all echo the same resentment, but their complaints are made in whispers; not one has the courage to openly rebel. What, I wonder to myself, do the men do on scrubbing day. I try to picture one of them on his hands and knees in a sea of brown mud. It is impossible. The next time I go for a supply of soft soap in a department where the men are working I take a look at the masculine interpretation of house cleaning. One man is playing a hose on the floor and the rest are rubbing the boards down with long-handled brooms and rubber mops.

"You take it easy," I say to the boss.

"I won't have no scrubbing in my place," he answers emphatically. "The first scrubbing day, they says to me 'Get down on your hands and knees,' and I says—'Just pay me my money, will you; I'm goin' home. What scrubbing can't be done with mops ain't going to be done by me.' The women wouldn't have to scrub, either, if they had enough spirit all of 'em to say so."

I determined to find out if possible, during my stay in the factory, what it is that clogs this mainspring of "spirit" in the women.

I hear fragmentary conversations about fancy dress balls, valentine parties, church sociables, flirtations and clothes. Almost all of the girls wear shoes with patent leather and some or much cheap jewelry, brooches, bangles and rings. A few draw their corsets in; the majority are not laced. Here and there I see a new girl whose back is flat, whose chest is well developed. Among the older hands who had begun work early there is not a straight pair of shoulders. Much of the bottle washing and filling is done by children from twelve to fourteen years of age. On their slight, frail bodies toil weighs heavily; the delicate child form gives way to the iron hand of labour pressed too soon upon it. Backs bend earthward, chests recede, never to be sound again.

My first experience is drawing to its close. I have surmounted the discomforts of insufficient food, of dirt, a bed without sheets, the strain of hard manual labour. I have confined my observations to life and conditions in the factory. Owing, as I have before explained, to the absorption of factory life into city life in a place as large as Pittsburg, it seemed to me more profitable to centre my attention on the girl within the factory, leaving for a small town the study of her in her family and social life. I have pointed out as they appeared to me woman's relative force as a worker and its effects upon her economic advancement. I have touched upon two cases which illustrate her relative dependence on the law. She appeared to me not as the equal of man either physically or legally. It remained to study her socially. In the factory where I worked men and women were employed for ten-hour days. The women's highest wages were lower than the man's lowest. Both were working as hard as they possibly could. The women were doing menial work, such as scrubbing, which the men refused to do. The men were properly fed at noon; the women satisfied themselves with cake and pickles. Why was this? It is of course impossible to generalize on a single factory. I can only relate the conclusions I drew from what I saw myself. The wages paid by employers, economists tell us, are fixed at the level of bare subsistence. This level and its accompanying conditions are determined by competition, by the nature and number of labourers taking part in the competition. In the masculine category I met but one class of competitor: the bread-winner. In the feminine category I found a variety of classes: the bread-winner, the semi-bread-winner, the woman who works for luxuries. This inevitably drags the wage level. The self-supporting girl is in competition with the child, with the girl who lives at home and makes a small contribution to the household expenses, and with the girl who is supported and who spends all her money on her clothes. It is this division of purpose which takes the "spirit" out of them as a class. There will be no strikes among them so long as the question of wages is not equally vital to them all. It is not only nature and the law which demand protection for women, but society as well. In every case of the number I investigated, if there were sons, daughters or a husband in the family, the mother was not allowed to work. She was wholly protected. In the families where the father and brothers were making enough for bread and butter, the daughters were protected partially or entirely. There is no law which regulates this social protection: it is voluntary, and it would seem to indicate that civilized woman is meant to be an economic dependent. Yet, on the other hand, what is the new force which impels girls from their homes into the factories to work when they do not actually need the money paid them for their effort and sacrifice? Is it a move toward some far distant civilization when women shall have become man's physical equal, a "free, economic, social factor, making possible the full social combination of individuals in collective industry"? This is a matter for speculation only. What occurred to me as a possible remedy both for the oppression of the woman bread-winner and also as a betterment for the girl who wants to work though she does not need the money, was this: the establishment of schools where the esthetic branches of industrial art might be taught to the girls who by their material independence could give some leisure to acquiring a profession useful to themselves and to society in general. The whole country would be benefited by the opening of such schools as the Empress of Russia has patronized for the maintenance of the "petites industries," or those which Queen Margherita has established for the revival of lace-making in Italy. If there was such a counter-attraction to machine labour, the bread-winner would have a freer field and the non-bread-winner might still work for luxury and at the same time better herself morally, mentally and esthetically. She could aid in forming an intermediate class of labourers which as yet does not exist in America: the hand-workers, the main d'oeuvre who produce the luxurious objects of industrial art for which we are obliged to send to Europe when we wish to beautify our homes.

The American people are lively, intelligent, capable of learning anything. The schools of which I speak, founded, not for the manufacturing of the useful but of the beautiful, could be started informally as classes and by individual effort. Such labour would be paid more than the mechanical factory work; the immense importation from abroad of objects of industrial art sufficiently proves the demand for them in this country; there would be no material disadvantage for the girl who gave up her job in a pickle factory. Her faculties would be well employed, and she could, without leaving her home, do work which would be of esthetic and, indirectly, of moral value.

I was discouraged at first to see how difficult it was to help the working girls as individuals and how still more difficult to help them as a class. There is perhaps no surer way of doing this than by giving opportunities to those who have a purpose and a will. No amount of openings will help the girl who has not both of these. I watched many girls with intelligence and energy who were unable to develop for the lack of a chance a start in the right direction. Aside from the few remedies I have been able to suggest, I would like to make an appeal for persistent sympathy in behalf of those whose misery I have shared. Until some marvelous advancement has been made toward the reign of justice upon earth, every man, woman and child should have constantly in his heart the sufferings of the poorest.

On the evening when I left the factory for the last time, I heard in the streets the usual cry of murders, accidents and suicides: the mental food of the overworked. It is Saturday night. I mingle with a crowd of labourers homeward bound, and with women and girls returning from a Saturday sale in the big shops. They hurry along delighted at the cheapness of a bargain, little dreaming of the human effort that has produced it, the cost of life and energy it represents. As they pass, they draw their skirts aside from us, the labourers who have made their bargains cheap; from us, the cooperators who enable them to have the luxuries they do; from us, the multitude who stand between them and the monster Toil that must be fed with human lives. Think of us, as we herd to our work in the winter dawn; think of us as we bend over our task all the daylight without rest; think of us at the end of the day as we resume suffering and anxiety in homes of squalour and ugliness; think of us as we make our wretched try for merriment; think of us as we stand protectors between you and the labour that must be done to satisfy your material demands; think of us—be merciful.

FACTORY WORK:
ANOTHER MIDDLE-CLASS IMPRESSION

Dorothy Richardson was another middle-class reporter who submerged herself in factory life. The following selection is from the introduction to the first extended description of her experiences, *The Long Day: The Story of a New York Working Girl as Told by Herself*, first published in 1905. Richardson's observations, those of a professional journalist, tend to be more vivid than van Vorst's. Richardson also had a less sentimental view of working women, but this reflects the differences in the workingwomen the two writers were describing as well as the differences between the authors' perspectives. Richardson was absorbed in the situation of newly arrived immigrants in Chicago and, in particular, New York, whereas van Vorst focused her attention on native-American working girls in Pittsburgh. The new immigrants from southern and eastern Europe, who formed an increasing share of the number of women in factories beginning in the 1880s, did suffer greater difficulties in adapting to the discipline of the factory and the dislocations of urban life than did native-American women, who had a higher degree of education and a stronger tradition of independent labor.

Important to Richardson's assessment of the dependent condition of workingwomen was her fear of the incursions of sexual licentiousness and prostitution among women who could not cope with the rigors of factory life. Her sense of the significance of prostitution was no doubt mistaken, but she was appropriately cognizant of the continuing problems of adjustment faced by new immigrants from preindustrial cultures. Her recognition of the difficulties of integrating new immigrants into industrial society was reflected also in her perception of unionization as an ideal for lending workingwomen an increased sense of identity. Thus, in contrast to van Vorst's prescription for women, hers was to develop a sense of awareness not as idealized women, but as dignified, independent workers.

Dorothy Richardson (1875–1955), a doctor's daughter from Prospect, Pennsylvania, began her career in 1896. She worked for the *Pittsburgh Dispatch*, Eugene V. Debs's *The Social Democrat*, and, beginning in 1899, the *New York Herald*. Leaving the *Herald* in 1909, she became a press agent for producer David Belasco and, later, Paramount Pictures.

In New York Factories

For obvious reasons, I have been obliged to give fictitious names to factories and shops in which I worked; and I have, in most cases,

From Dorothy Richardson, *The Long Day: The Story of a New York Working Girl as Told by Herself* (New York: Century Co., 1911), pp. 274–83 and 302–03.

substituted for the names of the streets where the factories were located the names of streets of like character.

The physical conditions, the sordid wretchedness of factory and workshop, of boarding- and lodging-house, I have not in any wise overstated.

As to moral conditions, I have not been in every instance so scrupulously truthful—that is, I have not told all the truth. For it is a truth which only too often will not bear even the suggestion of telling. Only in two or three instances—for example, in my account of Henrietta Manners—have I ventured to hint definitely at anything pertaining to the shame and iniquity underlying a discouragingly large part of the work-girls' world. In my magazine articles I was obliged to leave out all reference to this tabooed topic. The attitude of the public, especially the American public, toward this subject is a curious mixture of prudery and gallantry. It bridles at anything which impeaches the traditional honor and chastity of the working girl. The chivalry of American men—and my experience in workshop, store, and factory has proved to me how genuine and deep-rooted that chivalry is—combined with our inherent spirit of democracy, is responsible for the placing of the work-girl, as a class, in a light as false and ridiculous as that in which Don Quixote was wont to view the charms of his swineherd lady, Dulcinea. In the main, our notions of the woman who toils do more credit to our sentiments and to the impulses of our hearts than they do credit to our heads or to any serious desires we may cherish for her welfare. She has become, and is becoming more and more, the object of such an amount of sentimentality on the part of philanthropists, sociological investigators, labor agitators, and yellow journals—and a goodly share of journalism that prides itself upon not being yellow—that the real work-girl has been quite lost sight of. Her name suggests, according to their imaginations, a proud, independent, self-reliant, efficient young woman—a young woman who works for her living and is glad of it. One hardly dares criticize her, unless, indeed, it be to lecture her for an ever-increasing independence of her natural male protectors and an alleged aversion to babies.

That we should cling so tenaciously to this ideal is to our honor and glory. But fine words butter no parsnips; nor do our fine idealizations serve to reduce the quota which the working-girl ranks contribute to disreputable houses and vicious resorts. The factories, the work-shops, and to some extent the stores, of the kind that I have worked in at least, are recruiting-grounds for the Tenderloin and the "red light" districts. The [New York factories] send annually a large consignment of delinquents to their various and logical destinations. It is rare indeed that one finds a female delinquent who has not been in the beginning a working girl. For, sad and terrible though it be, the truth is that the majority of "unfortunates," whether of the specifically criminal or of the prostitute class, are what they are, not because they are inherently vicious, but because they were failures as workers and as wage-earners. They were failures as such, primarily, for no other reason than that they did not like to work. And they did not like to work, not because they are lazy—they are anything but lazy, as a rule—but because they did not know how to work.

Few girls know how to work when they undertake the first job, whether that job be making paper boxes, seaming corset-covers, or taking shorthand dictation. Nor by the term, "knowing how to work," do I mean, necessarily, lack of experience. One may have had no experience whatever in any line of work, yet one may know how to work—may understand the general principles of intelligent labor. These general principles a girl may learn equally well by means of a normal-school training or through familiarity with, and participation in, the domestic labor of a well-organized household. The working girl in a great city like New York does not have the advantage of either form of training. Her education, even at the best, is meager, and of housework she knows less than nothing. If she is city-born, it is safe to assume that she has never been taught how to sweep a room properly, nor how to cook the simplest meal wholesomely, nor how to make a garment that she would be willing to wear. She usually buys all her cheap finery at a cheap store, and such style and taste as she displays is "ready made."

Not having learned to work, either at school or at home, she goes to the factory, to the workshop, or to the store, crude, incompetent, and, worst of all, with an instinctive antagonism toward her task. She cannot work, and she does not work. She is simply "worked."

And there is all the difference in the world between "working" and "being worked." To work is a privilege and a boon to either man or woman, and, properly regulated, it ought to be a pleasure. To be worked is degrading. To work is dignified and ennobling, for to work means the exercise of the mental quite as much as the physical self. But the average working girl puts neither heart nor mind into her labor; she is merely a machine, though the comparison is a libel upon the functions of first-class machinery.

The harsh truth is that, hard as the working girl is "worked," and miserable as her remuneration is, she is usually paid quite as much as she is worth.

For her incompetency she is not entirely to blame; rather is it a matter of heredity and environment. Being a girl, it is not natural to her to work systematically. The workingwoman is a new product; in this country she is hardly three generations old. As yet she is as new to the idea of what it really means to work as is the Afro-American citizen. The comparison may not be flattering to our vanity, but, after a reading of Booker Washington's various expositions of the industrial abilities of the negro, I cannot but be convinced that the white workingwoman is in a corresponding process of evolution, so far as her specific functions for labor have been developed.

Conditions in the "Pearl," from the view-point of mere physical labor, were the most brutal in all my experience; but, from what I can learn, the "Pearl" is no worse than many other similar establishments. Young women will work in such places only as a last resort, for young women cannot work long under conditions so detrimental to bodily health. The regular workers are old women— women like Mrs. Mooney and her cronies. The steady workers at the "Pearl" were, with the exception of the "queen," all old women. Every day saw the arrival of a new force of young hands who were bound to "play out" at the end of three or four days' apprenticeship, if not sooner. I played out completely: I didn't walk a step for a week after I went home with Minnie Plympton that Saturday night. Which was all in accord with Mrs. Mooney's prediction the first day: "You won't last long, mind ye; you young uns never do. If you ain't strong as an ox it gits in your back and off ye go to the 'orspital; and if you're not able to stand the drivin', and thinks you're good-lookin', off you goes to the bad, sooner 'n stay here." . . .

That the responsibility for these conditions of moral as well as physical wretchedness is fundamentally attributable to our present socioeconomic system is a fact that has been stated so often before, and by writers who by right of specialized knowledge and scientific training are so much better equipped to discuss social economics than I may ever hope to be, that I need not repeat the axiom here. Nor would it be any more becoming for me to enter into any discussion of the various theories upon which the economists and the social reformers base their various projects for the reconstruction of the present system. Personally I have a strong prejudice in favor of the trades-union. I believe that workingwomen should awaken as quickly as possible to the advantages to be derived from organization of the industries in which they are employed. But I seem to be alone in my cherished desire. The women and girls I have worked with in New York do not view the trades-union as their more progressive and enlightened sisters of Chicago and the West generally choose to regard it. . . .

But, after all, the greatest factor in the ultimate development of the working girl as a wage-earning unit—the most potent force for the adjustment of all the difficulties besetting her at every turn, and for the righting of all her wrongs, social, economic, or moral—will be the attitude which she herself assumes toward the dispassionate consideration of those difficulties to be adjusted, and of those wrongs to be righted.

At the present time there is nobody so little concerned about herself and her condition as the workingwoman herself. Taking everything into consideration, and in spite of conditions which, to the observer viewing them at a distance great enough to get a perspective, seem irreconcilably harsh and bitter—in the face of all this, one must characterize the workingwoman as a contented, if not a happy woman. That is the great trouble that will have to be faced in any effort to alleviate her condition. She is too contented, too happy, too patient. But not wholesomely so. Hers is a contentment, a happiness, a patience founded, not in normal good health and the joy of living and working, but in apathy. Her lot is hard, but she has grown used to it; for, being a woman, she is patient and long-suffering. She does not entirely realize the tragedy of it all, and what it means to herself, or to her children perhaps yet to be born.

In the happy future, the working girl will no longer be content to be merely "worked." Then she will have learned to work. She will have learned to work intelligently, and, working thus, she will begin to think—to think about herself and all those things which most vitally concern her as a woman and as a wage-earner. And then, you may depend upon it, she will settle the question to please herself, and she will settle it in the right way.

THE KNIGHTS OF LABOR AND WOMEN WORKERS

During the late nineteenth century the only national union to take an active part in organizing women was the Knights of Labor. Motivated by an unusually idealistic desire to assist all workers, the Knights developed an interest in including women within its organizational ambit. However, their interest came largely after the union had begun its precipitous decline in 1886 in the wake of the Haymarket Riot. Their interest was focused largely on advancing the *political* rights of women. Obstacles were encountered in the attitudes toward women held by the male members. The following two statements, the first by the Knights' leading organizer of women and the second by Terence V. Powderly, another of their leaders, suggest some aspects of the effort of the Knights on behalf of workingwomen. Despite the limitations of the Knights' program, many of the women who led in organizing women workers during the next generation did acquire their first taste of unions and strikes during the efforts of the Knights to organize unskilled workers.

A REPORT OF THE GENERAL INSTRUCTOR
OF WOMAN'S WORK, 1889

. . . A few words about the Woman's Department. When I took a position at its head I fondly hoped to weld together in organization

From *Record of the Proceedings of the General Assembly of the Knights of Labor*, 1889 (Philadelphia: 1889), pp. 1–6.

such a number of women as would be a power for good in the present, and a monument to their honor in the relief it would establish for the women of the future. I was too sanguine, and I am forced to acknowledge that to fulfill my best hopes is a matter of impossibility; and I believe now we should, instead of supporting a Woman's Department, put more women in the field as Lecturers to tell women why they should organize as a part of the industrial hive, rather than because they are women. There can be no separation or distinction of wage-workers on account of sex, and separate departments for their interests is a direct contradiction of this, and also of that part of our declaration which says "we know no sex in the laws of Knighthood." Therefore, I recommend the abolition of the Woman's Department, believing, as I now do, that women should be Knights of Labor without distinction, and should have all the benefits that can be given to men—no more, no less—thereby making it incumbent upon all to work more earnestly for the general good, rather than for sex, Assembly or trade.

I am willing to serve this Order in any capacity they may deem me worthy; but I cannot stand at the head of something that— owing to the failure of the women to organize more thoroughly— does not exist except in name.

Year after year I have stood before you and recited the wrongs and indignities of women toilers. I have pictured their unhappy condition of being overworked and underpaid. I have dwelt upon the evils of the slop-shop and sweating system, and the hopeless misery of its victims. This time I have done none of this. Repetition is but a mockery to those who are suffering, and, until we can give them practical assistance by creating a demand for and purchasing only such goods as bear some indication of fairly-paid labor, it is useless to add to their miseries by exciting a hope that is never realized.

The only way in which [necessary] practical relief . . . can be given is by the members of organized labor making such a demand for its own products as to leave no room for the product of the slop shop, which, unfortunately, no law can stop, as all industrial affairs seem to be based on the hog-trough philosophy, where the weaker and smaller have to stand back until the big hogs are satisfied; then, if they cry out against such injustice, they are told they are conspirators and disturbers of the public peace. My advice to organized labor wherever found, or under whatever name, is to combine in creating a demand for each other's labeled goods, and thus deal the slop-shop and sweating system its death-blow. To do this successfully organization is essential.

Brother Knights of Labor, bend all your energies to organization. Organized effort by the majority means success. With only a minority it means defeat, hopelessness and despair. Let intelligence and justice encircle our every action until the great mass of earth's toilers be brought into the greatest and noblest of all conditions— the brotherhood and sisterhood of humanity—where an injury to one will be the concern of all.

Leonora M. Barry

The General Master Workman Recommends Equal Rights

Within the last two months I determined to learn the number of members who could vote if this Order should become a political party, as required by many of my most persistent correspondents. Early in the year the thought occurred to me to ask the entire Order to vote on the question, but that those who wished to form the party might have no further cause of complaint it was decided to ask only voters to act on my letter. In doing this those who are not voters were not forgotten. No matter how intelligent the non-voter may be, he or she would have no right to vote in favor of turning the Order into a party when the action taken could not be followed up at the polling booth. Neither should those who are voters decide that the Order should become a party in opposition to the wishes of those who are not. In my letter calling for the vote, it was distinctly stated that this action would not be binding. What was required was the sentiment of the Order. We know when the quarterly reports are in how many women are members of the Order, and can thus tell exactly how many members vote and how many do not. It was not a mere matter of sentiment that caused me to send out that

From *Record of the Proceedings of the General Assembly of the Knights of Labor*, 1890 (Philadelphia: 1890), p. 14.

letter, although many well-disposed persons seem to think that every member should vote. That would leave us just where we were before, and the same cry would continue to go up that the Order should become a party. I felt morally certain that the vote would be against turning the Order into a party. If all had voted, and the vote was in favor of a party, and but half of the number were voters, it would mislead the unthinking. That we have unthinking members is plainly manifest, or they would not clamor to vote on a question that they can only vote on in a sentimental way. We have had enough of sentiment; let us be practical. Woman is obliged to work the same as man. She contracts debts and pays bills; she owns property and she is swindled out of it; she has to obey laws and has to break them; she must look on and see rascals elected to office, but has no voice in their selection, although the evil results of their election will fall as heavily on her as on any one else. We ask in our Preamble for equal pay for equal work, but will never get it until we have manhood enough to place the weapon in the woman's hand with which to punish the offenders against law, decency, order and good government. I recommend that we change the twentieth clause in the Preamble to read:

To secure for both sexes equal rights.

That will place all members on an equality and will enable all to assist in making the law. Add to that another clause, reading as follows:

All members are requested to qualify as electors as quick as possible.

When we do this there will be nothing lacking in our Preamble, but until then we have no right to ask the woman member of the Order to stultify herself by voting on a simple question on which she cannot have a voice at the polls. Let us be manly enough to demand for her the same rights that man enjoys.

UNIONIZATION AND WOMEN:
A COMMON VIEWPOINT

The following selection presents attitudes toward women workers more characteristic of late nineteenth-century unions than the statements of the leaders of the Knights of Labor. In this complaint of a craft-union leader one finds classic arguments on behalf of home confinement for women, with the Victorian family advanced not as the cornerstone of capitalism but as a requisite for the success of the labor movement. Most craft unions had sought to restrict women since the late 1850s, and such unions accounted for the major part of union membership throughout the period of accelerating industrialization.

WOMEN AS BREADWINNERS: A NATURAL PHENOMENON?

The invasion of the crafts by women has been developing for years amid irritation and injury to the workman. The right of the woman to win honest bread is accorded on all sides, but with craftsmen it is an open question whether this manifestation is of a healthy social growth or not.

The rapid displacement of men by women in the factory and workshop has to be met sooner or later, and the question is forcing itself upon the leaders and thinkers among the labor organizations of the land.

Is it a pleasing indication of progress to see the father, the brother and the son displaced as the bread winner by the mother, sister and daughter?

Is not the evolutionary backslide, which certainly modernizes the present wage system in vogue, a menace to prosperity—a foe to our civilized pretensions?

Such are the pertinent queries forcing themselves at this moment upon economic consideration, and it is vain and unwise to evade the propositions and seek out a possible solution.

The growing demand for female labor is not founded upon philanthropy, as those who encourage it would have sentimentalists believe; it does not spring from the milk of human kindness. It is an insidious assault upon the home; it is the knife of the assassin, aimed at the family circle—the divine injunction. It debars the man, through financial embarrassment from family responsibility, and physically, mentally and socially excludes the woman equally from

From *American Federationist* 4 (October 1897): 186–87.

nature's dearest impulse. Is this the demand of civilized progress; is it the desires of Christian dogma?

If this be so, and their undesirability to restrain the evils emanating from its growing intensity conveys the belief, then they are fostering and assuming a responsibility, which cankerlike, must eat at their very vitals, and bring about a retribution terrible to contemplate.

Capital thrives not upon the peaceful, united, contented family circle; rather are its palaces, pleasures and vices fostered and increased upon the disruption, ruin or abolition of the home, because with its decay and ever glaring privation, manhood loses its dignity, its backbone, its aspirations.

The welfare and happiness of the many, consequently, are not in harmony with the ambitions of the few. The desires of men generally are for better social and domestic conditions, and to improve and perpetuate these a higher price for services rendered is essential.

To combat these impertinent inclinations, dangerous to the few, the old and well-tried policy of divide and conquer is invoked, and to our own shame, it must be said, one too often renders blind aid to capital in its warfare upon us. The employer in the magnanimity of his generosity will give employment to the daughter, while her two brothers are weary because of their daily tramp in quest of work. The father, who has a fair, steady job, sees not the infamous policy back of the flattering propositions. Somebody else's daughter is called in in the same manner, by and by, and very soon the shop or factory are full of women, while their fathers have the option of working for the same wages or a few cents more, or take their places in the large army of unemployed.

This briefly is the history of the female side of the industrial problem, and with all those years of bitter experience history goes on repeating itself.

College professors and graduates tell us that this is the natural sequence of industrial development, an integral part of economic claim.

Never was a greater fallacy uttered of more poisonous import. It is false and wholly illogical. The great demand for women and their preference over men does not spring from a desire to elevate humanity; at any rate that is not its trend.

The wholesale employment of women in the various handicrafts must gradually unsex them, as it most assuredly is demoralizing them, or stripping them of that modest demeanor that lends a charm to their kind, while it numerically strengthens the multitudinous army of loafers, paupers, tramps and policemen, for no man who desires honest employment, and can secure it, cares to throw his life away upon such a wretched occupation as the latter.

The employment of women in the mechanical departments is encouraged because of its cheapness and easy manipulation, regardless of the consequent perils; and for no other reason. The generous sentiment enveloping this inducement is of criminal design, since it comes from a thirst to build riches upon the dismemberment of the family or the hearthstone cruelly dishonored.

We can no longer afford to brush away with an impulse of mock gallantry the terrible evil that is threatening the land, the community, the home; and the best evidence, that at least some of us are perceptive enough to catch the real significance of the situation, is presentable from the fact that not a few of the trades, with a view to modifying its tendency, without harrassing its present victims, are looking into the matter—notably the machinists.

As masculine labor destroys the finer promptings and feelings of the sex, the necessary factors to happiness and prosperity, under the conjugal knot, are undermined, or they become totally undesirous of assuming domestic responsibility; and in either case our vaunted civilization receives a setback.

Whatever side this grave problem is viewed from, it is the same hideous, objectionable nightmare.

But somebody will say, would you have women pursue lives of shame rather than work? Certainly not; it is to the alarming introduction of women into the mechanical industries, hitherto enjoyed by the sterner sex, at a wage uncommandable by them, that leads so many into that deplorable pursuit.

It does not require one to be much of a philosopher to catch the demon peeping from beneath the veneered blessing.

by Edward O'Donnell, Secretary
Boston Central Labor Union

WOMEN AND THE RISE OF INDUSTRIAL UNIONISM

The following speech on behalf of the unionization of women was made by one of the leaders of a movement to organize women that gathered force during the first decade of the twentieth century. The expansiveness of the demand for labor was creating opportunities for workers in all sectors to advance their interests, both individual and collective, and certain groups of women coalesced into unions in which they were numerically predominant. The core of these workers were the new Jewish garment workers of New York, Chicago, and Philadelphia, whose ethnic cohesion overcame the inertia that always tended to retard the advance of unionization among women workers. As early as 1900, these workers had formed the local nuclei of what would become the International Ladies Garment Workers Union (ILGWU).

During the first decade of the century, the organization of women workers along industrial lines and across skill lines grew significantly, for a variety of reasons. The labor shortage of the period and the emergence of a more ethnically solid laboring class in certain industries were contributing factors to the success of industrial unionism. Also critical was the fundamental acceptance of the industrial system by the leadership of the union movement. In contrast to the leaders of the Knights of Labor a generation earlier, this new leadership was not motivated by the desire to restore an idyllic competitive commonwealth. Despite its rejection of the emphasis by the American Federation of Labor (AFL) on craft unionism, the new leadership accepted the philosophy of Samuel Gompers that industrial democracy would be attained primarily through the exercise of economic power and only secondarily through the invocation of political influence. Of additional importance was the critical support rendered by a group of highly respectable, upper middle-class women who provided links between the organizing women and established centers of power. These middle-class women were persuaded that the advance of all women required the unionization of workingwomen. Typifying this group of idealistic women was Mary Dreier Robins, the author of the speech reprinted here.

The daughter of a wealthy German immigrant and wife of a wealthy Klondike gold miner, Mary Dreier Robins enjoyed a life free from material obligations and chose to devote herself first to municipal reform and charitable enterprises—particularly to settlement house work with Jane Addams in Chicago—then to the promotion of the labor movement among women, and finally to the cause of women's suffrage. The reasons why she and a few other women of similar circumstances chose to align themselves with lower-class women, while most of their social circle maintained more limited horizons, are obscure. A well-educated, acutely intelligent woman whose desire for independence received consistent support from both her father and her husband, Mary Robins was free to develop a close association with Addams and such labor leaders as Mary Kenney O'Sullivan, Rose Schneiderman of the cap makers, and Agnes Nestor of the glove workers. These friendships fostered her intense sensitivity to the difficulties faced by workingwomen who were seeking dignity and independence under the prevailing assumptions of ideal womanhood. Her respectability suffered somewhat from her association with workingwomen and her implied criticism of Victorian morality; she was blackballed by the Chicago Women's City Club and vicious rumors were circulated that were designed to impugn her morality. Nonetheless, her wealth and position continued to demand respect and she placed this respect at the service of workingwomen through her long presidency (1907–21) of the National Women's Trade Union League (NWTUL).

Founded in 1903, the NWTUL first gained significant strength when it came to the assistance of New York shirtwaist makers during their strike of 1909–10. Under the leadership of Mary Robins and with the rising level of support for unions among garment workers, the membership of the NWTUL grew steadily after 1910 and soon achieved its goal of having "trade unionists in good standing" as a majority of its members. Even by 1910, there were eleven local leagues, a vigorous educational program, and more than 75,000 members. Partly as a consequence of the support of the NWTUL, the ILGWU successfully maneuvered through the first, critical years of a career that would take it to leadership among industrywide unions.

Mary Dreier Robins and the middle-class leadership of the NWTUL often have received criticism for being reluctant to work from within the labor movement and for attaching far too much importance to winning the suffrage. However, one should bear in mind that the established union leadership was fundamentally unwilling to cope with the unique problems of organizing women and that to a large extent the organizers of workingwomen who participated in the NWTUL had already been rebuffed by the American Federation of Labor. Furthermore, the favors women were able to extract from the AFL often came as a result of the respect that Gompers carried for Mary Robins and the skill with which she played on her connections with progressive politicians. Finally, in the light of the unusually strong opposition to women's suffrage in the United States, criticism of the NWTUL for its suffrage interest ought to be regarded with extreme caution.

MARY DREIER ROBINS ON THE VALUE OF UNIONS

Fellow Workers and Friends: We have met in this our Third Biennial Convention to consider and advance the solution of the greatest problem of this generation. Upon our ability as a people to answer to the demand for industrial justice, depends the future of America. The world-old struggle between human slavery and human freedom is being fought out in this age on the battlefields of industry. We are beginning to understand that unless we win industrial freedom we cannot long maintain either religious or political liberty. A free church and a free state cannot endure side by side with a despotic workshop. Men cannot work as serfs under a feudal despotism six days in the week and on the seventh live as freemen.

Present-day industrial conditions deny to thousands the bare right

From Mary Dreier Robins, "Presidential Address," *Life and Labor* 1 (September 1911): 278–80.

to work and require other thousands to work long hours for little pay. In shop and factory and mill all over our country women are working under conditions that weaken vitality and sap moral fibre—conditions that are destructive alike of physical health and mental and moral development. These conditions if permitted to continue will destroy the ideals and promise of our individual and national life. Long hours, small pay, despotic rules and foremen, overshadowed by the haunting fear of losing one's job, with consequent hunger, cold and bitter want, do not make for the development of free men and free women.

While our day's work is in the main directed to the immediate aspects and demands of this great struggle, we cannot act wisely nor understand its significance fully unless we keep in mind the underlying cause for these conditions. We should know why men and women must fight for bread—even in America. We should know why it is that the "bread line" lengthens in the richest city of the richest nation in the world. We should understand that there is a direct relation between the monopoly control of natural resources and our disinherited sisters in the sweatshop.

Surrounded as we are today in our cities by brick and mortar, stone and cement, and far from the living green things of the earth, it is difficult for us to remember the ancient commandment: "The profit of the earth is for all," and to recall that "the earth is to yield her increase in green herb for the service of men and bread to strengthen man's heart."

The nature of the attack of modern industrial despotism upon the integrity and promise of our individual and national life is such as makes a special call upon the women of our country, and it seems to have been reserved for this generation to work our new standards of social justice and develop a new basis for our industrial civilization. Freedom, maternity, education, and morality—all the blessed and abiding interests of childhood and the home—are in issue in this supreme struggle. All women who honor their sex and love their country should unite with us and our working sisters in the struggle for industrial freedom.

One of the chief social indictments of the nonunion workshop is its tendency to destroy originality and initiative among the workers.

Long hours under despotic control, high subdivision of labor with consequent monotony of toil tend to register permanent reactions of stolid submission, unreasoning repetition, and isolated personality in the minds of the workers. By the same token, the chief social gain of the union shop is not its generally better wages and shorter hours, but rather the incentive it offers for initiative and social leadership, the call it makes through a common industrial relationship and a common hope, upon the moral and reasoning faculties, and the sense of fellowship, independence, and group strength it develops. In every workshop of say thirty girls there is undreamed of initiative and capacity for social leadership and control—unknown wealth of intellectual and moral resource. The union brings into exercise these powers and uses them for the benefit of the group, thus stimulating and increasing the individual and group life. These mighty social powers that industry can engender and release for our social life are possible only under conditions of industrial democracy, i.e., in the union shop. Just as under a despotic church and a feudal state the possible power and beauty of the common people was denied expression, so under industrial feudalism the intellectual and moral powers of the workers are slowly choked to death, to the incalculable loss of the individual and the race. It is easy to kill; it requires a great spirit as well as a great mind to arouse the dormant energies, to vitalize them, and to make them creative forces for good. Who answers to the call?

A UNION LEADER: FANNIA M. COHN

One of the truly indigenous leaders of the ILGWU was Fannia M. Cohn. Born in Russia in 1888, she had entered the garment trades in New York as a teen-ager, joined the union in 1910, become chairman of the executive board of Local No. 41 in 1911, and served as a vice-president of the ILGWU from 1916–25. To Fannia Cohn, the ideal of unionizing workingwomen was compelling not simply as a means of improving material circumstances but as a way of enhancing their dignity, pride, and self-awareness. Depressed by the hostility of established trade unions and troubled by the lack of self-confidence often characteristic of workingwomen, she became convinced that the organization of women had to proceed separately from the organization of men and that educational programs designed to heighten women's self-perceptions had to be an integral part of the union movement. Consequently, she became a leader in promoting ILGWU educational programs, including lecture programs and evening classes within a workers' university. In 1916, she became organizing secretary of the Educational Committee of the national ILGWU and continued in a similar position when the committee became the Educational Department in 1923.

The following selection is a speech made by Fannia Cohn in 1917 that provides a clear statement of her idealistic sense of the mission of women's trade unionism. As is apparent from the selection, she was a fervent participant in the NWTUL. She believed that this was the most effective organization for obtaining support of the wider community and appreciated the assistance that the respectability of the organization provided in attracting young women to the labor movement. However, she attempted throughout her career to keep lines of communication open to the AFL and hoped that ultimately it would take a serious interest in organizing women. For example, she seized the occasion of the election of William Green to the presidency of the AFL in 1925 to write to him on behalf of greater AFL investment in the organization of women. (That letter follows the 1917 speech.) Typically, Green's response was warm but promised nothing by way of financial support.

A Union Officer Calls for Idealism

Madame Chairman and Fellow Delegates: We have within our organization about 50,000 women, and it may be interesting to you to know what is going on in that organization. We have carried on numerous strikes among workers of different trades that come under our jurisdiction. In the last eight months all the strikes we have

From Fannia M. Cohn, "International Ladies Garment Workers' Report," in *Sixth Biennial Convention Proceedings of the National Women's Trade Union League* (Chicago: Glennon & Kern Printers, 1917), pp. 36–38.

called have been among women. We have had more than twenty
organizers working among women only. With the cloak makers,
which are about 100 per cent organized, coming under our
jurisdiction, I hope within the next few years the International will
devote all its efforts to organizing women. We have 100,000
women who are unorganized working on different ladies' garments. . . .

From my report Madame Chairman, you can see that our
International Union carries the message of unionism and solidarity
among workers in every city and every state where there are ladies'
garments workers' unions, regardless of whether the members are
women or men.

It may be interesting to know that in our last convention of the
International an educational committee of five members was created,
with an allowance of $5,000 for the start. I cannot tell you what the
result of the work of that committee will be, because it is still
working out the problem. We elected an additional committee in
our last meeting, composed of three vice-presidents, and our only
woman vice-president is a member of that committee.

One of our largest local unions, and the largest women's local
union in the world, Local No. 25 of the Ladies' Waist Makers,
made an experiment on this line: They have an educational
department under the able leadership of Miss Julia Stuart Poyntz,
and one of the achievements of that department is the Unity House.
They have a winter Unity House and last summer a Unity House
was maintained in the Catskill mountains. In such a summer Unity
House each member can spend two weeks' vacation for $5 a week.
The fellowship that Unity House develops we cannot over value.

We had the Board of Education turn over to this Unity House an
entire school building, where the girls have their meetings, lectures,
and classes; where they can buy suppers for 10 cents each, provided
by the union. We hope in the near future the Ladies' Waist Makers'
Union will be able to have their own building, something like
clubrooms with a lunchroom attached. I think it is important to
introduce education in our unions, managed by the girls, of course.

To many trade union women and men the organization is an
economic proposition only. No doubt it is, but a union would be a

very dry affair if we discussed nothing outside of our trade. I think that is wrong. I do not see how we can get girls to sacrifice themselves—and it takes sacrifice to build up a union—unless we discuss something besides trade matters. Many of us suffered for years because we were the pioneers in our trade unions. There must be something more than the economic question, there must be idealism. You will always get people to do greater things and bigger things if you emphasize the idealistic side rather than the materialistic side.

Those who think the idealist can not be practical, and therefore successful within the labor movement, are mistaken. It is vision that makes us do great things.

To talk of democracy is not enough: democracy is judged by its actions and I wish we would talk less and practice democracy more within our unions. I do not think we are worse than other organizations, but I want that we should be better than other organizations, because this is a protest movement against industrial autocracy.

We must have free expression within our unions if we are to grow, especially at a time such as this. We are living in a transition stage when many of our old beliefs and hopes are being shattered and we will have to replace them with new ideals.

We are fighting for industrial democracy and freedom. How will we accomplish these changes that we expect, and that every honest and intelligent man and woman outside the labor movement expects us to accomplish? How can we accomplish these changes if we are not broad-minded, if we don't invite every working man and woman to say what they think about existing conditions? Let us open our doors to the newcomers; let us not concentrate power, it is dangerous. Keep everybody busy in the union, give everybody something to do, and then, and then only, will the union be effective; it will always move, it will always develop, it will never be stationary.

I am deeply impressed by this convention. I really consider it a privilege to be one of the delegates. The main thing that impresses me is the young sisters we have here with us. I am a little jealous about considering myself one of the old, for I am not, but still it fills one's heart with hope and joy to know that the work we are doing will be carried on by these young girls. It is a real pleasure to hear them discuss questions of the greatest importance. I see in that the vision of the future and the practical mind of the present.

I would invite our brother union men to come and learn something from these young girls. I challenge any of the men's organizations to say that their conventions are of greater interest or have a better spirit in them. That is the reason I am always in favor of a federation of women's unions where women are coming together to discuss the questions that interest them as women and workers, knowing their interests are not secondary but come first. I hope none of you will accuse me of trying to segregate the women workers from the men workers, on the contrary, I believe the women should go hand in hand with the men, and I believe this can be accomplished only when woman is man's equal on the industrial as well as the political field. And it is to bring about that glorious time we are assembled here to help build up the women's unions that will be equal to the men's unions.

Madame Chairman, may I tell you in all sincerity that I am very glad to be here, that I am very thankful to my international union for sending me as their delegate, and that I feel this convention will be to me, as to many others, an inspiration for further work. I thank you.

To WILLIAM GREEN

6 March 1925

My dear President Green,

I wish to call your attention to the fact that this communication is not official. I am not writing to you as an officer speaking for her organization. This is an appeal to the head of the American Labor Movement from a woman trade unionist.

I am impelled to write you after the attempt made by the A.F. of L. to devise ways and means of organizing working women brought no immediate results.

From Fannia M. Cohn Papers, by permission of Clarice Selub and Manuscripts and Archives Division, The New York Public Library, Astor, Lenox and Tilden Foundations.

We all realize the duty of the American Federation of Labor toward women workers. Whereas, the A.F. of L. and its affiliated unions consider that the organization of men is their concern, and it is carried on under their own auspices, they do not follow this out when it comes to the organization of women.

When the deplorable conditions of the unorganized working woman are to be considered, a conference is called by many ladies' organizations who have no connection with the labor movement, and they are the ones to decide "how to improve the conditions of the poor working woman."

By this time we realize that women have come into this industry for good, whether from choice or from necessity, and this points to the fact that women will more and more become a factor in industry.

Some unions may succeed in keeping women out of their organizations for a while, but they cannot keep them out of industry. And what we need most is organization amongst women. I am conscious of the difficult task in organizing women into trade unions, but this should only increase our efforts in this field.

The organization of women is not merely a moral question, but also an economic one. Men will never be certain with their conditions unless the conditions of the millions of women are improved.

The old theory of the impossibility of organizing women will not solve this problem. Instead, men and women trade unionists will have to make a joint effort to organize the unorganized women by carrying on an educational campaign amongst them, and by enlisting the cooperation of men members of trade unions.

To achieve any results it will be necessary to make a study of women in industry, length of employment, the conditions under which they work, and most important of all, of their psychology, such research will be helpful to the trade unions in the industries in which women are employed. And women in the labor movement think that this task should be undertaken by the American Federation of Labor.

I, as a woman who has dedicated her life to the cause of labor, am eager to have this research done by the American Labor Movement through the A.F. of L. instead of leaving it to other organizations who have different purposes in view.

I take the liberty of writing you about the matter, because I am convinced that you, too, are interested in solving this problem of the organization of women into trade unions.

With best personal wishes for a successful administration, I am,

Sincerely and Fraternally Yours,

Fannia M. Cohn

A UNION LEADER: JENNIE MATYAS

One of the young women who was involved in the formative years of the ILGWU was Jennie Matyas (born in 1895). During the 1930s she became a very prominent union organizer of the ILGWU in San Francisco, and in 1941 she became vice-president of the national union. But it is her career during the second and third decades of the century that is most interesting for the ways in which it is representative of those who were the union rank and file. Matyas attended her first union meeting in 1912 and by 1916 had become a shop leader.

The following reading, drawn from an extensive interview with her that was conducted in 1955, pertains to that early career. Of particular interest is Jennie Matyas's conversion to trade unionism. There was little in her background to indicate, in an obvious way, that she would become an enthusiast. Emigrating from Transylvania in 1905, her family brought little in the way of political convictions and possessed a relatively low level of religious consciousness. They had been a Jewish family surrounded by Catholic neighbors, had faced no apparent discrimination in their village, and had emigrated alone. In New York, the family proved highly frugal, rapidly paying back the cost of their ocean passage, and Jennie found she was an extremely successful worker. Assessment of the appeal of the message of union organizers—given the character of industrial conditions and opportunities for women—for young women such as Jennie Matyas is left to the reader.

Also of note in the reminiscences of Jennie Matyas are her

suggestions of the extent to which the newly committed thought of themselves as socialists. Although an older generation of organizers either had serious reservations about socialism or obscured their ideological persuasions to avoid inviting middle-class hostility, women organizers who came to intellectual maturity during the 1910s were more apt to consider themselves socialists and to be less reluctant to develop an interest in socialist political alternatives. However, given the vagueness of their socialism, their emphasis on enhancing the dignity of labor, and their powerful interest in winning the suffrage for women, they found that they shared much common ground with those women, such as most of the middle-class leadership of the NWTUL, who tended to accept the fundamental presumptions of capitalism.

Finally, this testimony suggests some of the difficulties that the ILGWU endured during the 1920s. Faced by high unemployment within the garment industry, by the increasing apathy of the AFL, and by heightened middle-class hostility toward unionism, the ILGWU found its membership declining and its locals bitterly divided over almost every issue of strategy. Some local leaders were radicalized by the reversals that had followed the high idealism of the preceding decade and turned for inspiration to the apparently more promising Russian experience. This widened the gap between themselves and those, like Jennie Matyas, who rejected the concept of the dictatorship of the proleteriat and, believing in the fundamental responsiveness of American institutions to the needs of labor, were reluctant to seek dramatic political change. Unemployed, or disillusioned, or unwilling to endure the stress of internecine warfare, or reluctant to accept the victory of an opposing faction, many of the local leaders dropped out of the industry and out of the movement. (Matyas used the opportunity to advance her education.) Their exodus, along with the tendency of liberals within the ILGWU to unite with conservative AFL leaders such as Samuel Gompers and William Green in opposition to the Communists, reduced even further the interest of organized labor in providing women workers with equal opportunity. Some of the dropouts, like Jennie Matyas, would return when the Great Depression and New Deal provided the basis of support for a revivified union movement.

At that point, the political and personal disagreements that had seemed so important during the early 1920s became, at least for a period, simply academic, as a result of the dynamic growth of industrial unionism along the lines pioneered by the ILGWU.

RECOLLECTIONS OF JENNIE MATYAS

Matyas: . . . I didn't have any feeling of Semitism or anti-Semitism, until I grew up. Later, when I left my immediate friends and environment, I began to feel that there was such a thing as anti-Semitism, because for some strange reason that I couldn't understand, people didn't recognize that I was Jewish and would say things to me that sort of put me on the spot. If I called them on it and told them that I was Jewish, it would be embarrassing to them and so I would keep quiet and then rebel at the thought that I had to listen to something that I thought was unjust. I thought the situation was unjust to the other persons too because if they had known that I was Jewish, they probably wouldn't have said what they did. There I was. It was quite a dilemma.

Q: In your family were there views such as Socialism?

Matyas: Oh no, good gracious me. We had never heard the term until we came to this country. After I went to work, one of my brothers was told that he had to leave the home because he had adopted what seemed like some form of Socialism. Anyhow, my father thought he was a rebellious type of boy; he didn't say his prayers as often as he should, so my father told him he would either have to mend his ways or leave home. Much to my mother's sorrow, he chose to leave home. I subsequently heard that he became a Socialist. The word sounded very terrible to me and I thought, "Oh, what a nice boy he would be if only he hadn't adopted that awful philosophy."

Q: The family believed in the status quo?

From "Jennie Matyas and the ILGWU" (Berkeley: Regional Oral History Office, Bancroft Library, University of California, 1957), pp. 23–90, by permission of Jennie Matyas Charters.

Matyas: Oh yes. If we believed in anything at all. We were so busy making a living that there wasn't much thought. We believed in God and the justice that God dispensed and one didn't question. I remember one time I did put a few questions to my father, not about God but about a certain ritual that I couldn't quite understand. And he stamped his foot and pounded the table, "One mustn't ask questions." It was ungodly to ask questions.

Q: Have you remained Orthodox?

Matyas: Well, I was Orthodox until I went to teach Sunday school. You see, when I believe in something, I believe in it very hard and when I lose the belief, I lose it. I taught Sunday school and when I heard myself teaching the story of Jacob and his ladder, somehow it didn't quite make sense to me. I hadn't learned to see things figuratively and I just lost my belief in conventional religion.

Q: What eventually happened to your other brothers and sisters?

Matyas: This brother who had to leave home, I don't know where he is. I would like very much to know.

When I went to work finally . . . I went to work the day I was fourteen. That is, I went to work legally when I was fourteen. I worked in the summer before that and did a lot of commercial homework before that, but when I went to work officially, then of course, I came in contact with someone who tried to get me to join a union which I thought must be very dreadful. I heard street meetings and I stopped and listened and I was told the speakers were Socialists. I listened very eagerly to know what Socialism was and I remember I heard one of the speakers say, "All we're asking for is bread and butter." And I went away very disgusted because he talked for an hour on his right to have bread and butter. "Why wouldn't bread alone be sufficient?" I was between fourteen and fifteen at the time and butter seemed a terrific luxury to me.

When I was asked to join a union by one of the women who worked in the factory where I worked, I said, "A union, what is that?" She tried to tell me but she wasn't too articulate about it. I said, "Well, would the boss like it if I joined the union?" She said, "For Pete's sakes, don't ever let him know. You'd lose your job and I'd lose mine." Well, I thought about it and thought about it and finally I thought, "Well, maybe it makes sense." I didn't take it too seriously; my ambition in life was to get to be a good worker because being the oldest daughter, it was my job to do the dressmaking for the family.

Q: When this woman asked you to join a union, did you join?
Matyas: Not for quite awhile. No. I didn't think that was a very good idea at first.

After I found a job in a dress factory, I became a "learner" and I'd work for another worker. That was the custom in those days. Subcontracting, it was called. An operator would take on as many learners as he could get. He couldn't pay less than $3.50 a week, and in my case again, it became $3.20 a week. This operator would keep a learner on one operation because it became profitable to him. He was a pieceworker. The learner would become very proficient in one operation and would stay there. Well, I'd be very eager to learn more and more and as soon as I got so I knew one operation, I'd quit my job. He'd give me a raise. Maybe he'd bring me up to $4 or even up to $5. I'd quit my job and look for another job as a learner again so that I'd learn another operation, though I had to start at $3.50 again. Finally I got to the point where I really knew how to work and I could hold a job on my own.

I remember one time, I was very daring, and I thought I'd try for a job on my own, to make the whole garment. I got the job and I was frightened day after day; I thought I'd lose my job. My mother was very concerned over the fact that I had a job on my own. I thought, "Oh, if only I could make as much as $8 a week, wouldn't that be wonderful." And my mother kept asking me day after day how much I would get. I said, "Mother, you know they never tell you until the end of the week. I don't know, maybe I'll get $8. I think I'm managing all right." Well, finally the week was up and I went to my employer, praying I would get $8 a week, and I asked him how much I would get and he said, "Well, what do you think you're worth?" I said, "I don't really know, but what do you think I'm worth?" He said, "Well, I tell you, you're not too bad. I'll start you on $11 a week and see what happens." I had to control my excitement so he wouldn't see that I didn't really expect that much.

I almost ran home. I was worried all the way home. What if I told my mother I was getting so much and she began to count on it and plan on a higher standard of living. I knew I couldn't hold a job that paid so well and I didn't want to get her prepared for a standard I was afraid I couldn't live up to. Finally, when I got home, mother said, "How much are you going to get?" And I said quickly, "Well, I'm-getting-$11-a-week-but-don't-count-on-it. It's-sure-not-to-last." (laughter)

Well, it lasted for awhile but when I got so I thought I would like to learn a little more, I quit that job and went to work somewhere where they made a better quality garment and actually I got to the point where I became a sample maker and worked with the designer in a very large factory. I arrived at the point where I was treated magnificently and where I got a nice wage because my work was so topnotch.

Q: You sound like the ideal employee.

Matyas: Well, I was considered a very reliable and dependable employee, but I was very disturbed by how the other people were being treated. I realized that, individually, nobody could do anything about it. The long hours we would work. My superiors spoke in my presence because

I was a sample maker and they thought surely my sympathies were not with the ordinary workers because here I was picked out to be a topnotch worker. . . .

Q: How old were you at that time?

Matyas: A little over fifteen. I made progress fast because I worked at it very hard.

Well, when I saw all that, I realized that no one could do anything individually to change conditions and that conditions would just have to be changed. And so when one of the workers asked me again whether I would go to a union meeting, I did, but it was surreptitious. The boss was not allowed to find out. The union was very poor at this time. I think it was in 1912 or 1913. . . .

You asked me what the functions of a shop chairlady were. In addition to keeping the records, it was also essential to build the morale of each shop and you'd have individual shop meetings. In addition to that, you'd have daily so-called mass meetings of all the workers that met in that particular hall. You'd have them in the general assembly to get the report of what was going on from day to day and those days you'd have the very best outside speakers.

Fiorello La Guardia was one of our outside speakers in the 1916 strike. At that time I didn't know who LaGuardia was, except that he was a very fiery somebody and he stood up there and talked very entertainingly and convincingly. He kept turning around and would say, "As Jennie here says. . . ." And I thought, "Now, isn't that funny. He doesn't know me. How does he know my name? How does he know what I say?" I felt tremendously flattered. For all I know, it may have been an oratorical device.

But in these assembly meetings I was always the presiding person, naturally, and introduced the other speakers. And I had always said, and believed, that we would not go back to work until we got all our demands. Well, when the agreement came and it was so far short of our original demands, my childish mind just couldn't get the importance of it and I couldn't see that a wonderful beginning was actually made.

Q: You couldn't go back to your original shop when you finally did go back to work, could you?

Matyas: No. The employer wouldn't have me and I recognized the fairness of that because I had chosen not to go back to work and he put somebody else on the job. I didn't contest his decision not to rehire me.

I didn't think it would be hard for me to find another job because by this time I was a very good worker and I thought there was always room for a good worker. I began to look for other jobs and I got them very easily, but unfortunately, I had worked up popularity as a hall chairlady and, as I came into a shop, I'd work for a day or two until somebody would say unwittingly, "Oh, there's Jennie. Don't you remember Jennie?" And the employer would find out who Jennie was and with no reason whatsoever, Jennie was just out of a job. It took me about two years before I succeeded in overcoming that. It was a very trying thing for the family, but I somehow took it for granted as one of the prices one paid for progress. I didn't feel at all abused about it. My dream was that someday nobody would have to pay a price for wanting to abolish misery and poverty, but it was hard to persuade my mother. She knew we needed the money desperately.

Q: Did you continue active in the union?

Matyas: Oh yes, always.

Q: What were your functions?

Matyas: When the strike was on, I was a member of the general strike committee. When the strike was over, I was a member of the executive committee of my local, and the grievance committee. When I finally did find a job, I was elected a shop steward. I was always elected a shop steward before very long and I was always quite willing to accept the responsibility. . . .

Q: I wanted to ask you about the leaders of the union. What origin were they?

Matyas: Most of the leadership of the union was Jewish and Italian, and most of them were great idealists and had come from Europe in search of this wonderful America, this land of freedom, and when they came here they found abuse in our industry, sweatshopism. A book by Sholem Asch called *East River* gives a picture of conditions in our industry at a given time, of sweatshopism.

Q: Was it your impression that the leaders were radicals? Were they anarchists as they were charged with being?

Matyas: I didn't know any anarchists. I had heard of anarchists and had met some, but anarchism just didn't interest me. I couldn't visualize any country without a government. Perhaps it was a nice dream, for all I knew, but the thought of human beings so perfect that no government was essential just never made any sense to me. Socialists, on the other hand, did not seem unreasonable to me. They seemed extremely idealistic.

Q: You mentioned in an earlier interview that your family was against Socialism.

Matyas: Oh, my family was desperately against Socialism.

Q: How did you make this transition, into thinking Socialism was an ideal . . . ?

Matyas: At first I had more or less a child's concept of Socialism. I had heard a great many Socialist speakers on street corners. Of course, eventually I learned that the aims of Socialists were to have social ownership of the socially necessary industries, so that production would be for use, not for profit, and so that poverty would be abolished. And it made sense.

Q: Did you learn about this through the union leaders?

Matyas: No, not so much through the union leaders, although I knew that most of the union leaders were Socialists. They were more concerned with the immediate problems of the union, although I knew that fundamentally they had a

Socialist approach. I began to read books like William Morris's *News from Nowhere* and Bellamy's *Looking Backward* and [they] had a great effect on me.

I had a vision of a beautiful world.

Q: Did you go to Socialist party meetings?

Matyas: Yes, although I didn't join the Socialist party at that time. I wasn't old enough and I wasn't going to join the young people's Socialists because that would brand me as being young and I wouldn't admit that. Being young never had any premium for me. My desire always was to be grown-up, so the responsibility I carried would be in keeping with my age. I liked being trusted with responsibility.

Q: Were the Socialist meetings very large?

Matyas: Some were large and some were small. The district meetings were very small; the general membership meetings were large. When I finally joined, when I was 18 years old, I soon became a member of the executive committee and the central committee. It was just taken for granted that I was a full-fledged person. The leadership in those days was very idealistic, just as in the union. Morris Hillquit, who was a brilliant corporation attorney, was one of the members of the executive committee and Algernon Lee of the Rand School, who was a great ideal of mine.

Q: Did you meet many people from the unions at the Socialist meetings?

Matyas: Yes, I think pretty nearly everybody belonged to a union. I don't recall that they were from my union.

Q: But many of the shop members with whom you associated were not Socialists?

Matyas: Oh no. The members of the shops of my union were like a cross section of any community. The cross section of any community in this country was not Socialist. We rolled up a big Socialist vote once or twice nationally, but never enough to elect a Socialist in many cities. There were Socialist mayors here and there, and members of

municipal councils, but the Socialists were never a party
that could elect members to power.

Q: As a shop steward, did you try to encourage people to
          become Socialists?

Matyas: I don't recall that I did. I'm very certain it was known that
          I was a Socialist, but it had nothing to do with my
          function as a shop steward.

Q: I remember your saying that you had met Eugene Debs.
          What were your impressions of him?

Matyas: Oh yes, that was a wonderful thing. I was as faithful a
          Socialist party member as I was a union member, and I
          thought the Socialist party was the vehicle through which
          we would search for a better world and the union was the
          vehicle through which we would abolish immediate
          abuses, so the two had to go hand in hand. So I was very
          active in the Socialist party and was in on the inner
          circles. Whenever anyone outstanding came to town, I
          was there. I was always considered the child prodigy
          because of my devotion and assumption of responsibility.

          This time Eugene Victor Debs was slated to come to a
          meeting by the Socialist party against the declaration of
          war in 1916. Eugene Debs was very peace loving and
          antiwar. That was like having a great hero, almost a god,
          come to New York City. When he arrived there were
          several private coffee cup sessions and I was always in on
          them. One time I remember being just thrilled when he
          asked me what I was doing and I told him I was a
          member of my union. He had a little talk with me over
          coffee, very informal, and he put his arm around me and
          said, "Little girl, how I wish you could do the work you
          ought to do. You will when the world becomes a better
          world." I was in heaven. I thought, "This great man
          thinks there is something in me which will help to make a
          better world."

          Then we had a great mass meeting at which he was the
          speaker. I sat in the audience and I saw this tall, lanky,
          idealistic human being who leaned forward as though his

very inner soul spoke to us. He said, "When I think of the cold, grey, glittering steel thrust into the warm, quivering flesh of man, I recoil with horror." And war to me was a terrible, terrible, personal thing. And I became even more strongly antiwar after that time.

To me Socialism was the way we would bring the Golden Rule into being. Oh, the shock that came to me when I read George Bernard Shaw who said, "Don't do unto others as you would like to be done by. Tastes differ." . . .

Q: Did you find in the early 1920's that membership was falling off?

Matyas: I think membership was falling off a great deal. Of course, people had no money to pay dues with. But we came back eventually. The effect of the Russian revolution was even worse on our membership.

Q: When did you first become aware of the effects of the Russian revolution on your union?

Matyas: The effects on our union started in the early 1920's.

Q: I know that the Communist International actually organized a drive to take over American unions.

Matyas: Yes. My acquaintance with it was in the early 20's. I was naive and never believed anything bad until I came into contact with it personally. One time I went to another union on behalf of some cause or other. To my amazement, I saw a sign on the door that said, "Meeting of Members of Local 22." Well, I was a member of Local 22, so I went in. I saw that it was a meeting of some of our members, but the speakers, who were also members, were saying such strange and dreadful things that I just couldn't believe them. They were encouraging revolution against the union itself and against the union leadership.

In those days they were very crude. I heard a woman, Ida Rothstein, later Ida Roth, who was just recently killed in an automobile accident, say, "Is there no spunk in among the people here? In Paris you ought to hear how members talk to their union leaders. They spit in their eyes." I couldn't begin to tell you the shock it was. The language was so crude and out of keeping with anything I had heard and the thought of that kind of disloyalty didn't make sense. I didn't hear any issues discussed, just the virtues of being rebellious.

Q: Did they label themselves Communists?

Matyas: No. I hadn't heard of a separate group in our union that labeled itself anything. There evidently was a growing group which I think subsequently labeled itself the Needle Trades Alliance.

I think it kept growing more and more and William Z. Foster became the leader, in the trade union field, of all of the Alliances. I think these so-called Alliances were more active in the needle trades than anywhere else. They always find it easier to work in unions that are already liberal than in strong and conservative unions. They didn't go to many of the other A.F. of L. unions because they wouldn't have had a chance.

Q: But Socialists are notoriously anti-Communist?

Matyas: Oh, terrifically. But in the union we weren't Socialists; we were unionists who believed in democracy so strongly that we thought everyone naturally had a right to his opinion. The opinions were absolutely crazy and we had to show them up, but we thought they had a right to their opinion. We soon realized their opinions were poisonous and vile and very unscrupulous and the aim was to wreck our organization. There were leaders in our union who recognized that. I belonged to the group that found it very difficult to accept the theory that stupid as anyone was, he could not be allowed to express his opinion. I felt one couldn't go out and fight a fellow worker, ruinous as he was. You could fight your boss, because it was fighting opposite interests, but to fight a fellow worker was emotionally impossible for me. There was a group of us women who felt that way. We didn't really truly understand that these people, who called themselves progressives, they never called themselves Communists even then. . . .

I couldn't fight them, but I couldn't go with them either because they were so stupid and so bad. I realized that their work was very destructive. I couldn't quite understand how serious it was, but I knew it was very bad.

Q: I have a note here that Juliet Poyntz became an active member of the Russian secret service.

Matyas: Yes. I didn't know that. None of us knew that. As a matter of fact, when we later learned about it, I was the most shocked person in the whole world. To us, she was just this wonderfully handsome person with a lovely character. She was teaching at Barnard College. She was very interested in helping us to become interested in educational activities. I remember Juliet Poyntz, in addition to wanting members to be interested in the education movement, also wanted members to be more active even in the regular, local union functions. Of course, I sort of worked with Juliet Poyntz. I'm not sure if I worked with her or just kept admiring her. She was very beautiful and so intelligent.

Q: Was she openly a Communist?

Matyas: Not at the time. 1915, nobody knew anything about Communism. To me she was just somebody from Barnard College, this grand and lovely lady who was interested enough in the working-class movement to come and be with us.

Q: When did you learn she was with the Russians?

Matyas: Oh, not until I left the union. She had already been gone from us years and years before that. . . .

Q: What did you do, in the early 1920s, when you felt you could not fight the destructive element but you couldn't go along with them either?

Matyas: I ran away. I had always wanted desperately to get an education. After I quit school, I went to night school, but then my activity in the union kept me from it. I did continue to take classes in English for awhile, one night a week. Eventually even my class in English had to go by the board, because it was so important to give everything to the organization. To get a regular certificate of elementary school graduation and then a high school certificate, going at night, would take at least ten years. Ten years would be the end of the world. There was so much work to do that education began to assume a selfish aspect to me.

Q: And now you decided to go back to school?

Matyas: Now I decided here was my chance. If I couldn't go with these idiots and I couldn't fight them, I would just go to school. And a lot of my colleagues who felt as I did went out. Some got married; some went into some or another little business. They couldn't stay in the union and not be on one side. . . .

CLASS INTERESTS PLACED ABOVE WOMEN'S RIGHTS

More committed to the primacy of class struggle than the founders of industrial organization among women was Mary Harris Jones, or "Mother" Jones (1830–1930), as she was called by her contemporaries. A widowed dressmaker who lost all her possessions in the 1871 Chicago fire, she accidentally became an organizer for the Knights of Labor and by the first decade of the century had emerged as a prominent organizer for the United Mine Workers in Alabama, Pennsylvania, West Virginia, and Colorado. She expressed no sensitivity to the interests of women as a disadvantaged class and, in fact, urged women to ignore "women's" problems. In her fervent, evangelical organizing efforts she ignored women workers and in her Socialist politics looked with trepidation on the prospect of women's suffrage, which she believed—certainly correctly in the short run—would prove to be a conservative force.

Mother Jones has attracted a great deal of interest in recent years as an inspiring example of courageous, independent womanhood. However, largely as a result of the potency of economic class consciousness characteristic of unionism in the extractive industries of the West, her implicit conception of ideal womanhood differed in no significant way from that of the typical male rank-and-file trade unionist of the AFL. The following selection indicates her position on the suffrage.

"You Don't Need a Vote to Raise Hell"

I came to New York to raise funds for the miners' families. Although they had gone back beaten to work, their condition was pitiful. The women and children were in rags and they were hungry. I spoke to a great mass meeting in Cooper Union. I told the people after they had cheered me for ten minutes, that cheering was easy. That the side lines where it was safe, always cheered.

"The miners lost," I told them, "because they had only the constitution. The other side had bayonets. In the end, bayonets always win."

I told them how Lieutenant Howert of Walsenberg had offered me his arm when he escorted me to jail. "Madam," said he, "will you take my arm?"

"I am not a Madam," said I. "I am Mother Jones. The government can't take my life and you can't take my arm, but you can take my suitcase."

I told the audience how I had sent a letter to John Rockefeller, Junior, telling him of conditions in the mines. I had heard he was a good young man and read the Bible, and I thought I'd take a chance. The letter came back with "Refused" written across the envelope. "Well," I said, "how could I expect him to listen to an old woman when he would not listen to the President of the United States through his representative, Senator Foster."

Five hundred women got up a dinner and asked me to speak. Most of the women were crazy about women suffrage. They thought that Kingdom-come would follow the enfranchisement of women.

"You must stand for free speech in the streets," I told them.

From Mary Harris Jones, *The Autobiography of Mother Jones* (Chicago: Charles H. Terr & Co., 1925), pp. 202–04.

"How can we," piped a woman, "when we haven't a vote?"

"I have never had a vote," said I, "and I have raised hell all over this country! You don't need a vote to raise hell! You need convictions and a voice!"

Some one meowed, "You're an anti!"

"I am not an anti to anything which will bring freedom to my class," said I. "But I am going to be honest with you sincere women who are working for votes for women. The women of Colorado have had the vote for two generations and the workingmen and women are in slavery. The state is in slavery, vassal to the Colorado Iron and Fuel Company and its subsidiary interests. A man who was present at a meeting of mine owners told me that when the trouble started in the mines, one operator proposed the women be disfranchised because here and there some woman had raised her voice in behalf of the miners. Another operator jumped to his feet and shouted, 'For God's sake! What are you talking about! If it had not been for the women's vote the miners would have beaten us long ago!' "

Some of the women gasped with horror. One or two left the room. I told the women I did not believe in women's rights nor in men's rights but in human rights. "No matter what your fight," I said, "don't be ladylike! God Almighty made women and the Rockefeller gang of thieves made the ladies. I have just fought through sixteen months of bitter warfare in Colorado. I have been up against armed mercenaries, but this old woman, without a vote, and with nothing but a hatpin, has scared them.

"Organized labor should organize its women along industrial lines. Politics is only the servant of industry. The plutocrats have organized their women. They keep them busy with suffrage and prohibition and charity."

V

Women in the Services:
Home and Office

During the period of acceleration in industrialization and urbanization that followed the Civil War, the most expansive economic opportunities for women were in service employment. As is the case today, the services encompassed a vast range of employments—from jobs characterized by low productivity to those performed by highly trained professionals. Despite the increasing significance of women professionals among all service workers through the 1920s, the women working in lower-paying, lower-productivity jobs remained far more numerous. In this section the experience of those women who worked in all but the most professional of service occupations is explored.

DOMESTIC SERVICE: THE BLACK EXPERIENCE

Until the 1940s, the majority of women employed in service jobs were domestic servants. Among those domestics a disproportionate share were black women, particularly during the late nineteenth century, who simply continued to perform the kind of service they had given under slavery. These black women faced discrimination in their efforts to enter the ranks of the new service workers in offices and stores, but because they often had to support their families as the primary breadwinner, they took whatever work was available in the lowest-status, lowest-paying service occupations.

During the late nineteenth and early twentieth centuries the demand for domestics was greatest in the cities of the Northeast and the Great Lakes states. This demand, together with the unwilling-ness of women who had recently immigrated from Europe to undertake domestic service as a lifetime occupation, the opportuni-ties available to these new immigrants in other employments, and the discrimination faced by blacks in the South, resulted in a substantial flow of black women to northern cities long before World War I. Indeed, the first massive opportunities for blacks in northern cities were for women in domestic service, and in some cities black women were as much as 40 per cent more numerous than black men before World War I. It is possible that the first black women to arrive in northern cities formed an unusually high percentage of the prostitutes in those cities. Jane Addams pointed out in *A New Conscience and an Ancient Evil* (New York: Macmillan, 1913) that the employment bureaus that advanced travel fare to migrants were often found to be associated with pimps. Those bureaus placed migrant women in their debt, arranged lodging in a house owned by a pimp, and thereby provided a means to ease young women into prostitution. Facilitating the exploitation was the reluctance of courts to give credit to the testimony of black women when it was given against white men.

The following is a firsthand account by a domestic servant representative of the lives of those who remained in the South. Such servants did forgo the higher wages they might have earned in northern cities, but they found recompense in a greater measure of social security by working in the cities of the upper South.

A Black Domestic

I am a negro woman, and I was born and reared in the South. I am now past forty years of age and am the mother of three children. My husband died nearly fifteen years ago, after we had been married about five years. For more than thirty years—or since I was ten years old—I have been a servant in one capacity or another in white

From Anonymous (A Negro Nurse), "More Slavery at the South," *The Independent* 72 (25 January 1912): 196–200.

families in a thriving Southern city, which has at present a population of more than 50,000. In my early years I was at first what might be called a "house-girl," or better, a "house-boy." I used to answer the doorbell, sweep the yard, go on errands, and do odd jobs. Later on I became a chambermaid and performed the usual duties of such a servant in a home. Still later I was graduated into a cook, in which position I served at different times for nearly eight years in all. During the last ten years I have been a nurse. I have worked for only four different families during all these thirty years. But, belonging to the servant class, which is the majority class among my race at the South, and associating only with servants, I have been able to become intimately acquainted not only with the lives of hundreds of household servants, but also with the lives of their employers. I can, therefore, speak with authority on the so-called servant question; and what I say is said out of an experience which covers many years.

To begin with, then, I should say that more than two-thirds of the negroes of the town where I live are menial servants of one kind or another, and besides that more than two-thirds of the negro women here, whether married or single, are compelled to work for a living,—as nurses, cooks, washerwomen, chambermaids, seam-stresses, hucksters, janitresses, and the like. I will say, also, that the condition of this vast host of poor colored people is just as bad as, if not worse than, it was during the days of slavery. Though today we are enjoying nominal freedom, we are literally slaves. And, not to generalize, I will give you a sketch of the work I have to do—and I'm only one of many.

I frequently work from fourteen to sixteen hours a day. I am compelled by my contract, which is oral only, to sleep in the house. I am allowed to go home to my own children, the oldest of whom is a girl of 18 years, only once in two weeks, every other Sunday afternoon—even then I'm not permitted to stay all night. I not only have to nurse a little white child, now eleven months old, but I have to act as playmate or "handy-andy," not say governess, to three other children in the home, the oldest of whom is only nine years of age. I wash and dress the baby two or three times each day; I give it its meals, mainly from a bottle; I have to put it to bed each night;

and, in addition, I have to get up and attend to its every call between midnight and morning. If the baby falls to sleep during the day, as it has been trained to do every day about eleven o'clock, I am not permitted to rest. It's "Mammy, do this," or "Mammy, do that," or "Mammy, do the other," from my mistress, all the time. So it is not strange to see "Mammy" watering the lawn in front with the garden hose, sweeping the sidewalk, mopping the porch and halls, dusting around the house, helping the cook, or darning stockings. Not only so, but I have to put the other three children to bed each night as well as the baby, and I have to wash them and dress them each morning. I don't know what it is to go to church; I don't know what it is to go to a lecture or entertainment or anything of the kind; I live a treadmill life; and I see my own children only when they happen to see me on the streets when I am out with the children, or when my children come to the "yard" to see me, which isn't often, because my white folks don't like to see their servants' children hanging around their premises. You might as well say that I'm on duty all the time—from sunrise to sunrise, every day in the week. I am the slave, body and soul, of this family. And what do I get for this work—this lifetime bondage? The pitiful sum of ten dollars a month! And what am I expected to do with these ten dollars? With this money I'm expected to pay my house rent, which is four dollars per month, for a little house of two rooms, just big enough to turn round in; and I'm expected, also to feed and clothe myself and three children. For two years my oldest child, it is true, has helped a little toward our support by taking in a little washing at home. She does the washing and ironing of two white families, with a total of five persons; one of these families pays her $1.00 per week, and the other 75 cents per week, and my daughter has to furnish her own soap and starch and wood. For six months my youngest child, a girl about thirteen years old, has been nursing, and she receives $1.50 per week but has no night work. When I think of the low rate of wages we poor colored people receive, and when I hear so much said about our unreliability, our untrustworthiness, and even our vices, I recall the story of the private soldier in a certain army who, once upon a time, being upbraided by the commanding officer because the heels of his shoes were not polished, is said to have replied: "Captain, do you expect all the virtues for $13 per month?"

Of course, nothing is being done to increase our wages, and the way things are going at present it would seem that nothing could be done to cause an increase in wages. We have no labor unions or organizations of any kind that could demand for us a uniform scale of wages for cooks, washerwomen, nurses, and the like; and, for another thing, if some negroes did here and there refuse to work for seven and eight and ten dollars a month, there would be hundreds of other negroes right on the spot ready to take their places and do the same work, or more, for the low wages that had been refused. So that, the truth is, we have to work for little or nothing or become vagrants! And that, of course, in this State would mean that we would be arrested, tried, and despatched to the "State Farm," where we would surely have to work for nothing or be beaten with many stripes!

Nor does this low rate of pay tend to make us efficient servants. The most that can be said of us negro household servants in the South—and I speak as one of them—is that we are to the extent of our ability willing and faithful slaves. We do not cook according to scientific principles because we do not know anything about scientific principles. Most of our cooking is done by guesswork or by memory. We cook well when our "hand" is in, as we say, and when anything about the dinner goes wrong, we simply say, "I lost my hand today!" We don't know anything about scientific food for babies, nor anything about what science says must be done for infants at certain periods of their growth or when certain symptoms of disease appear; but somehow we "raise" more of the children than we kill, and, for the most part, they are lusty chaps—all of them. But the point is, we do not go to cooking-schools nor to nurse-training schools, and so it cannot be expected that we should make as efficient servants without such training as we should make were such training provided. And yet with our cooking and nursing, such as it is, the white folks seem to be satisfied—perfectly satisfied. I sometimes wonder if this satisfaction is the outgrowth of the knowledge that more highly trained servants would be able to demand better pay! . . .

Another thing—it's a small indignity, it may be, but an indignity just the same. No white person, not even the little children just learning to talk, no white person at the South ever thinks of addressing any negro man or woman as Mr., or Mrs., or Miss. The women are called, "Cook," or "Nurse," or "Mammy," or "Mary Jane," or "Lou," or "Dilcey," as the case might be, and the men are called "Bob," or "Boy," or "Old Man," or "Uncle Bill," or "Pate." In many cases our white employers refer to us, and in our presence, too, as their "niggers." No matter what they call us—no matter what they teach their children to call us—we must tamely submit, and answer when we are called; we must enter no protest; if we did object, we should be driven out without the least ceremony, and, in applying for work at other places, we should find it very hard to procure another situation. In almost every case, when our intending employers would be looking up our record, the information would be given by telephone or otherwise that we were "impudent," "saucy," "dishonest," and "generally unreliable." In our town we have no such thing as an employment agency or intelligence bureau, and, therefore, when we want work, we have to get out on the street and go from place to place, always with hat in hand, hunting for it. . . .

You hear a good deal nowadays about the "service pan." The "service pan" is the general term applied to "left-over" food, which in many a Southern home is freely placed at the disposal of the cook, or, whether so placed or not, it is usually disposed of by the cook. In my town, I know, and I guess in many other towns also, every night when the cook starts for her home she takes with her a pan or a plate of cold victuals. The same thing is true on Sunday afternoon after dinner—and most cooks have nearly every Sunday afternoon off. Well, I'll be frank with you, if it were not for the service pan, I don't know what the majority of our Southern colored families would do. The service pan is the mainstay in many a home. Good cooks in the South receive on an average $8 per month. Porters, butlers, coachmen, janitors, "office boys" and the like, receive on an average $16 per month. Few and far between are the colored men in the South who receive $1 or more per day. Some mechanics do; as, for example, carpenters, brick masons, wheelwrights, blacksmiths, and the like. The vast majority of negroes in my town are serving in menial capacities in homes, stores and offices. Now taking it for granted, for the sake of illustration, that the husband receives $16 per month and the wife $8. That would be $24 between the two. The chances are that they will have anywhere from five to thirteen children between them. Now, how far will $24 go toward housing and feeding and clothing ten or twelve persons for thirty days? And, I tell you, with all of us poor people the service pan is a great institution; it is a great help to us, as we wag along the weary way of life. And then most of the white folks expect their cooks to avail themselves of these perquisites; they allow it; they expect it. I do not deny that the cooks find opportunity to hide away at times, along with the cold "grub," a little sugar, a little flour, a little meal, or a little piece of soap; but I indignantly deny that we are thieves. We don't steal; we just "take" things—they are a part of the oral contract, expressed or implied. We understand it, and most of the white folks understand it. Others may denounce the service pan, and say that it is used only to support idle negroes, but many a time, when I was a cook, and had the responsibility of rearing my three children upon my lone shoulders, many a time I have had occasion to bless the Lord for the service pan! . . .

THE STATUS OF DOMESTIC SERVICE

American women never have accepted domestic service as an attractive form of employment; those who perform such work have always done so largely because they were unable to find other means of securing an income. As a result of the distaste with which domestic service is regarded, even vast numbers of new immigrants and the migration of blacks to northern cities could not satisfy the demand by middle-class families for servants. The general scarcity of labor characteristic of the American economy guaranteed that the scorn attached to domestic service would set wages substantially above the productivity of service labor. In turn, the premium attached to domestic service encouraged a movement led by manufacturers and practitioners of the emerging field of home economics to increase the productivity of household labor and to dignify housework, or at least that performed by middle-class housewives.

The following selection, from the first systematic study of domestic service, suggests more precisely the way in which domestics viewed their work. It is interesting, despite the mechanization, electrification, and specialization of household work in our modern economy, to observe the similarity of contemporary complaints raised about housework.

DISADVANTAGES OF DOMESTIC SERVICE

The question was asked of employees, "What reasons can you give why more women do not choose housework as a regular employment?" The reasons assigned may be classified as follows:

Pride, social condition, and unwillingness to be called servants	157
Confinement evenings and Sundays	75
More independence in other occupations	60
Too hard and confining	42
Other work pays better	42
Lack of consideration by mistresses	38
Hours too long	38
Do not like housework	19
Do not know how to do housework	12
Can live at home by working in shops	11
Girls are too lazy	8
Health considerations	8
Girls are too restless	6
Too few privileges	6
Hard work, little pay	5
Other occupations easier	4
Different tastes	4
Bad character of some reflects on others	3

From Lucy Maynard Salmon, *Domestic Service* (New York: Macmillan Co., 1911), pp. 141–50.

Receive no encouragement	3
Too lonely and meals alone	3
Constant change in work	3
Shop work cleaner	2
No chance for promotion	2
Miscellaneous reasons, one each	11
Total	562

Some of these and other reasons demand a more detailed explanation.

The first industrial disadvantage is the fact that there is little or no opportunity for promotion in the service nor are there opening out from it kindred occupations. An ambitious and capable seamstress becomes a dressmaker and mistress of a shop, a successful clerk sets up a small fancy store, the trained nurse by further study develops into a physician, the teacher becomes the head of a school; but there are no similar openings in household employments. Success means a slight increase in wages, possibly an easier place, or service in a more aristocratic neighborhood, but the differences are only slight ones of degree, never those of kind. "Once a cook, always a cook" may be applied in principle to every branch of the service. The only place where promotion is in any way possible is in hotel service. Those women who would become the most efficient domestics are the ones who see most clearly this drawback to the occupation.

The second disadvantage is the paradoxical one that it is possible for a capable woman to reach in this employment comparative perfection in a reasonably short time. Table service is a fine art which many waitresses never learn, but it is easily mastered by one who "mixes it with brains." One illustration of this is the superior service given at summer resorts by college students without special training. The proper care of a room is understood by few maids, but the comprehension of a few simple principles enables an intelligent woman soon to become an expert. The work of a cook involves much more, but because many persons cook for years without learning how to provide a single palatable and nourishing dish, it does not follow that the art cannot be readily acquired. This fact taken in connection with the previous one unconsciously operates to prevent a large number of ambitious women from becoming domestics.

A third disadvantage is the fact that "housework is never done." In no other occupation involving the same amount of intelligent work do the results seem so literally ephemeral. This indeed is not the true statement of the case—mistresses are learning slowly that cooking is a moral and scientific question, that neatness in caring for a room is a matter of hygiene, and that table service has aesthetic possibilities. But if it has taken long for the most intelligent part of society to understand that the results of housework are not transient, but as far-reaching in their effects as are the products of any other form of labor, it cannot be deemed strange that domestics as a class and those in other occupations complain "in housework there's nothing to show for your work."

A fourth disadvantage is the lack of organization in domestic work. The verdict from the standpoint of the statistician has been quoted. A domestic employee sums up the question from her point of view; she says, "Most women like to follow one particular branch of industry, such as cooking, or chamber work, or laundry work, because it enables one to be thorough and experienced; but when these are combined, as a general thing the work is hard and never done."

A fifth disadvantage is the irregularity of working hours. This is a most serious one, since the question is complicated not only by the irregularity that exists in every family, but also by the varying customs in different families. The actual working hours of a general servant may vary from one instance of five hours in Kansas to another of eighteen hours in Georgia. They sometimes vary in the same city from seven to seventeen hours. It is a difficult matter to ascertain with the utmost definiteness, but a careful examination of all statements made seems to show that the actual working hours are ten in the case of thirty-eight per cent of women employees, thirty-seven per cent averaging more than ten hours, and twenty-five per cent less than this. The working hours for men average somewhat longer than the hours for women, while there are slight differences in the various classes of servants; but they are of too indefinite a character to be specially noted.

Many of these differences are inherent in the composition of the family, and can never be removed; many of them are accidental and their number could be lessened were employers so inclined; many of them grow out of necessarily differing standards of living. This is seen where one family of ten employs one general servant and another family of ten employs eleven servants. . . . The one afternoon each week with generally one or more evenings after work is done is not sufficient compensation.[1] It is the irregularity in the distribution of working time rather than the amount of time demanded that causes dissatisfaction on the part of employees. No complaint is more often made than this, and the results of the investigation seem to justify the complaint. To a young woman therefore seeking employment the question of working hours assumes the aspect of a lottery—she may draw a prize of seven working hours or she may draw a blank of fourteen working hours; she cannot be blamed for making definite inquiries of a prospective employer regarding the size of the family and the number of other servants employed.

A sixth disadvantage closely connected with the preceding is the matter of free time evenings and Sundays. This objection to housework is frequently made;[2] it is one that can never be wholly obviated since the household machinery cannot stop at six o'clock and must be kept in order seven days in the week, but were society so inclined, the objection could be lessened.

1. "You are mistress of no time of your own; other occupations have well-defined hours, after which one can do as she pleases without asking any one."

2. "Women want the free use of their time evenings and Sundays."

"If I could bear the confinement I would go into a mill where I could have evenings and Sundays."

"Sunday in a private family is usually anything but a day of rest to the domestic, for on that day there are usually guests to dinner or tea or both, which means extra work."

"I wouldn't mind working Sundays if it wasn't for the extra work."

"I suppose the reason why more women choose other work is, they would rather work all day and be done with it, and have evenings for themselves."

"Some families have dinner at three o'clock Sundays and lunch at eight or nine, and that makes it very hard for girls."

A seventh difficulty is presented to the American-born girl when she realizes that she must come into competition with the foreign born and colored element.[3] Although much of this feeling is undoubtedly unreasonable, it is not peculiar to domestic service. The fact must be accepted, with or without excuse for it.

Another disadvantage that weights with many is the feeling that in other occupations there is more personal independence. This includes not only the matter of time evenings and Sundays, which they can seldom call unconditionally their own, but there is a dislike of interference on the part of the employer, either with their work or with their personal habits and tastes. This interference is often hard to bear when the employer is an experienced housekeeper—it is intolerable in the case of an inexperienced one. The "boss" carpenter who himself knew nothing about the carpenter's trade would soon have all his workmen arrayed against him; in every occupation an employee is unwilling to be directed except by his superior in knowledge and ability.[4]

3. "A great many very ignorant girls can get housework to do, and a girl who has been used to neatness and the refinement of a good home does not like to room with a girl who has just come from Ireland and does not know what neatness means."

"In——that have much colored help and do not have white help, so the white girls think any other work is better than housework."

"In California self-respecting girls do not like to work with Chinamen—they do not know how to treat women."

"Before the introduction of Chinese labor a young girl never lost social caste by doing housework; but since this element came, household service as an occupation has fallen in the social scale."—Employer.

"When a native American girl goes out to housework she loses caste at once, and can hardly find pleasure in the foreign immigrants that form a majority of servants, and who make most of the trouble from the ignorance and preconceived notions of America."—Employer.

4. "The reason for dislike of housework is the want of liberty, and the submission which girls have to submit to when they have to comply with whatever rules a mistress may deem necessary. Therefore many girls go into mechanical pursuits, that some of their life may be their own."

"Girls in housework are bossed too much."

"There are too many mistresses in the house when the mother and grown-up daughters are all at home."

"Most of us would like a little more independence, and to do our work as we please."

"In housework you receive orders from half a dozen persons, in a shop or factory from but one."

It seems unreaonable to expect domestic service to be an exception to this universal rule. But even experienced housekeepers often do not realize how difficult it is for one person to work in the harness of another, and by insisting on having work done in their own way, even by competent servants, they sometimes unconsciously hinder the accomplishment of their own ends. There is also connected with this the preference for serving a company or a corporation rather than a private individual. It is hard to explain this feeling except on general grounds of prejudice, but the belief undoubtedly exists that there is more personal independence connected with work in a large establishment than there is in serving an individual. There is often a similar feeling of independence in working in families employing a large number of servants, or in those occupying a high station in life.

The industrial disadvantages of the occupation are best summed up by a young factory operative who was for a time in domestic service. In answer to the question, "Why do girls dislike domestic service?" she writes:

In the first place, I don't like the idea of only one evening a week and every other Sunday. I like to feel that I have just so many hours' work to do and do them, and come home and dress up and go out or sit down and sew if I feel like it, and when a girl is in service she has very little time for herself, she is a servant. In the second place, a shop or factory girl knows just what she has to do and can go ahead and do it. I also think going out makes a girl stupid in time. She gets out of style, so to speak. She never reads and does not know what is going on in the world. I don't mean to say they all get stupid, but it makes gossips of girls that if they worked in shops or factories would be smart girls. Then I think shop or factory girls make the best wives. Now I don't mean all, but the biggest part of them, and the cleanest housekeepers. The domestic after she gets married gets careless. She don't take the pride in her home that the shop-girl does. She has lived in such fine houses that her small tenement has no beauty for her after

"A man doesn't let his wife and daughters and sons interfere in the management of his mill or factory—why does a housekeeper let everybody in the house boss?"

the first glow of married life is over. She don't try either to make her home attractive or herself, and get discouraged, and is apt to make a man disheartened with her, and then I think she is extravagant. She has so much to do with before she is married and so little to do with after she don't know how to manage. She can't have tenderloin steak for her breakfast and rump roast for her dinner, and pay the rent and all other bills out of $12 a week—and that is the average man's pay, the kind of man we girls that work for a living get. Of course I don't mean to say the domestics don't have a good time, they do; some of them have lovely places and lay up money, but after all, what is life if a body is always trying to see just how much money he or she can save?"

The industrial disadvantages of the occupation certainly are many, including as they do the lack of all opportunity for promotion, the great amount of mere mechanical repetition involved, the lack of organization in the service, irregularity in the working hours, the limitation of free time evenings and Sundays, competition with the foreign born and the negro element that seems objectionable to the American born, and the interference with work often by those less skilled than the workers themselves. The industrial disadvantages, however, form but one class of the two that weigh most seriously against the occupation. The social disadvantages will be discussed in the following chapter.

CONQUEST OF THE OFFICE

During World War I women filled the nation's offices as clerks, stenographers, and, most importantly, as typists. However, the primary victories in expanding office opportunities for working-women had already been won. More than a generation earlier women had found wide employment as office clerks, replacing men in government offices during the Civil War. These women retained their jobs after the war, and then, during the 1870s, competed with men for similar clerking and stenographic positions in the private sector. Unopposed by craft unions and willing to perform this skilled work for lower wages than men, women gradually came to predominate in office clerking and stenography. The assumption of these jobs by women was by no means automatic or painless to the women involved. During the years of significant transition, before World War I, women had had to compete with determination and shrewdness to wrest new job opportunities from men.

An extremely influential magazine in encouraging women to compete with men, particularly in the area of stenography, was the *Business Woman's Journal.* Founded in 1889 in New York by Mary F. Seymour, an entrepreneur in the creation of secretarial schools for women, the magazine labored to provide workingwomen with information and encouragement that would reduce the number of women "who are crowding into the ranks of unskilled labor, by pointing out new occupations." Mary Seymour's feature articles emphasized the acquisition of office skills, publicized new job opportunities, informed women of changes in the law that would affect their status, offered advice on "practical fashions," provided news on pertinent developments in education, and lent ample space to "physical culture and hygiene," particularly to medical evidence and argument to the effect that women were creatures durable in body and fully equal to men in their intellectual capacities. The two readings offered here are typical articles from the magazine: a sketch of the first woman typist and tactical advice to women office workers. As should be clear from the selections, Mary Seymour's practical advice often suggested respect for the prevailing belief in the intellectual inferiority of women. Was her advice sound? An answer to that ought to consider that the stereotyping of secretarial roles as women's work was more than a generation away—a product of World War I and the 1920s. To Mary Seymour, the assumption by women of new and real economic opportunities seemed only the beginning of upward movement in the marketplace, and she believed women would soon be able to convince men of their equality. The restriction of women to lower-productivity office work and the underlying intensification of pressures tending to shore up Victorian ideals of family life and womanhood may well have been difficult for anyone to predict.

THE FIRST EXPERT TYPE-WRITER OPERATOR

The other day I met Mrs. M. A. Saunders, a lady famed fifteen years ago as one of the first women who dared to step out and travel down town for the purpose of earning an honest livelihood in the walks generally presumed to belong by right of possession and long continued occupancy to the sterner sex. She was then a young woman, and enthusiastic, with a surplus amount of energy and ambition. The type-writer offered her a field and business which seemed to suit her exactly. In one month, by constant practice of five hours a day, she could write sixty words a minute, and was then offered a position by the Type-writer Company (at that time consisting of the firm of Locke, Yost & Bates), of General Agent or Traveling Pioneer; she traveled all over the West and has the honor of having arranged the first keyboard of the Remington type-writer and sold and inaugurated the use of the first type-writers in the Western cities, among them St. Louis, Cincinnati, Chicago, Indianapolis, etc. Her ability as a talker and also an operator was widely known, and her discouragements and trials were of course numerous, as the machine as then put upon the market was very poor compared with our splendidly manufactured machines of to-day. Some of her experiences were very amusing, after the anxiety caused by the then present disturbing influences had passed away. For instance, a machine was sent to a large banking house in this city, and she was explaining its merits, its speed, perfection of construction, etc. (for at that time, you understand, it was a very difficult matter to make people believe that the type-writer in the hands of an expert was faster than the pen), when suddenly the machine broke down. She covered up her discomfiture by explaining that probably they had sent the wrong machine down, and hurrying away to have the right one shipped, thus bridged over the difficulty pro tem.

At another time, a lawyer told her to have the "thing" taken away; she remarked, "How can you lose so much of your valuable time, when every hour you write is half an hour and more wasted;" he said, "What do you mean by that?" "Well, I can write on that machine twice or thrice faster than you can with your pen." "Ah." said he, "I can hardly believe that." "Will you purchase the machine if I can prove it by writing your name, which I never heard of before three times, while you write it with the pen once?" "Yes," said he, "I will." No sooner said than done, and the delighted lawyer immediately called for his check-book and wrote a check for $125, the then price for the All Capital machine.

Mrs. Saunders, after three years of this life, decided she would prefer to settle down in the City; so she obtained her present position of Corresponding Clerk in the Brooklyn Life Insurance Company. At that time she was only a type-writer, but having a good deal of spare time on her hands, she studied stenography, and also brushed up her knowledge of book-keeping. As the head book-keeper was taken ill and died about two years later, she applied for the vacancy which was accorded to her at an advanced salary. She now not only attends to all the correspondence, and double entry book-keeping, but examines all the policies, has charge of the Real Estate accounts, etc. She is very fond of her work, is kept very busy, and she is paid well for her services.

Her greatest value lies in her ability to write on the type-writer from dictation accurately and at the rate of eighty-five words per minute. So capable is she in this respect that her employers use but little short-hand, preferring to dictate directly to the type-writer, and thus have the letter for immediate perusal. If any changes are desirable, they can be made and the letter re-written at once.

This lady is of course no longer young, having served faithfully for fifteen years; but though her hair show lines of silver her enthusiasm has not diminished. She is one of the staunchest friends of the type-writer, and of working women, and is always ready, when the opportunity offers, to lend a hand in assisting others to obtain the independence which she enjoys.

HOMELY HINTS TO YOUNG WOMEN IN BUSINESS

Never ask for your services more, and never accept for them less, than they are actually worth. If you demand more compensation than you are capable of earning you will either not be engaged at all or will be dismissed as soon as some one can be found to take your place. If you accept less than you know your experience and ability ought to command, you will throw out of employment some one else who is only capable of earning a small salary. . . . When the skilled artisan will *accept* the salary of the unskilled, the employer does not hesitate to avail himself of such an opportunity, and the bread is thus taken out of the mouths of those whose workmanship is estimated on a lower scale.

Never chat during business hours. Remember, that although you may not be occupied at the time, others in the office with you are, and your conversation will be very likely to disturb them. Employ your leisure hours *in reading or study* and you will be surprised to see how much you can thus add to your stock of knowledge.

Be as lady-like in your office as you would be in a parlor; and above all things avoid undue familiarity with the clerks with whom you may be associated. Treat them always with kindness and be ever ready to do them a favor, but remember that familiarity breeds contempt. The dignified and refined manners of the young ladies who first entered the different kinds of business awakened respect and made a place for others. Do not by your artless behavior in public offices destroy the good opinions which have thus been earned. Do not treat as a social friend a young man you may chance to meet in business until you have the approval of your friends, or your association with him has been sufficiently long to prove his worth.

Never accept gifts or other attentions from your employer unless he has introduced you to the members of his family, and you have been received on a social equality by them. He may invite you to entertainments with the kindest motives, but remember that in accepting his attentions you are exposing yourself to criticism and

From *The Business Woman's Journal* 1 (March–April 1889): 50–52.

will lose much of the respect of others to which you are entitled.

In your association with men in business, above all things strive to command their respect.

Do not receive letters or social calls at your place of business. Although you may have leisure for this purpose, such calls will probably be an annoyance to those with whom you are associated in business. In a printing office or in a manufactory, at noon, business ceases and the employees are given an hour for lunch, but in most offices where ladies are employed, the machinery of business continues all day. . . .

Never use the telephone for your personal business, except in cases of absolute necessity. You may be alone in the office of your employer, and a little chat with a friend through the telephone may not, at that time, interfere in the slightest degree with the interest of *your* employer, but what do you know of the engagements of the young lady at the other end of the wire. . . .

The fact that employers do not complain of anything of this kind is not a proof that they are satisfied. Many of them dislike exceedingly to find fault with the refined and lady-like girls in their employ, and rather than do this, will either bear their annoyance in silence or, which is more often the case, conclude to dismiss the young woman in fault and hire a young man. . . .

We do not mean by these remarks to imply that young ladies are not quite as trustworthy as young men. On the other hand, the statement that they are far more trustworthy than young men has frequently been made to the writer by employers. For this reason, my dear girls, I want you to keep up the record. We do not feel responsible for the conduct of the young men; but we must remember that the employment of women has not yet in popular estimation ceased to be an experiment, and that the mistakes made by a *few* are recorded against us all.

A man who at some time had in his employ a giddy girl, who was in the habit of spending her leisure time in chatting with the clerks, can never be convinced that this is not the common habit of all women in business, unless previously he had employed one who had been a valuable assistant. If a young man in his employ proves troublesome or incompetent, he dismisses him and employs another.

It never occurs to him to say: "I will never employ a young man again, young men are idle and incompetent, you cannot depend on them." Yet these are just the kind of arguments that are used against women, when any one of them makes a mistake. Women have not, in popular estimation, reached the heights where they can be considered individuals. We have not yet attained the dignity of having our work estimated as that of Ellen, Sarah, or Jane. We still belong to the inconglomerate mass called "women" and must stand and fall together.

When the standard of womanhood has been raised so high that men will not say, when some woman of their acquaintance makes a mistake or has done some foolish unbusinesslike act: "Oh! These women." When we have advanced to such a position that we may be judged as individuals, then the responsibilities which rest upon our shoulders will be lighter; but under present conditions, and in every act of our lives, let us all remember that on each of us rests the responsibility of sustaining the dignity of all.

VI

Women in the Services:
The Professions

Service occupations, including those that have been open, in varying degrees, to women, contain a range of activities that is extraordinary by any measure. In this section the opportunities available to women in some of the more highly skilled of these occupations will be assessed, focusing on teaching, medicine, and law. But this category of high-skill employments ought not to be seen as firm or constant in its definition. For example, some might question the level of skills that prevailed in teaching for much of the nineteenth century; others might suggest that nursing and midwifery should be given visibility in the high-skill category; and still others might want to include the performing arts, specifically acting. A case might also be made that philanthropy, in which women have played a role of some significance, is a high-skill service.

The point is that all of these occupations did, at some point, offer opportunities to women for personal advancement. The reasons for, and character of, the success or failure of women in those occupations are significant to the history of women in the marketplace. However, the professions that have attracted the most women and have been of the greatest influence in shaping American social development are singled out for special attention here.

Not only have the service occupations open to women been highly diverse, but the trends in some of them have witnessed extremes in participation by women. For example, during the late colonial period midwifery existed as a highly expansive area for female employment, with many women attending programs of study in obstetrics, such as at William Shippen's innovative Philadelphia hospital, founded in 1765. However, the high monetary returns that a growing urban middle class brought to the practice of obstetrics attracted men in increasing numbers to midwifery, and by 1800 they appeared to have monopolized the better opportunities. Although midwifery continued to be significant in the West, by 1840 in the East the male midwives had turned their discipline into an arm of medicine. Through the control of medical schools they reduced the participation of women even further. Nursing, in contrast, began as an occupation dominated by men, and it was not until the Civil War created an extreme shortage of male nurses that women penetrated the profession in any numbers. Despite the fact that the skills of the new nurses were high, particularly in comparison with the skill level of much orthodox medicine at the time, the opening of the occupation to women (indeed, its transformation into "women's work") was followed by the sustained entry of educated women who reduced wages below what productivity justified.

Law and medicine, although they underwent fundamentally similar trends, became open to women in different ways and in varying degrees, as the selections that follow will reveal. One point of comparison ought to be mentioned here: during the nineteenth century the entry of women into law was substantially more difficult than into medicine. In entering law, women faced a profession that was highly organized and protected by firm governmental sanctions. Medicine, however, was loosely structured and more pliant to the aspirations of women. Thus, although there were almost 9,000 women doctors by 1910, that year found fewer than 1,500 women in the legal profession. However, medicine, like teaching, was in far less demand than was law and that fact, coupled with the lack of barriers to entry, resulted in economic returns that were far lower for women doctors and teachers than for women lawyers. Once again, it must be emphasized that women's experience in the marketplace has varied widely for occupation, region, era, and the individual.

THE PROPERTY RIGHTS OF MARRIED WOMEN

Critical to the legislative needs of many of the independent women professionals of the nineteenth century were the acts dealing with married women's property. Mississippi passed the first legislation designed to protect the property rights of married women in 1839 but the act was narrow in scope and designed simply to protect family estates of planters who lacked sons. It was New York, in 1848, which passed the first comprehensive act. The reading which follows is its text.

It was no coincidence that the year of the property act was also the year of the women's rights convention at Seneca Falls, New York. The New York victory was in large part a response to the application of democratic ideology to the legal position of women; to the force of a developing body of equity law, with eighteenth-century roots, that expanded rights of married women; to the desire of a rapidly growing number of middle- and upper-class women for future protection in the event of the death or incapacitation of their husbands; and to the concern of middle-class reformers such as New York's Ernestine L. Rose, a Polish immigrant and committed Owenite, for protecting the interests of lower-class married women who lacked the resources to use the common law to their advantage. But, as was typical of so many institutional innovations that allowed women to develop social independence, this breakthrough was accomplished only when the men in power became convinced that the legal change would advance their interests. In particular, beside rationalizing common law practices, the act promised to protect wealthy but insecure men in the event of bankruptcy (by preserving their wives' assets intact) and to guarantee to heavily landed family heads, often of Dutch descent, that their estates would not be squandered by dissolute sons-in-law (by enabling their daughters to hold their assets independently).

Despite the motives behind the property-right enactments and the failure of the acts to give married women full legal equality, they did constitute victories on behalf of independent women, especially professional women. Those victories should be seen as the working out not only of a fundamental labor scarcity but also of a potent democratic ideology and the interests of an emergent urban middle class.

To Protect the Property of Married Women

The people of the State of New York, represented in Senate and Assembly, do enact as follows:

I. The real and personal property of any female who may hereafter marry, and which she shall own at the time of her marriage, and the rents, issues and profits thereof, shall not be subject to the disposal of her husband nor be liable for his debts and shall continue her sole and separate property as if she were a single female.

II. The real and personal property and the rents, issues, and profits thereof of any female now married shall not be subject to the disposal of her husband; but shall be her sole and separate property as if she were a single female except so far as the same may be liable for the debts of her husband heretofore contracted.

III. It shall be lawful for any married female to receive by gift, grant, device, or bequest, from any person other than her husband and to hold to her sole and separate use, as if she were a single female, real and personal property and the rents, issues and profits thereof, and the same shall not be subject to the disposal of her husband, nor be liable for his debts.

IV. All contracts made between persons in contemplation of marriage shall remain in full force after such marriage takes place.

THE DESIGNATION OF TEACHING AS "WOMEN'S WORK"

In the 1820s, women began entering the profession of teaching in massive numbers. Well educated for their day but lacking in opportunities, they had found themselves, in effect, underemployed.

Passed by the New York State Legislature, 7 April 1848.

The expansion of the common schools created unusual opportunities for these young women because school boards lacked enough funds to provide a wage adequate to continue to attract men. The boards became enthusiastic about the prospect of employing women. The rapidity of the change in employment patterns is suggested by the data presented by Horace Mann, the secretary of the Massachusetts Board of Education, in the following selection.

The saving provided by the employment of women teachers led school boards to campaign actively for the services of young women, and no educational leader was more active and articulate in this regard than Horace Mann. His appeal to young women who might enter teaching and to taxpayers to reassure them about the trend is one of the first full-blown descriptions of women as having a disposition uniquely suited to the profession of teaching. This kind of description, of course, contributed to the popular identification of teaching, particularly in the lower grades, as women's work. This conception came to its cultural peak during the late nineteenth century, just when the nation's commitment to an investment in education was assuming its modern dimensions and character. For women, this identification meant that although teaching jobs would be abundant, those jobs would be considered professional opportunities of relatively low status—compared with medicine and law, for example—and therefore would merit relatively low compensation.

During the years of the transformation, especially during the 1840s, the lower status accorded women was extremely painful. Women brought demands for equal pay for equal services to teacher associations but found themselves facing discrimination in gaining access to their leadership. By the 1870s women had gained some leverage over the local and state associations, but by then men formed only a small minority of teachers (except in the high schools) and wages had begun to appear more uniform, albeit low. Then, in contrast with medicine and law, when specialization, centralized state licensing, and professional schools came to teaching (from the 1880s through the 1920s), women were in position to have easy access to the changing profession. Accordingly, women filled the normal schools (the first one founded by Horace Mann in 1839) and fully participated in professional activities. Following the 1920s, largely as a result of modernization, the wages of teachers tended to improve markedly (despite the Great Depression), to the point where, by the 1960s, teaching in the public schools became distinctly attractive to men as well as women and it appeared that men and women were competing on unusually equal terms. However, women continued to face discrimination through the limitation of opportunities in institutions of higher learning, where faculties were dominated by professions that had undergone nineteenth-century development more similar to that of medicine or law.

Horace Mann on the Employment of Female Teachers

One of the most extraordinary changes which have taken place in our schools, during the last seven years, consists in the great proportionate increase in the number of female teachers employed. In 1837 the number of male teachers in all our public schools was 2370; of females, 3591. In the school year 1843–4 it was males, 2529; females, 4581. Increase in the number of male teachers, 159; female increase, 990. During the same time, the number of schools in the State has increased only 418.

This change in public sentiment, in regard to the employment of female teachers, I believe to be in accordance with the dictates of the soundest philosophy. Is not woman destined to conduct the rising generation, of both sexes, at least through all the primary stages of education? Has not the Author of nature pre-adapted her, by constitution, and faculty, and temperament, for this noble work? What station of beneficent labor can she aspire to, more honorable, or more congenial to every pure and generous impulse? In the great system of society, what other part can she act, so intimately connected with the refinement and purification of the race? How otherwise can she so well vindicate her right to an exalted station in the scale of being; and cause that shameful sentence of degradation by which she has so long been dishonored, to be repealed? Four-fifths of all the women who have ever lived, have been the

From Horace Mann, *Eighth Annual Report of the Board of Education* (Boston: Datton & Wentworth, State Printers, 1845), pp. 60–62.

slaves of man,—the menials in his household, the drudges in his field, the instruments of his pleasure; or at best, the gilded toys of his leisure days in court or palace. She has been outlawed from honorable service, and almost incapacitated, by her servile condition, for the highest aspirations after usefulness and renown. But a noble revenge awaits her. By a manifestation of the superiority of moral power, she can triumph over that physical power which has hitherto subjected her to bondage. She can bless those by whom she has been wronged. By refining the tastes and sentiments of man, she can change the objects of his ambition; and with changed objects of ambition, the fields of honorable exertion can be divided between the sexes. By inspiring nobler desires for nobler objects, she can break down the ascendency of those selfish motives that have sought their gratification in her submission and inferiority. All this she can do, more rapidly and more effectually than it can ever be done in any other way, unless through miracles, by training the young to juster notions of honor and duty, and to a higher appreciation of the true dignity and destiny of the race.

The more extensive employment of females for educating the young, will be the addition of a new and mighty power to the forces of civilization. It is a power, also, which, heretofore, to a very great extent, has been unappropriated; which has been allowed, in the administration of the affairs of men, to run to waste. Hence it will be an addition to one of the grandest spheres of human usefulness, without any subtraction from other departments;—again without a loss. For all females,—the great majority,—who are destined, in the course of Providence, to sustain maternal relations, no occupation or apprenticeship can be so serviceable; but, in this connection, it is not unworthy of notice, that, according to the census of Massachusetts, there are almost eight thousand more females than males belonging to the State.

But if a female is to assume the performance of a teacher's duties she must be endowed with high qualifications. If devoid of mental superiority, then she inevitably falls back into that barbarian relation, where physical strength measures itself against physical strength. In that contest, she can never hope to succeed; or, if she succeeds, it will be only as an Amazon, and not as a personification of moral power. Opportunities, therefore, should be everywhere opened for the fit qualification of female teachers; and all females possessing in an eminent degree, the appropriate natural endowments, should be encouraged to qualify themselves for this sacred work. Those who have worthily improved such opportunities, should be rewarded with social distinction and generous emoluments. Society cannot do less than this, on its own account, for those who are improving its condition; though for the actors themselves, in this beneficent work, the highest rewards must forever remain where God and nature have irrevocably placed them,—in the consciousness of well-doing.

Could public opinion, on this one subject, be rectified, and brought into harmony with the great law of Christian duty and love, there are thousands of females amongst us, who now spend lives of frivolity, of unbroken wearisomeness and worthlessness, who would rejoice to exchange their days of painful idleness for such ennobling occupations; and who, in addition to the immediate rewards of well-doing, would see, in the distant prospect, the consolations of a life well-spent, instead of the pangs of remorse for a frivolous and wasted existence.

OPENING MEDICINE TO WOMEN

The medical profession offered considerable opportunities to the large class of well-educated women that had developed by the late nineteenth century. That was so for a number of related reasons. In the first place, in the nineteenth century, medicine was by no means tightly regulated by its practitioners. Practice by heretical doctors who were able to attract a clientele was rather common. Although orthodox physicians often won public sanction for the licensing procedures of their state medical societies, state governments were by no means vigorous in preventing the practice of new, unlicensed disciplines or in requiring the prescription of a licensed physician for the purchase of drugs. In the second place, there was great room for improvement in nineteenth-century medical practices and the general public was quite cognizant of that fact. Although orthodox physicians had expanded their knowledge of anatomy since the late eighteenth century, they were enthusiastic about massive bloodletting, cupping, purging, sweating, blistering, and the use of large doses of dangerous drugs, especially calomel and opium, for a wide range of maladies. Consequently, they cured few and undoubtedly killed many who would have recovered rather well on their own. Thirdly, in the eighteenth century, with the increasing specialization of roles within the family, women, particularly in New England, had begun to acquire a great deal of experience in an indigenous folk medicine that relied very heavily on herbal therapeutics. During the nineteenth century there appeared almanacs and do-it-yourself handbooks to assist them in these arts. Indeed, even in the late nineteenth century, people probably relied more on informal family remedies than on the services of trained physicians. A final factor contributing to the entry of women into formal medicine was the rise of a substantial demand for the services of women doctors. Two very different groups of women sought medical services from women: those influenced by the Victorian modesty which led them to be prudish about their bodies and those who sought liberation from the confinement of that orthodox Victorian medical thought that emphasized the fragility of the female sex. Thus, experienced in the application of empirically-tested cures and taking advantage of public distrust of established doctors, women were able to enter medicine in relatively large numbers, particularly after the emergence of the specialized demand for women doctors.

The first sizeable entry of women into the marketplace of medicine was during the 1840s and 1850s as the heretical sect of homeopathy spread in America and, like other such sects, attracted more female practitioners than did regular medicine. Its theory held that diseases could be cured by drugs that would produce in the healthy the symptoms of the ill. Although it effected no more cures than orthodox medicine, its emphasis on infinitesimal doses reduced the kill rate of orthodox medicine. Its concern for moderation also made it more compatible with traditional folk medicine. Consequently, homeopathy enjoyed very considerable popularity at mid-century and attracted a large number of female practitioners—17 per cent of the almost 2,000 students in homeopathic medical schools in 1900 (the high-water year of the sect).

At the same time that women entered homeopathy they also entered orthodox medicine and tended to take up specialities and practice that involved treatment of women and children. By 1900, almost 10 per cent of all students in nonhomeopathic medical schools were women and women physicians in the nation numbered more than 5,000. By 1910, there would be well over 8,000 women physicians in the United States. The entry of women into regular medical practice was by no means smooth, but the way was established by a handful of exceptionally talented and motivated women. One of those was Elizabeth Blackwell (1821–1910), who received the first orthodox medical degree earned by a woman in the United States (in 1849 from Geneva College, later part of Syracuse University). Her description of her entry into the profession, along with some of her correspondence to her sister Emily, who was one of the first women trained in obstetrics, follows here.

Supported by a strong family commitment to equal educational opportunities for women, and highly motivated by the ideals of the women's rights movement of the 1840s, Blackwell chose regular medicine as a career objective. This required two years of teaching for the acquisition of adequate savings for tuition, extensive correspondence with leading doctors that often subjected her to professional ridicule, application to twenty-nine medical schools, and a test of her enormous resources of patience, poise, and tact during her years at Geneva. After specialized training in Europe (and the loss of an eye), she returned to New York where, in 1853, having been rejected by established physicians, she established a pioneer dispensary for poor women and children. She proceeded to found a hospital staffed entirely by women, to train nurses for Civil War service, and, then, after the Civil War, to establish, with her sister, a separate medical college for women in New York—the Woman's Infirmary Medical School—that proved to be a leader in setting standards for women's medical schools throughout the nation. Thus, although she did not advance the scientific frontiers of medicine she did significantly increase opportunities for women, both through her own example, including her specialization in health and hygiene for women, and through her efforts in medical education.

The gains by women in the medical profession that had been so apparent in 1910 were not amplified in subsequent decades. Thus, in 1940, despite continued population growth, the number of women physicians was actually substantially less than had been the case a generation earlier. During the 1910s, before the impact of the Great Depression in reducing all opportunities for women and the influence of the new Victorianism of the 1920s in changing the self-perceptions of women, the structure of medical education was beginning to change, with the result of restricting opportunities for women. In the face of the increasing scale of laboratory and hospital facilities necessary for a modern medical education and the waning popularity of the marginal disciplines, small women's medical colleges were unable to attract sufficient resources and either failed or merged into larger universities. The result was that a smaller number of medical schools came to dominate admissions and these medical schools did not change their policies—which is to say that they admitted very few women. As for the Blackwells' Women's Infirmary Medical School, it closed when Cornell University's medical school opened its doors in New York in 1899.

Pioneer Work in Medicine

. . . I had not the slightest idea of the commotion created by my appearance as a medical student in the little town. Very slowly I perceived that a doctor's wife at the table avoided any communication with me, and that as I walked backwards and forwards to college the ladies stopped to stare at me, as at a curious animal. I afterwards found that I had so shocked Geneva propriety that the theory was fully established either that I was a bad woman, whose designs would gradually become evident, or that, being insane, an outbreak of insanity would soon be apparent. Feeling the unfriendliness of the people, though quite unaware of all this gossip, I never

From Elizabeth Blackwell, *Pioneer Work in Opening the Medical Profession to Women* (New York: Longmans, Green & Co., 1895), pp. 69–73, 171–73, and 200–05.

walked abroad, but hastening daily to my college as to a sure refuge, I knew when I shut the great doors behind me that I shut out all unkindly criticism, and I soon felt perfectly at home amongst my fellow-students.

The following extracts from my journal of those days show how any early difficulties were successfully overcome:

November 9 [1847]

My first happy day; I feel really encouraged. The little fat Professor of Anatomy is a capital fellow; certainly I shall love fat men more than lean ones henceforth. He gave just the go-ahead directing impulse needful; he will afford me every advantage, and says I shall graduate with éclat. Then, too, I am glad that they like the notoriety of the thing, and think it a good "spec."

November 10

Attended the demonstrator's evening lecture—very clear—how superior to books! Oh, this is the way to learn! The class behaves very well; and people seem all to grow kind.

November 11

Anatomy very interesting to-day; two admirable demonstrations. Dr. Webster, full of enthusiasm, told us of Godman, who was converted to phrenology by reading a work against it, in order to cut it up.

November 15

To-day, a second operation at which I was not allowed to be present. This annoys me. I was quite saddened and discouraged by Dr. Webster requesting me to be absent from some of his demonstrations. I don't believe it is his wish. I wrote to him hoping to change things.

November 17

Dr. Webster seemed much pleased with my note, and quite cheered me by his wish to read it to the class to-morrow, saying if they were all actuated by such sentiments the medical class at

Geneva would be a very noble one. He could hardly guess how much I needed a little praise. I have no fear of the kind students.

November 20

In the amphitheatre yesterday a little folded paper dropped on my arms as I was making notes; it looked very much as if there were writing in it, but I shook it off and went on quietly with my notes. Some after-demonstration of a similar kind produced a hiss from the opposite side of the room. I felt also a very light touch on my head, but I guess my quiet manner will soon stop any nonsense.

November 22

A trying day, and I feel almost worn out, though it was encouraging too, and in some measure a triumph; but 'tis a terrible ordeal! That dissection was just as much as I could bear. Some of the students blushed, some were hysterical, not one could keep in a smile, and some who I am sure would not hurt my feelings for the world if it depended on them, held down their faces and shook. My delicacy was certainly shocked, and yet the exhibition was in some sense ludicrous. I had to pinch my hand till the blood nearly came, and call on Christ to help me from smiling, for that would have ruined everything; but I sat in grave indifference, though the effort made my heart palpitate most painfully. Dr. Webster, who had perhaps the most trying position, behaved admirably.

November 24

To-day the Doctor read my note to the class. In this note I told him that I was there as a student with an earnest purpose, and as a student simply I should be regarded; that the study of anatomy was a most serious one, exciting profound reverence, and the suggestion to absent myself from any lectures seemed to me a grave mistake. I did not wish to do so, but would yield to any wish of the class without hesitation, if it was their desire. I stayed in the ante-room whilst the note was being read. I listened joyfully to the very hearty approbation with which it was received by the class, and then entered the amphitheatre and quietly resumed my place. The Doctor told me he felt quite relieved.

No further difficulty ever afterwards occurred.

December 4

Dr. Webster sent for me to examine a case of a poor woman at his rooms. 'Twas a horrible exposure; indecent for any poor woman to be subjected to such a torture; she seemed to feel it, poor and ignorant as she was. I felt more than ever the necessity of my mission. But I went home out of spirits, I hardly know why. I felt alone. I must work by myself all life long.

Christmas Day

Bright and gay with sleighs. The lake looks most beautiful, the mist rising from it in arches, the sky a brilliant blue, and the ground covered with snow. I received my Christmas Annual with great joy; and having purchased 25 cents' worth of almonds and raisins, I had quite a cosy time reading it.

Sunday, January 16 [1848]

A most beautiful day; it did me good. The text impressed itself on me—"Thou wilt keep him in perfect peace whose mind is stayed on Thee." I felt happy and blessed. Ah! If the Almighty would always shine on me, how strong I should be! "The Lord God is a sun and shield; the Lord will give grace and glory; no good thing will He withhold from them that walk uprightly. . . ."

To Her Sister

November 20, 1850

Dear E.,

I want to talk to you seriously about the future—that is to say, my medical future. It has been a heavy, perplexing subject to me on what system I should practise, for the old one appeared to me wrong, and I have even thought every heresy better; but since I have been looking into these heresies a little more closely I feel as dissatisfied with them as with the old one. We hear of such wonderful cures continually being wrought by this and the other thing, that we forget on how small a number the novelty has been exercised, and the failures are never mentioned; but on the same principle, I am convinced that if the old system were the heresy, and the heresy the established custom, we should hear the same wonders related of the drugs. Neither hydropathy nor mesmerism are what their enthusiastic votaries imagine them to be. At Gräfenberg I could not hear of one case of perfect cure, and unfortunately the undoubtedly great resources of cold water are not so developed and classified as to enable a young practitioner to introduce it, professedly, into his practice. Mesmerism has not converted me since watching its effects on patients. I do wish most heartily that I could discover more of the remedial agency of magnetism, for my conviction is that it ought to be powerfully beneficial in some cases; and as I find they have a magnetic dispensary here in London, I shall certainly try and attend it frequently. I am sorry that I have been unable hitherto to attend more to homoeopathy, the third heresy of the present time, but I am trying now to find out opportunities. Here I have been following now with earnest attention, for a few weeks, the practice of a very large London hospital, and I find the majority of patients do get well; so I have come to this conclusion— that I must begin with a practice which is an old-established custom, which has really more expressed science than any other system; but nevertheless, as it dissatisfies me heartily, I shall commence as soon as possible building up a hospital in which I can experiment; and the very instant I feel sure of any improvement I shall adopt it in my practice, in spite of a whole legion of opponents. Now E., future partner, what say you—is it not the only rational course? If I were rich I would not begin private practice, but would only experiment; as, however, I am poor, I have no choice. I look forward with great interest to the time when you can aid me in these matters, for I have really no medical friend; all the gentlemen I meet seem separated by an invincible, invisible barrier, and the women who take up the subject partially are inferior. It will not always be so; when the novelty of the innovation is past, men and women will be valuable friends in medicine, but for a time that cannot be. I spend now about three or four hours each day in the wards, chiefly medical, diagnosing disease, watching the progress of cases, and accustoming my ear to the stethoscope. Already, in this short time, I feel that I have made progress, and detect sounds that I could not distinguish on my entrance. I advise you, E., to familiarise yourself with the healthy sounds of the chest. When you go home, auscultate all the family; you will find quite a variety in the sounds, though all may be healthy persons. Lay a cloth over the chest and listen with the ear simply; it is as good as a stethoscope with clean people. I wish I could lend you my little black stethoscope that I brought from the Maternité.

I have been disappointed in one thing here—the Professor of Midwifery and the Diseases of Women and Children wrote me a very polite note, telling me that he entirely disapproved of a lady's studying medicine, and begging me to consider that his neglecting to give me aid was owing to no disrespect to me as a lady, but to his condemnation of my object.

By-the-by, I must tell you of a scientific explanation of the toughness of meat which I obtained from Mr. Paget's lecture the other morning; it arises from cooking meat during the rigor mortis! Would not that be a delicate suggestion for a squeamish individual? . . .

New York, May 12, 1854

I need not tell you with what interest and hope I look forward to your Edinburgh news. The prospect is very good. . . . One of the most difficult points I have to contend with here is the entire absence of medical sympathy; the medical solitude is really awful at times; I should thankfully turn to any educated woman if I could find one. . . . Pray bear in mind to collect all the information you can about maternity, the relation of the sexes, and kindred subjects. We have a vast field to work in this direction, for reliable information is desperately needed in the world on these topics. I feel as if it were peculiarly our duty to meet this want. There is much vain thought given to these matters here. An active set of people are making desperate efforts to spread their detestable doctrines of "free love" under scientific guise, placing agents with the advertisements of their books worded in the most specious and attractive manner at the doors of the conventions now being held here; on the other hand, equally misleading publications are brought out in opposition.

Such teaching is utterly superficial and untrustworthy, and consequently misleading. We want facts, scientifically accurate observations, past and present, on all that bears on these matters. . . .

You remember the pamphlet sent me by Dr. Sims of Alabama.
He is now here, determined to establish a hospital for the special
treatment of women's diseases; he is enlisting much support, and
will, I think succeed. He seems to be in favour of women studying
medicine. I think I shall help him in any way I can. . . .

I have at last found a student in whom I can take a great deal of
interest—Marie Zackrzewska, a German, about twenty-six. Dr.
Schmidt, the head of the Berlin midwifery department, discovered
her talent, advised her to study, and finally appointed her as chief
midwife in the hospital under him; there she taught classes of about
150 women and 50 young men, and proved herself most capable.
When Dr. Schmidt died, the American Minister advised her to
come to New York; but here the German doctors wanted her to
become a nurse. In desperation she consulted "The Home for the
Friendless," where they advised her to come to me. There is true
stuff in her, and I shall do my best to bring it out. She must obtain a
medical degree. . . .

July 24 [1854]

Don't be discouraged. There is no doubt about our losing many
opportunities because of our sex, but you must also bear in mind the
disadvantages all students labour under, unless in exceptional cases.
Crowded together in masses, they only see at a distance the most
interesting cases; the complete study is reserved for the physician or
his constant attendant. I remember expressing my impatience while
in the Maternité at the restrictive rules there, and M. Blot said,
"What you wish for are only enjoyed by the few who occupy the
most favoured positions." Yet I gained, in spite of all difficulties, a
great deal, and in accelerating ratio the longer I stayed. I remember
that it seemed to me I had gained more in my fourth month at the
Maternité than in the whole three preceding ones. Now I say this
because I don't want you to over-estimate the worth of pantaloons.
Disguise in France or elsewhere would by no means give you all you
need; if the disguise were complete you would just be reduced to the

level of the common poor student, and would be, I think, quite disappointed. It needs also that influential men should take an interest in you, and give you chances quite beyond the ordinary run. I know that at St. Bartholomew's I would not have exchanged my position for that of the simple student, though I would gladly for the clinical clerk or interne's position. Now you can do nothing in France, except by special medical influence. Your time is limited, and you cannot wait for examinations and promotions as an ordinary student. You ask me what I did, and what can be done as a lady. I entered the Maternité, dissected at l'Ecole des Beaux-Arts alone, employed a répétiteur who drilled me in anatomy and smuggled me into the dead-house of La Charité at great risk of detection, where I operated on the cadavre. I once made the rounds of his wards in the Hôtel-Dieu with Roux, heard his lectures, and saw his operations. I attended lectures on medical generalities at the College of France and Jardin des Plantes. I believe that was all in the way of Parisian study. I applied to Davenne, Director-General of the hospitals, for permission to follow the physicians—refused; applied to Dubois and Trousseau to attend lectures at the Ecole de Médecine—refused; Trousseau advising me to disguise. You see I had no introductions, no experience. I went into the Maternité soon after going to France, and came out with a sad accident, not inclined to renew the battle, not well knowing how and with a promising chance opened to me in London. I should do differently now. I should get the most influential introduction I could; I should tell them just what I wanted, find which hospitals would be most suited to my purpose, and if by putting on disguise I could get either an assistant's post or good visiting privilege, I would put it on. I don't believe it would be a disguise at all to those you were thrown with, but it would be a protection if advised by intelligent men, and would make them free to help you. I should avoid crowds, because you gain nothing in them; I don't think either the lectures at l'Ecole de Médecine or the great hospital visits, where from one to five hundred students follow, would be of any use. It is in a more private and intimate way, and in hospitals where many students do not go, that you might gain. I know no one in a position to give you more valuable letters than Dr. Simpson, if he is disposed to. You ask me what I saw at the

Maternité, but I find my notes imperfect; I have only noted down nine versions, &c. But I think the most important thing in the Maternité is the drilling in the more ordinary labours, for only where the finger is thoroughly trained can you detect varieties. The cases you send me are very interesting, and I am very glad you have made such full notes, as they will be useful hints in future solitary practice. Don't be in a hurry to leave Dr. S., for I fear you will nowhere else find a good drilling in that department. I shall see how far I can make your notes available from time to time in my own practice. With regard to my own clientele, I shall have advanced 50 dollars over last year; slow progress, but still satisfactory, as it is reliable practice, not capricious success. Only think, the thermometer has been up to 102 in some of the rooms down town! We have had three days' "spells" this July that seem to me a little beyond anything I have ever had to endure.

November 13 [1854]

I shall be very anxious to know what you do in Paris. I almost doubt the propriety of your entering the Maternité, or rather I hope that the necessity may be obviated by your finding other openings. That Dubois is somewhat of an old fox, and will, I presume, at once advise your entrance, to get rid of any responsibility; but I would not think of doing so until I had seen all the others and tried for better openings. I think you could get sufficient midwifery at the Ecole de Médecine, where the midwives have the night cases; the association would be unpleasant from the character of the women, but it would leave you your freedom. You have done excellently in Edinburgh, and nothing could be more satisfactory than the way you leave. I think, however, before going to Paris you had certainly better see Dr. Oldham of Guy's; he is disposed to be friendly, and if he chose might greatly help you. It would seem as if it would be well to pursue your English studies before the Parisian; if you could follow Doctors Burrows and Baly in medicine at St. Bartholomew's, and Oldham at Guy's, you would do well. I am very glad you are collecting special medical statistics; we shall find them very serviceable in lecture or pamphlet form. It will be necessary next year to make an active effort for the dispensary, and I think a few lectures would be very important. My conviction becomes constantly stronger that you will return, and my plans for the future all involve that fact. A pleasant circumstance occurred to my German, Dr. Zackrzewska. I arranged a Cleveland course for her, and she entered two weeks ago; she met a very friendly reception, and found that Dr. Kirkland is in correspondence with Professor Muller of Berlin, and he had mentioned her in some of his letters in such high terms, that the faculty told her, if she would qualify herself for examination in surgery and chemistry and write an English thesis, that they would graduate her at the end of this term. Of course she is studying with might and main, and will, I have no doubt, succeed; so we may reckon on a little group of three next year. That will be quite encouraging.

THE MEDICAL CAREER OF A PROGRESSIVE WOMAN

Once women won their initial battle for acceptance into the orthodox medical profession, they found that the prevailing level of medical education, even in the best schools, was often rather inadequate. Most programs were extremely brief, very rarely more than two years in length, frenetically practical, intensely commercial, and poorly taught. Consequently, particularly after 1870, American women joined the flood of practitioners who turned to European universities, particularly in Germany, Austria, and Switzerland, to improve their skills and to develop an effective speciality. Zurich was the first university to accept Americans and almost one-half of the students accepted initially were women.

One of the women traveling abroad was Alice Hamilton, daughter of a well-to-do Michigan family, who studied in Leipzig and Munich in 1895. Despite sophisticated European training she, like a number of other new women doctors, was far more moved by the social imperatives posed by modern industrialization. She discovered that in America before World War I medicine was offering vital and exciting opportunities for an independent woman with a social conscience. The following selection from Alice

Hamilton's autobiography describes her entry into a pioneering career in the field of industrial medicine.

ALICE HAMILTON AND INDUSTRIAL MEDICINE

By the autumn of 1896 our year in Europe was over and we came home. Edith had a position waiting for her. She became headmistress of the Bryn Mawr School in Baltimore. Because no position awaited me I went with her for a winter's work in the Johns Hopkins Medical School. In spite of my year in Germany, nobody seemed to want my services. The demand for trained bacteriologists and pathologists did not begin 'til some years later, and the only thing to do was to keep on fitting myself for a career and hoping that some day an opening would come.

Those were the great days of the Johns Hopkins Medical School. I met there not only my former teachers, W. H. Howell and J. J. Abel, but William Welch, Simon Flexner, William Osler, Howard Kelly, John Finney, Franklin Mall, Lewellys Barker. Exciting as it is to work in a foreign laboratory there is something satisfying in returning to one's own country and one's own language, in every sense of that phrase. Baltimore was not gay and colorful as were Munich and Frankfurt, but the men I worked with accepted me without amusement or contempt or even wonder, and I slipped into place with a pleasant sense of belonging. . . .

My regular work, which was pathological anatomy, was done under Simon Flexner. It was really pure enjoyment. He gave me two cases to work up and helped me to have them published. It was Dr. Flexner who first taught me that important part of research, the thorough and critical review of all that has been written on one's problem and the scrupulous care one must use to give credit where credit is due. . . .

That was the last year of student life for me—the delightful life at once free from responsibility and full of varied interests. Although I dipped into it again for short periods, at the University of Chicago

From *Exploring the Dangerous Trades: The Autobiography of Alice Hamilton* (Boston: Little, Brown and Co., 1943), pp. 51–54 and 115–21.

and the Institut Pasteur in Paris, it was not the same, for it was only an interlude in my real work. My first job was offered to me that summer, to teach pathology in the Women's Medical School of Northwestern University in Chicago. I accepted it with thankfulness, not only because it meant employment in my own field, but because it was in Chicago. At last I could realize the dream I had had for years, of going to live in Hull House.

Agnes put this idea in my mind. Neither of us had heard much about social reform in our sheltered youth. Free trade and civil service reform were the only movements we heard discussed at home. My father took Godkin's *Nation*; its program of reform, which meant integrity and expert knowledge in civil office, taxation for revenue only, no tariff protection for special interests, satisfied him completely. Fort Wayne had no slums, there was no unemployment; the problem of poverty was individual in each case: it was due either to misfortune, which called for charity, or to shiftlessness, which called for stern measures. The first appeal we ever heard for the righting of a wrong outside our own country was in a speech at school in Farmington on the Hindu child widows.

During the two years in Fort Wayne, however, between Farmington and Ann Arbor, Agnes came across Richard Ely's books. She was fired with enthusiasm for his program of Socialism and won me over to it easily. We began then to read about the settlement movement. Now it happened that in the spring before I went to Germany, Jane Addams came to Fort Wayne to speak in the Methodist Church. She was already famous, though Hull House was not more than six years old. Norah brought the exciting news to Agnes and me, and we three went to hear her in the evening. I cannot remember my first impressions; they blend into the crowd of impressions that came in later years. I only know that it was then that Agnes and I definitely chose settlement life. Years later we carried out our resolve: Agnes went to the Lighthouse in Philadelphia and I found myself a resident of Hull House.

When I look back on the Chicago of 1897 I can see why life in a settlement seemed so great an adventure. It was all so new, this exploring of the poor quarters of a big city. The thirst to know how the other half lives had just begun to send people pioneering in the unknown parts of American life. Now, when we have floods of books and plays on every aspect of that life, from Southern sharecroppers to Pennsylvania coal miners, from Scandinavian farmers in the Northwest to the Cajun fisher folk of Louisiana, it is hard to believe that when Miss Addams came to Chicago the first book of that kind was still to be written. Jacob Riis brought out his *How the Other Half Lives* in 1891. It was in the early nineties that Walter Wyckoff, a Princeton graduate, did what was then unheard of: he took to the road as a casual laborer and wrote of his hopeless quest for jobs. So to settle down to live in the slums of a great city was a piece of daring as great as trekking across the prairie in a covered wagon. . . .

It was also my experience at Hull House that aroused my interest in industrial diseases. Living in a working-class quarter, coming in contact with laborers and their wives, I could not fail to hear tales of the dangers that workingmen faced, of cases of carbon-monoxide gassing in the great steel mills, of painters disabled by lead palsy, of pneumonia and rheumatism among the men in the stockyards. Illinois then had no legislation providing compensation for accident or disease caused by occupation. (There is something strange in speaking of "accident and sickness compensation." What could "compensate" anyone for an amputated leg or a paralyzed arm, or even an attack of lead colic, to say nothing of the loss of a husband or son?). . .

At the time I am speaking of Professor Charles Henderson was teaching sociology in the University of Chicago. He had been much in Germany and had made a study of German sickness insurance for the working class (the *Krankenkassen*), a system which aroused his admiration and made him eager to have some such provisions made in behalf of American workmen. The first step must be, of course, an inquiry into the extent of our industrial sickness, and he determined to have such an inquiry made in Illinois. Governor Deneen was then in office and Henderson persuaded him to appoint an Occupational Disease Commission, the first time a state had ever undertaken such a survey. Dr. Henderson had some influence in selecting the members and, as he knew of my great interest in the subject, he included me in the group of five physicians who, together with himself, an employer, and two members of the State Labor Department, made up the commission. We had one year only for our work, the year 1910.

We were staggered by the complexity of the problem we faced and we soon decided to limit our field almost entirely to the occupational poisons, for at least we knew what their action was, while the action of the various kinds of dust, and of temperature extremes and heavy exertion, was only vaguely known at that time. Then we looked for an expert to guide and supervise the study, but none was to be found and so I was asked to do what I could as managing director of the survey, with the help of twenty young assistants, doctors, medical students, and social workers. As I look back on it now, our task was simple compared with the one that a state nowadays faces when it undertakes a similar study. The only poisons we had to cover were lead, arsenic, brass, carbon monoxide, the cyanides, and turpentine. Nowadays, the list involved in a survey of the painters' trade alone is many times as long as that.

But to us it seemed far from a simple task. We could not even discover what were the poisonous occupations in Illinois. The Factory Inspector's office was blissfully ignorant, yet that was the only governmental body concerned with working conditions. There was nothing to do but begin with trades we knew were dangerous and hope that, as we studied them, we would discover others less well known. My field was to be lead, Dr. Emery Hayhurst took brass, Drs. G. Apfelbach and M. Karasek, carbon monoxide in the steel mills. Caisson disease[1] had appeared in the state, in connection chiefly with the construction of tunnels in Chicago, and Dr. Peter Bassoc undertook the study of the 161 cases of this disease which had occurred up to this date. Dr. George Shambaugh contributed a chapter on boiler makers' deafness and Drs. F. Lane and J. D. Ellis one on the rhythmic oscillation of the eyes of coal miners, known as nystagmus.

1. This is a disease caused by work in compressed air when the return to normal air pressure is too quick. The air absorbed by the body under pressure expands if that pressure is released too suddenly and this causes damage, especially in the delicate tissues of the brain and the spinal cord. Violent pain in the limbs (known as "the bends") and brain disturbances (called the blind staggers) result if the worker goes too quickly into the open air. He is protected now by being made to pass slowly through a series of decompression chambers.

While we were visiting plants, we set our young assistants to reading hospital records, interviewing labor leaders and doctors and apothecaries in working-class quarters, for we must unearth actual instances of poisoning if our study was to be of any value. Thus I was put on the trail of new lead trades, some of which I had never thought of—for instance, making freight-car seals, coffin "trim," and decalcomania papers for pottery decoration; polishing cut glass; brass founding; wrapping cigars in so-called tinfoil, which is really lead. Hospital records yielded cases from these and from many other jobs which were not mentioned in foreign textbooks.

One case, of colic and double wristdrop, which was discovered in the Alexian Brothers' Hospital, took me on a pretty chase. The man, a Pole, said he had worked in a sanitary-ware factory, putting enamel on bathtubs. I had not come across this work in the English or the German authorities on lead poisoning, and had no idea it was a lead trade, but the factory was easy to reach on the near West Side and I stopped in to ask about the man's work. The management assured me that no lead was used in the coatings and invited me to inspect the workroom, where I found six Polish painters applying an enamel paint to metal bathtubs. So ignorant was I that I accepted this as the work of enameling sanitary ware, and did not even notice that all the men were painting the outsides of the tubs. I did note the name of the paint and went to the factory which produced it, but there I was told that enamel paint is free from lead. Completely puzzled, I made a journey to the Polish quarter to see the palsied man and heard from him that I had not even been in the enameling works, only the one for final touching up. The real one was far out on the Northwest Side. I found it and discovered that enameling means sprinkling a finely ground enamel over a red-hot tub where it melts and flows over the surface. I learned that the air is thick with enamel dust and that this may be rich in red oxide of lead. A specimen of it which I secured from a workman, who said he often took some home to his wife for scouring pans and knives, proved to contain as much as 20 per cent soluble lead—that is, lead that will pass into solution in the human stomach. Thus I nailed down the fact that sanitary-ware enameling was a dangerous lead trade in the United States, whatever was true of England and Germany.

OPENING LAW TO WOMEN

Like many of the women who entered law during the mid and late nineteenth century, Myra Colby Bradwell (1831–94) was powerfully motivated by the ideal of social equality for women and had family connections that allowed her to overcome the legal barriers to her practicing the profession. Throughout her life, from her childhood in a strongly abolitionist family (they were close friends of Elijah Lovejoy), to her work on the Sanitary Commission during the Civil War, and to her assistance in organizing the American Woman Suffrage Association in 1869, she was closely in touch with feminist ideas and programs. Her marriage in 1852 to a poor farmer's son who used the law as a vehicle to rapid financial and political success (he was elected a Cook County judge in 1861) created an appreciation for the social leverage of the law. She proceeded to study law under her husband's guidance. In 1868, relying on his political influence, she obtained a charter that allowed her to establish and become president of a weekly legal newspaper, the *Chicago Legal News*, and a legal publishing firm, the Chicago Legal News Company. Both enterprises thrived, and, through editorial capacities applied to the most widely read legal publication in the Midwest, Myra Bradwell became a significant intellectual force in the development of law in her region.

Myra Bradwell had to draw on her husband's political assets, for Illinois did not allow women to be licensed to practice the law. In 1869, after establishing her successful business enterprises, she attempted to open the legal profession in Illinois, applying for admission to the state bar. (The first woman admitted to the bar in the United States was Arabella Mansfield, in 1869, in Iowa.) She was refused and proceeded to take her case all the way to the Supreme Court, which, in 1873, upheld the judgment of the lower court. The opinion of the Illinois court is reprinted here. It presents the grounds typically advanced to deny women access to the legal profession. However, the majority opinion of the Supreme Court ignored these arguments. The Court simply denied Myra Bradwell's claim to protection under the national citizenship provided by the Fourteenth Amendment, thereby leaving the setting of standards for women's entry into the professions up to individual states. (See *Bradwell* v. *State of Illinois*, 83 U.S. Reports 130 [1872].)

In her work as an editor-publisher, Myra Bradwell developed a firm sense of her intellectual superiority and felt no compulsion to apply for regular admission to the bar, although the Illinois legislature passed an act in 1872 guaranteeing women equal access to the professions and the Illinois State Bar Association made her an honorary member in the same year. Instead, with the support of her husband, she developed a firm determination to remove all legal barriers to women. The results included the passage of Illinois legislation assuring married women the right to their own earnings (1869); guaranteeing a widow some interest in her husband's estate; allowing women to hold school offices; and making women eligible for offices of notary public (1875). Finally, in 1890, the Illinois Supreme Court, acting on her 1869 motion, admitted her to the practice of law and two years later the United States Supreme Court admitted her to practice before it.

Setting aside its unusual distinction, Myra Bradwell's legal career was quite similar to that of the other women who entered the legal profession in the late nineteenth century. Many lacked formal legal education because the universities began to admit them to their law schools only in the 1890s, and then did so in a very limited fashion. Most women lawyers functioned without formal admission to the practice of the law, often supporting a husband's career. Even if they did achieve formal professional acceptance, they usually supported themselves through salaried positions, generally with insurance companies or governmental agencies, rather than through independent practice. Women lawyers almost always practiced civil, rather than criminal law, and most often pursued office, rather than court, practice. A large, but unmeasured, portion of the women admitted to the bar never practiced law, preferring instead informal legal assistance to organizations ranging from the WCTU to the WTUL or, like Arabella Mansfield, the pursuit of other careers, particularly teaching.

Myra Bradwell Before the Illinois Supreme Court

Mr. Justice Lawrence delivered the opinion of the Court:

At the last term of the court, Mrs. Myra Bradwell applied for a license as an attorney at law, presenting the ordinary certificates of character and qualifications. The license was refused, and it was stated, as a sufficient reason, that under the decisions of this court, the applicant, as a married woman, would be bound neither by her express contracts, nor by those implied contracts, which it is the policy of the law to create between attorney and client.

Since the announcement of our decision, the applicant has filed a printed argument, in which her right to a license is earnestly and ably maintained. Of the qualifications of the applicant we have no doubt, and we put our decision in writing in order that she, or other persons interested, may bring the question before the next legislature.

The applicant, in her printed argument, combats the decision of this court in the case of *Carpenter* v. *Mitchell*, 50 Ill. 470, in which we held a married woman was not bound by contracts having no relation to her own property. We are not inclined to go over again the grounds of that decision. It was the result of a good deal of deliberation and discussion in our council chamber, and the confidence of the present members of this court in its correctness cannot easily be shaken. We are in accord with all the courts in this country which have had occasion to pass upon a similar question, the Supreme Court of Wisconsin, in *Conway* v. *Smith*, 13 Wis. 125, differing from us only on the minor point, as to whether, in regard to contracts concerning the separate property of married women, the law side of the court would take jurisdiction.

As to the main question, the right of married women to make contracts not affecting their separate property, the position of those who assert such right is, that because the legislature has expressly removed the common law disabilities of married women in regard to holding property not derived from their husbands, it has, therefore,

From 55 Illinois 535 (1869).

by necessary implication, also removed all their common law disabilities in regard to making contracts, and invited them to enter, equally with men, upon those fields of trade and speculation by which property is acquired through the agency of contracts. The hiatus between the premise and conclusion is too wide for us to bridge. It may be desirable that the legislature should relieve married women from all their common law disabilities. But to say that it has done so, in the act of 1861, the language of which is carefully guarded, and which makes no allusion to contracts, and does not use that or any equivalent term, would be simple misinterpretation. It would be going as far beyond the meaning of that act as that act goes beyond the common law in changing the legal status of women. The act itself is wise and just, and therefore entitled to a liberal interpretation. This we have endeavored to give it in the cases that have come before us, but we do not intend to decide that the legislature has gone to a length in its measure of reform for which the language it has carefully used furnishes no warrant.

It is urged, however, that the law of the last session of the legislature, which gives to married women the separate control of their earnings, must be construed as giving to them the right to contract in regard to their personal services. This act had no application to the case of *Carpenter* v. *Mitchell*, having been passed after that suit was commenced, and we were unmindful of it when considering this application at the last term. Neither do we now propose to consider how far it extends the power of a married woman to contract, since, after further consultation in regard to this application, we find ourselves constrained to hold that the sex of the applicant, independently of coverture, is as our law now stands, a sufficient reason for not granting this license.

Although an attorney at law is an agent, as is claimed by the applicant's argument, when he has been retained to act for another, yet he is also much more than an agent. He is an officer of the court, holding his commission, in this State, from two of the members of this court, and subject to be disbarred by this court for what our statute calls "mal-conduct in his office." He is appointed to assist in the administration of justice, is required to take an oath of office, and is privileged from arrest while attending courts.

Our statute provides that no person shall be permitted to practice as an attorney or counsellor at law without having previously obtained a license for that purpose from two of the justices of the Supreme Court. By the second section of the act, it is provided that no person shall be entitled to receive a license, until he shall have obtained a certificate from the court of some county of his good moral character, and this is the only express limitation upon the exercise of the power thus entrusted to this court. In all other respects it is left to our discretion to establish the rules by which admission to this office shall be determined. But this discretion is not an arbitrary one, and must be exercised subject to at least two limitations. One is, that the court should establish such terms of admission as will promote the proper administration of justice; the second, that it should not admit any persons or class of persons who are not intended by the legislature to be admitted, even though their exclusion is not expressly required by the statute.

The substance of the last limitation is simply that this important trust reposed in us should be exercised in conformity with the designs of the power creating it. Whether, in the existing social relations between men and women, it would promote the proper administration of justice, and the general well being of society, to permit women to engage in the trial of cases in court, is a question opening a wide field of discussion upon which it is not necessary for us to enter.

It is sufficient to say that, in our opinion, the other implied limitation upon our power, to which we have above referred, must operate to prevent our admitting women to the office of attorney at law.

If we were to admit them, we should be exercising the authority conferred upon us in a manner which, we are fully satisfied, was never contemplated by the legislature. Upon this question, it seems to us neither this applicant herself, nor any unprejudiced and intelligent person, can entertain the slightest doubt.

It is to be remembered that at the time this statute was enacted, we had, by express provision, adopted the common law of England, and, with three exceptions, the statutes of that country passed prior to the fourth year of James the First, so far as they were applicable to our condition.

It is to be also remembered that female attorneys at law were unknown in England, and a proposition that a woman should enter the courts of Westminster Hall in that capacity, or as a barrister, would have created hardly less astonishment than one that she should ascend the bench of Bishops, or be elected to a seat in the House of Commons.

It is to be further remembered that when our act was passed, that school of reform, which claims for women participation in the making and administering of the laws had not then arisen, or, if here and there a writer had advanced such theories, they were regarded rather as abstract speculations than as an actual basis for action. That God designed the sexes to occupy different spheres of action, and that it belonged to men to make, apply, and execute the laws, was regarded as an almost axiomatic truth.

It may have been a radical error, but that this was the universal belief certainly admits of no denial. A direct participation in the affairs of government, in even the most elementary form, namely, the right of suffrage, was not then claimed, and has not yet been conceded, unless recently, in one of the newly settled territories of the West.

In view of these facts, we are certainly warranted in saying, that when the legislature gave to this court the power of granting licenses to practice law, it was with not the slightest expectation that this privilege would be extended equally to men and women. Neither has there been any legislation since that period, which would justify us in presuming a change in the legislative intent. Our laws, today, in regard to women, are substantially what they have always been, except in the change wrought by the acts of 1861 and 1869, giving to married women the right to control their own property and earnings.

Whatever, then, may be our individual opinions as to the admission of women to the bar, we do not deem ourselves at liberty to exercise our power in a mode never contemplated by the legislature, and inconsistent with the usages of courts of the common law, from the origin of the system to the present day.

But it is not merely an immense innovation in our own usages, as a court, that we are asked to make. This step, if taken by us, would mean that, in the opinion of this tribunal, every civil office in this State may be filled by women; that it is in harmony with the spirit of our constitution and laws that women should be made governors, judges, and sheriffs. This we are not yet prepared to hold.

In our opinion, it is not the province of a court to attempt, by giving a new interpretation to an ancient statute, to introduce so important a change in the legal position of one-half the people. Courts of justice were not intended to be made the instruments of pushing forward measures of popular reform. If it be desirable that those offices which we have borrowed from the English law, and which, from their origin, some centuries ago, down to the present time, have been filled exclusively by men, should also be made accessible to women, then let the change be made, but let it be made by that department of the government to which the constitution has entrusted the power of changing the laws.

The great body of our law rests merely upon ancient usage. The right of a husband in this State to the personal property of his wife, before the act of 1861, rested simply upon such usage, yet who would have justified this court, if prior to the passage of that act, it had solemnly decided that it was unreasonable that the property of the wife should vest in the husband, and this usage should no longer be recognized? Yet was it not as unreasonable that a woman by marriage should lose the title of her personal property, as it is that she should not receive from us a license to practice law? The rule in both cases, until the law of 1861, rested upon the same common law usage, and could have pleaded the same antiquity.

In the one case it was never pretended that this court could properly overturn the rule, and we do not see how we could be justified should we disregard it in the other.

The principle can not be too strictly and conscientiously observed, that each of the three departments of the government should avoid encroachment upon the other, and that it does not belong to the judiciary to attempt to inaugurate great social or political reforms. The mere fact that women have never been licensed as attorneys at law is, in a tribunal where immemorial usage is as much respected as it is and ought to be in courts of justice, a sufficient reason for declining to exercise our discretion in their favor, until the propriety of their participating in the offices of State and the administration of public affairs shall have been recognized by the law-making department of the government,—that department to which the initiative in great measures of reform properly belongs.

For us to attempt, in a matter of this importance, to inaugurate a practice at variance with all the precedents of the law we are sworn to administer, would be an act of judicial usurpation, deserving of the gravest censure. If we could disregard, in this matter, the authority of those unwritten usages which make the great body of our law, we might do so in any other, and the dearest rights of person and property would become a matter of mere judicial discretion.

But it is said the twenty-eighth section of chapter 90 of the revised statutes of 1845 provides that, whenever any person is referred to in the statute by words importing the masculine gender, females, as well as males, shall be deemed to be included.

But the thirty-sixth section of the same chapter provides that this rule of construction shall not apply when there is anything in the subject or context repugnant to such construction. That is the case in the present instance.

In the view we have taken of this question, the argument drawn by the applicant from the constitution of the United States has no pertinency.

In conclusion, we would add that, while we are constrained to refuse this application, we respect the motive which prompts it, and we entertain a profound sympathy with those efforts which are being so widely made to reasonably enlarge the field for the exercise of woman's industry and talent. While those theories which are popularly known as "woman's rights" can not be expected to meet with a very cordial acceptance among the members of a profession, which, more than any other, inclines its followers, if not to stand immovable upon the ancient ways, at least to make no hot haste in measures of reform, still, all right minded men must gladly see new spheres of action opened to woman, and greater inducements offered her to seek the highest and widest culture.

There are some departments of the legal profession in which she can appropriately labor. Whether, on the other hand, to engage in the hot strifes of the bar, in the presence of the public, and with momentous verdicts the prizes of the struggle, would not tend to destroy the deference and delicacy with which it is the pride of our ruder sex to treat her, is a matter certainly worthy of her consideration.

But the important question is, what effect the presence of women as barristers in our courts would have upon the administration of justice, and the question can be satisfactorily answered only in the light of experience. If the legislature shall choose to remove the existing barriers, and authorize us to issue licenses equally to men and women, we shall cheerfully obey, trusting to the good sense and sound judgment of women themselves, to seek those departments of the practice in which they can labor without reasonable objection.

Application denied.

A DETERMINED ASSAULT UPON THE BAR

During the 1870s, in particular, throughout the northern states well-educated middle-class women, motivated by feminist ideals, often having participated in some aspect of the war effort, and cognizant of the potential of the law for advancing their personal ambitions, sought entry into law schools and the legal profession. The District of Columbia became a focal point for the activity of women who wanted to enter law schools and legal practice because of the many women who had held jobs there during the Civil War as government clerks and the lack of a compacted, elite group of local law firms conducting government business.

The woman who staked out the first ground in the nation's capital for the practice of law by women was Belva Ann Bennett McNall

Lockwood (1830–1917). The following reading offers her recollections of that pioneering experience. Subsequently, she worked to provide women employees in government with equal pay for equal work, participated in the National Women's Suffrage Association, and worked for liberalization of the laws specifying the property rights of married women.

How Belva Lockwood Became a Lawyer

. . . All my leisure hours were employed in study. And now, possessing myself of an old copy of the Four Books of Blackstone's *Commentaries*, I gave myself daily tasks until I had read and reread them through. In the midst of these labors I committed the indiscretion so common to the women of this country, and, after fifteen years and more of widowhood, married the Rev. Ezekiel Lockwood, on the 11th of March, 1868.

But this marriage did not cure my mania for the law. The school was given up, and during the following year I read Kent's *Commentaries*, occupying all the spare moments in the midst of my domestic work. In the autumn of 1869, on the opening of the Columbian College Law Class, I attended with my husband, by invitation of its President, Dr. Samson, the opening lecture of the course, delivered by him. I also went to the second lecture, and before the third presented myself for matriculation in the class and offered to pay the entrance fee. This was refused, and I was thereupon informed that the question of my admission would be submitted to the faculty. One week, two weeks, elapsed, when one day I received a letter running thus:

Columbian College, Oct. 7, 1869

[To] Mrs. Belva A. Lockwood:

Madam,

The Faculty of Columbian College have considered your request to be admitted to the Law Department of this institution,

From Belva Lockwood, "My Efforts to Become a Lawyer," *Lippincotts Monthly Magazine*, vol. 87 (February 1888): 215–29.

and after due consultation, have considered that such admission would not be expedient, as it would be likely to distract the attention of the young men.

Respectfully,

Geo. W. Samson, Pres.

I was much chagrined by this slap in the face, and the inference to be drawn from it, that my rights and privileges were not to be considered a moment whenever they came in conflict with those of the opposite sex. My husband counselled that I should keep silence about it, as his relations with Dr. Samson, as ministers and co-laborers in the same church, had hitherto been friendly. But the truth would out. The newspaper men got hold of it, as newspaper men will, and came to me and demanded to see the letter, declaring that the action of Dr. Samson was a matter of public interest. My husband protested; but I read them the letter, retaining the original, which I still have.

Next year the National University Law School was opened, and, ostensibly as a part of its plan to admit women to membership on the same terms as young men, I was invited, with other ladies, to attend the classes, and gladly accepted. At its first session, fifteen ladies matriculated, partly as a novelty, I suppose, but certainly without any adequate idea of the amount of labor involved. Many of them left with the close of the first quarter; but some continued through the year, and a few of them held on until the middle of the second year. Only two persons, Lydia S. Hall and myself, completed the course. At first, besides the regular class recitations, we were admitted to the lectures with the young men, although the recitations had been separate. This was a compromise between prejudice and progress. It was not long before there commenced to be a growl by the young men, some of them declaring openly that they would not graduate with women. The women were notified that they could no longer attend the lectures, but would be permitted to complete the course of studies. As Commencement day approached, it became very evident that we were not to receive our diplomas, nor be permitted to appear on the stage with the young men at graduation. This was a heavy blow to my aspirations, as the diploma would have been the entering wedge into the court and saved me the weary contest which followed.

For a time I yielded quite ungracefully to the inevitable, while Lydia S. Hall solaced herself by marrying a man named Graffan and leaving the city. She was not a young woman at that time, but a staid matron past forty; and after her departure I entirely lost sight of her, and suppose she became "merged," as Blackstone says, in her husband. I was not to be squelched so easily.

I asked a member of the bar, Francis Miller, Esq., to move my admission to the bar of the Supreme Court, D.C., which he did, some time in the latter part of July, 1872, and I was referred to the examining committee for report. I at once hunted up the committee and asked for the examination. It was with evident reluctance that the committee came together for the examination, which was quite rigid and lasted for three days. I waited for weeks after this, but the committee did not report. Thereupon I entered complaint of their action to the Supreme Justice, David K. Cartter, and another committee was appointed. It was Judge Cartter who one year before, in the revision of the Laws of the District of Columbia, knowing that some women in the District were preparing for admission to the bar, had asked that the rule of court be so amended as to strike out the word "male," and it had been done, so that this disability no longer stood in my way. The new committee, like the old one, examined me for three days, but would not report. They were opposed to the innovation. The age of progress that had to some extent softened and liberalized the judges of the District Supreme Court had not touched the old-time conservatism of the bar. I was blocked, discouraged, pro tempore, but had not the remotest idea of giving up.

Desperate enough for any adventure, I now, at the request of Theodore Tilton, went on a canvassing and campaigning tour through the Southern States in the interest of the *New York Tribune* and *Golden Age*, and of Horace Greeley, whom the Liberal Republicans had nominated for the Presidency in July, 1872. My trip was a reasonably successful one, but it did not elect Greeley.

After the political sky had cleared, I made my appearance at a course of lectures in the Georgetown College Law Class; but when a call was made by the Chancellor for the settlement of dues my money was declined, and I was informed by a note from the Chancellor, a few days later, that I could not become a member of the class. I then turned my attention to Howard University, and for a time attended the lectures in that institution; but the fight was getting monotonous and decidedly one-sided. Some of the justices of the peace in the District, and Judge William B. Snell of the Police Court, had notified me that I would be recognized in their respective courts as attorney in the trial of any case in which I chose to appear; and Judge Olin had recognized me in the Probate Court in the District. I had even ventured to bring suit on a contract in a justice court. This procedure was considered so novel that it was telegraphed all over the country by the Associated Press.

I now grew a little bolder, and to a certain extent desperate, and addressed the following letter to President Grant, then President ex officio of the National University Law School:

> No. 432 Ninth Street, N.W.
> Washington, D.C., September 3, 1873

To His Excellency U. S. Grant, President U.S.A.:

Sir,

You are, or you are not, President of the National University Law School. If you are its President, I desire to say to you that I have passed through the curriculum of study in this school, and am entitled to, and demand, my diploma. If you are not its President, then I ask that you take your name from its papers, and not hold out to the world to be what you are not.

> Very respectfully,
> Belva A. Lockwood

This letter contained about as much bottled-up indignation as it was possible for one short missive to conceal under a respectful guise. I received no direct answer, but next week I was presented by the Chancellor of the University, W. B. Wedgewood, with my diploma duly signed, and a few days after I was admitted to the bar.

On my admission, the clerk remarked, "You went through

to-day, Mrs. Lockwood, like a knife. You see the world moves in our day." Justice Cartter said, "Madam, if you come into this court we shall treat you like a man." Justice Arthur McArthur remarked, "Bring on as many women lawyers as you choose: I do not believe they will be a success." These comments did not affect me, as I already had my hands full of work, and cases ready to file in anticipation of my admission. My friends had confidence in my ability; and the attention that had been called to me in the novel contest I had made not only gave me a wide advertising, but drew towards me a great deal of substantial sympathy in the way of work. Besides this, I had already booked a large number of government claims, in which I had been recognized by the heads of the different Departments as attorney: so that I was not compelled, like my young brothers of the bar who did not wish to graduate with a woman, to sit in my office and wait for cases. I have been now fourteen years before the bar, in an almost continuous practice, and my experience has been large, often serious, and many times amusing. I have never lacked plenty of good paying work; but, while I have supported my family well, I have not grown rich. In business I have been patient, painstaking, and indefatigable. There is no class of case that comes before the court that I have not ventured to try, either civil, equitable, or criminal; and my clients have been as largely men as women. There is a good opening at the bar for the class of women who have taste and tact for it.

But neither my ambitions nor my troubles ceased with my admission to the District bar. On or about the 1st of April, 1874, having an important case to file in the Court of Claims, I asked one A. A. Hosmer, a reputable member of the bar of that court, to move my admission thereto, having previously filed with the clerk my power of attorney in the case, and a certificate from the clerk of the District Court of my good standing therein, as required by the rule of that court.

At precisely twelve o'clock the five justices of that dignified court marched in, made their solemn bows, and sat down. Without ceremony, after the formal opening of the court by the clerk, and the reading of the minutes of the last session, my gracious attorney moved my admission. There was a painful pause. Every eye in the

court-room was fixed first upon me, and then upon the court; when
Justice Drake, in measured words, announced, "Mistress Lockwood, you are a woman." For the first time in my life I began to
realize that it was a crime to be a woman; but it was too late to put
in a denial, and I at once pleaded guilty to the charge of the court.
Then the chief justice announced, "This cause will be continued for
one week." I retired in good order, but my counsel, who had only
been employed for that occasion, deserted me, and seemed never
afterwards to have backbone enough to keep up the fight.

On the following week, duly as the hand of the clock approached
the hour of twelve, I again marched into the court-room, but this
time almost with as much solemnity as the judges, and accompanied
by my husband and several friends. When the case of Lockwood was
reached, and I again stood up before that august body, the solemn
tones of the chief justice announced, "Mistress Lockwood, you are a
married woman!" Here was a new and quite unexpected arraign-
ment, that almost took my breath away for the moment; but I
collected myself, and responded, with a wave of my hand towards
my husband, "Yes, may it please the court, but I am here with the
consent of my husband," Dr. Lockwood at the same time bowing to
the court. My pleading and distressed look was of no avail. The
solemn chief justice responded, "This cause will be continued for
another week."

Seeing that a fierce contest was imminent, I forthwith employed a
member of this bar, one Charles W. Horner, to appear and plead my
cause. He was a man who loved justice, and who feared neither the
court nor conservatism. He prepared an able argument, presented it
to the court on the following Monday, and, after patient attention,
was allowed to file the same with the clerk, while the cause of
"Lockwood" was continued for one more week. Next Monday,
Judge Peck, who had been sitting in the cause, had died; and of
course there was an adjournment for another week. Upon the
convening of the court at this time the cause was given to Judge
Nott to deliver the opinion of the court; and three weeks were
devoted to this work. I had time to reflect, to study up on my law, to
ponder upon the vast disparity between the sexes, and, if I had

possessed any nice discrimination, to see the utter folly of my course. But I would not be convinced.

Three weeks later, I was again present on the solemn assembling of that court. It took Judge Nott one hour and a half to deliver his opinion, which closed as follows:

> The position which this court assumes is that under the laws and Constitution of the United States a court is without power to grant such an application, and that a woman is without legal capacity to take the office of attorney.

Of course this was a squelcher, and with the ordinary female mind would have ended the matter; for it was concurred in without a dissenting voice by the four other judges on that august bench. But I was at this time not only thoroughly interested in the law, but devoted to my clients, anxious that their business should not suffer, and determined to support my family by the profession I had chosen. My cases and my powers of attorney were filed in the court, and there was nothing to prevent me from taking the testimony, which I did, and preparing the notices and motions which my clients filed. Nevertheless I found that I was working continuously at a disadvantage, and that my clients lacked the confidence in me that I would have commanded had I stood fairly with the court.

I had another important case in course of preparation to file in the Court of Claims, and in order to bridge over the disability under which I stood with the court, I took an assignment of the claim. But in this I hardly succeeded better. The case was that of Webster M. Raines *et ux.* against the United States, and my assignment covered only one-third of it. I appeared in *propria persona,* and attempted to argue my own case. The chief justice declared that I was not the assignee, although the original claimant appeared in court and declared that I was, and stated also his desire to have me represent his portion of the case. It was no use. When I arose to explain my position, the court grew white at my audacity and imperturbability, and positively declined to hear me. Then I hired a lawyer to represent me in the case,—a male attorney, who had been a judge on the bench. He occupied the court for three days in saying very badly what I could have said well in one hour. This was some little revenge; but he lost my case, and I at once appealed it to the United States Supreme Court, hoping that before the case would be reached in that court I should have had the three years of good standing in the court below, and thus become entitled to admission thereto under the rule, which reads, "Any attorney in good standing before the highest court of any State or Territory for the space of three years shall be admitted to this court when presented by a member of this bar." I read the rule over carefully and repeatedly, to make sure that it included me, and asked myself, Why not? Was not I a member of the bar of the Supreme Court of the District of Columbia in good standing? Had I not been such for three years? The law did not say "any man," or "any male citizen," but "any attorney."

Patiently, hopefully, I waited. At last, in October, 1876, full of hope and expectation, and in company with the Hon. A. G. Riddle, whom I had asked to introduce me, I presented myself before the bar of the United States Supreme Court for admission thereto. Again I had reckoned without my host. My attorney made the presentation, holding my credentials in his hand. Those nine gowned judges looked at me in amazement and dismay. The case was taken under advisement, and on the following Monday an opinion rendered, of which the following is the substance: "As this court knows no English precedent for the admission of women to the bar, it declines to admit, unless there shall be a more extended public opinion, or special legislation." No pen can portray the utter astonishment and surprise with which I listened to this decision. My reverence for the ermine vanished into thin air. I was dazed, and kept repeating to myself, "No English precedent! How about Queens Eleanor and Elizabeth, who sat in the *aula regia* and dispensed the duties of chief chancellor of the English realm in person? How about Anne, Countess of Pembroke, who was hereditary sheriff of Westmoreland, and who at the assizes at Appleby sat with the judges on the bench?" "A more extended public opinion,"—how was I to make it? "Special legislation,"—how was I to obtain it, with a family to support, and a sick husband on my hands? I went home, and again took up the thread of my law cases before the District bar, but determined not to let this matter rest.

What next? When Congress assembled in December, I appealed to the Hon. Benjamin F. Butler to draft and introduce in that body a bill for the admission of women to the bar of the United States Supreme Court. This was my first bid for the special legislation. The bill was carefully drawn, introduced, recommended by the House Judiciary for passage, debated, and ingloriously lost on its third reading.

The following year a second bill, drafted, at my suggestion, by Hon. Wm. G. Lawrence, fared even worse than the first, and died almost before it was born.

During all these years of discouragement I was indefatigable in the prosecution of my cases before the bar of the District, and had won some reputation as a lawyer. My husband, after three years of total prostration, died, April 23, 1877. In the autumn of 1877 some of the newspaper men of Washington, who had begun to be interested in the long and unequal contest that I had waged, asked me what I intended to do next. "Get up a fight all along the line," I replied. "I shall ask again to be admitted to the bar of the Supreme Court; I shall myself draft a bill and ask its introduction into both Houses of Congress; and, as I have now a case to be brought in the Federal court in Baltimore, *Royuello* v. *Attoché*, I shall ask admission to the bar of the Federal court at Baltimore." This latter claim had been sent to me from the city of Mexico, and was for fifty thousand dollars. "Very well," said they: "we are going to help you out this time." And they did.

I prepared and asked the Hon. John M. Glover to introduce into the House of Representatives, in December, 1877, the following bill:

Be it enacted by the Senate and House of Representatives of the United States of America in Congress assembled:

That any woman duly qualified who shall have been a member of the highest court of any State or Territory, or of the Supreme Court of the District of Columbia, for the space of three years, and shall have maintained a good standing before such Court, and who shall be a person of good moral character, shall, on motion, and the production of such record, be admitted to practise before the Supreme Court of the United States.

I was soon called to make an argument before the House Committee on the Judiciary, after which the bill was favorably reported without a dissenting voice, and passed the House early in the session by two-thirds majority.

On reaching the Senate, it was referred to the Senate Judiciary and committed to the Hon. Aaron A. Sargent, of California. Conceiving that the bill as it passed the House was not broad enough, he amended it, but his amendment was lost, and the Judiciary Committee made an adverse report on the bill. I had done a great deal of lobbying and had used a great many arguments to get the bill through, but all to no avail. With consummate tact, Mr. Sargent had the bill recommitted, but it went over to the next session. I worked diligently through the second session of the Forty-fifth Congress for the passage of my bill, but the Judiciary Committee made a second adverse report on the bill, and this time Mr. Sargent had the forethought to have the bill calendared, so that it might come up on its merits.

But another misfortune overtook me: Mr. Sargent was taken ill before my bill was reached, and compelled to go to Florida for his health. What was I to do now? Here was my work for years about to be wrecked for want of a foster-mother in the Senate to take charge of it. I knew pretty well the status of every member of that body, for I had conversed with all of them, both at this and at the previous session; and in this extremity I went to the Hon. Joseph E. McDonald, of Indiana, and besought him to take charge of the bill. At first he declined, because, as he said, it was Mr. Sargent's bill, and, when I insisted, he bade me go to the Hon. George F. Hoar. I found that gentleman somewhat unwilling to take the entire responsibility of the bill. I was not satisfied to leave anything that I ought to do undone, and so returned to Mr. McDonald, told him that I feared Mr. Sargent's health was such that he would not return in time, and besought him to take upon himself the responsibility of urging and securing the passage of the bill, saying that Senator Hoar would assist him, and Senator Sargent also, when he returned. From the time he assumed this responsibility Senator McDonald was vigilant in the interest of the bill, and, as the Forty-fifth Congress drew to a close, used what influence he could to get the bill up. It was in a precarious position. A single objection would carry it over. When it was about to be reached, I grew anxious, almost desperate,—called out everybody who was opposed to the bill, and begged that it might be permitted to come up on its merits, and that a fair vote might be had on it in the Senate.

I have been interested in many bills in Congress, and have often appeared before committees of Senate and House; but this was by far the strongest lobbying that I ever performed. Nothing was too daring for me to attempt. I addressed Senators as though they were old familiar friends, and with an earnestness that carried with it conviction. Before the shadows of night had gathered, the victory had been won. The bill admitting women to the bar of the United States Supreme Court passed the Senate on the 7th of February, 1879. It was signed by the President, Rutherford B. Hayes, some days later.

On the 3d of March, 1879, on motion of the Hon. A. G. Riddle, I was admitted to the bar of the United States Supreme Court. The passage of that bill virtually opened the doors of all the Federal Courts in the country to the women of the land, whenever qualified for such admission. I was readily admitted to the District Courts of Maryland and Massachusetts after this admission to the Supreme Court.

On the 6th of March, 1879, on motion of the Hon. Thomas J. Durant, I was admitted to the bar of the United States Court of Claims. Thus ended the great struggle for the admission of woman to the bar. Most of the States in the Union have since recognized her right thereto, and notably the State of Pennsylvania, as in the case of Carrie B. Kilgore, who has recently been admitted to the Supreme Court of the State.

VII

Women as Consumers

The heightened specialization of the woman's economic role within the family that was associated with the rise of the Victorian concept of ideal womanhood included increasing attention to the tasks of household management. A significant part of those tasks were necessarily involved with consumption. In the late nineteenth century, the rising incomes of rapidly proliferating middle-class families, the development of greater variety and choice in available products, the extensive use of mass advertising and national brands, the availability of consumer durables designed to save household labor, and the spread of the modern department store all augmented the necessity for greater expertise applied to consumption, particularly that practiced by urban families. Expertise demanded specialization, and responsibility for that specialization fell to women as housewives.

The process whereby women acquired that responsibility was in part simply a logical, convenient extension of the household chores already allocated to them. But quite possibly, at work, as well, were negative connotations that some nineteenth-century Americans attached to consumption, thereby supporting the delegation of that task to women. That is, in the popular literature, not to mention in political rhetoric, "consumers" often received invidious comparison with "producers." To be sure, much of this cultural emphasis reflected the economic problems of rural America in the last decades of the century, but we should be careful not to underestimate the power of romantic ideas to nineteenth-century Americans of all walks of life. Furthermore, the separation of income-generating work from the household with advancing urbanization made household expenditures more difficult to justify as "investment" designed to support a family enterprise. However, in another, and probably more characteristic Victorian analysis, the delegation of consumption to women did not mean the allocation of an inferior task to inferior people, but rather the allocation of a function critical to family saving and, indeed, even to upward mobility—a function requiring frugality and sobriety—to individuals of unusually high spirituality. Many women visibly promoted this conception of consumption: they included women as diverse as the antifeminist Catherine Beecher, who extolled the high virtue of housekeeping in *The American Woman's Home* (1869); the militant women of the Women's Christian Temperance Union, who sought to restrict the consumption of American men; and those practical chemists who pioneered home economics, or domestic science.

By the first decade of the twentieth century, middle-class women had, to a significant extent, become identified as professional consumers. Although largely unorganized, they possessed very great power in the marketplace. Already they had contributed to pure food and drug legislation, on both federal and state levels; their influence was ready to shape the market, already emergent before World War I, for the consumer goods that put electricity to the service of the household; and they were prepared to play a critical role in the mobilization for World War I.

WOMEN AS TAXPAYERS

An often-ignored, but important phase of the activities of women as consumers has been their consumption of services provided by governments: education, transportation, sanitation, national defense, and so on. Today, such purchases are often made directly in the form of fees and charges. But, until the 1920s, the nation's public revenue system consisted almost exclusively of taxes. Thus, those who purchased government services did so, in effect, through tax payments. As is suggested in the following section, during the nineteenth century women were significant as payers of both excise and property taxes. But, of course, until the passage of the Nineteenth Amendment women lacked any electoral control over the disposition of their tax contributions, except in the handful of states that allowed them to vote in all elections and in the few others that permitted them to vote in school board elections. In effect, women were required to purchase government services without having any direct influence over the delivery of those services. This point appears in the following reading as the basis of an attractive argument on behalf of women's suffrage and, indeed, the argument appeared in all of the suffrage campaigns, particularly in state contests. Historians, however, have not credited the argument with much influence in the winning of women's suffrage.

TAXATION OF WOMEN IN MASSACHUSETTS

The women of Massachusetts, like the colonists one hundred years ago, are taxed every year by Congress millions of dollars, without either their consent or the consent of their Representatives. We may say to them, as King George's ministers said to the colonists, You are as much represented in Congress as the 85,387 adult males in the State who are also disfranchised. . . . They will reply, Because you have wronged other people is no reason why you should tyrannize over us; and these men may, if they please, all become voters,—we cannot. We may again say to them, We tax you, as the Constitution authorizes us to do, "for the common defence and general welfare of the United States." (Const. art. I, sec. 8.) They will reply, We prefer to judge for ourselves about what is or is not for the general welfare. We utterly deny your right to take our property for any purposes, unless we deem it to be for the general welfare. And what must we answer to these replies? What can we answer? Can we do any thing more than admit the fact, that, whether we judge of the rightfulness of the taxation of women by Congress, by the principles acted upon by our fathers at the risk of their lives, or the principles which we have ourselves adopted in our fundamental law, every such act is one of simple

From William I. Bowditch, *Taxation of Women in Massachusetts*, rev. ed. (Cambridge, Mass.: John Wilson & Son, 1875), pp. 17–69.

tyranny? Taxation without representation is tyranny, according to the principles of the fathers and the Declaration of Independence, though the persons taxed be women. Our fathers risked death rather than pay a tax of threepence a pound on tea. We, their sons, have taxed the women of the land 25 cents for every pound of tea they consumed. If our fathers were right in resisting the attempt to extract a miserable threepence, what must we think of ourselves?

Besides the indirect taxation of the women of Massachusetts by the General Government,—a taxation which the very rich are obliged to submit to, and the very poor cannot escape,—all those who have a certain amount of property are directly taxed here. Each year a state, county, and town or city tax is levied on them.

In 1871, the House of Representatives directed the Tax Commissioner to ascertain and report to the Legislature the number of females taxed directly, those who had property taxed to husbands, guardians, or trustees, and also the corporation taxes paid by them. The Report (House Document, No. 428) states that 33,961 women were taxed, and that they paid $1,927,653.11. The whole tax raised that year (Aggregate of Polls, Property, Taxes, &c., assessed May, 1871, p. 25) was $22,063,946. So that in 1871 the women paid more than one-twelfth of all the sums raised by taxation in all the towns and cities of the Commonwealth. Of the whole sum thus raised, $782,753 was assessed upon polls. Deducting this, it appears that the women really paid very nearly one-eleventh of the entire tax on property in 1871. . . .

In the 163 places from which I have received returns, the whole tax paid was $21,089,409, or more than four-fifths of the whole sum raised in the State. If from this sum we deduct $526,604 paid by polls, we have $20,562,805 as the whole tax on property in these places. Of this latter sum, the women paid $1,966,601, or .095 per cent. We may, therefore, from these returns, and from those of 1871, consider it as clearly proved that the women of the State, taken as a whole, pay certainly one-eleventh, and probably one-tenth, or even more, of all the tax on property in the State.

Disregarding the 21 towns from which I have no returns as to the number of women taxed, I find that 18,775 women paid $1,934,638 in taxes, or an average of $103 and the equivalent of 51 polls for each woman. The cities of Boston, Chelsea, and Newton, and the town of Brookline, all clustered together, paid $13,079,436, or more than one-half the whole tax of the State. Of this sum ($13,079,436) 8,447 women paid $1,448,479, or a little more than one-tenth of the whole tax,—being an average of $171. . . .

There is another fact connected with the taxation of women which, being a man, I am ashamed to point out, but which yet cannot be passed over in silence; and that is the inexpressible meanness of the thing. We men save at least two millions of dollars every year from our own burdens by this act of injustice.

If, as we have seen, the women no doubt pay more than one-eleventh of the whole tax on property, every man of property in the State saves more than one-eleventh of his taxes by the taxation of women. The cities and towns pay more than half the taxes levied in the State, and the women pay more than one-ninth of the whole. So that one-half the men of property in the State save every year more than one-ninth of their taxes, by compelling the women who have no votes with which to protect themselves to pay the amount. . . .

But aside from and beyond all the considerations that have hitherto been urged against the direct taxation of women, we deny the right thus to tax them.

By the Constitution (part 2, ch. I, art. 4) the General Court has, it is true, power to impose and levy proportional and reasonable assessments, rates, and taxes upon all the inhabitants of and persons resident and estates lying within the said Commonwealth;" but the Bill of Rights (art. 23) declares that "no subsidy, charge, tax, impost, or duties ought to be established, fixed, laid, or levied under any pretext whatsoever, without the consent of the people or their representatives in the Legislature."

Miss Sarah E. Wall, duly qualified to vote in every respect, except sex, was taxed in Worcester, and refused to pay her tax. No report is given of any argument in the Supreme Court on either side. She appeared for herself, and W. A. Williams for the collector. The whole opinion of the Court is contained in these two short paragraphs:—

"By the Constitution of Mass. ch. I, sec. I, art. 4, the Legislature has power to impose taxes upon all the inhabitants of and persons resident and estates lying within the said Commonwealth. By the laws passed by the Legislature in pursuance of this power and authority, the defendant is liable to taxation, although she is not qualified to vote for the officers by whom the taxes were assessed.

"The Court, acting under the Constitution, and bound to support it and maintain its provisions faithfully, cannot declare null and void a statute which has been passed by the Legislature in pursuance of an express authority conferred by the Constitution." (*Wheeler* v. *Wall,* 6 Allen Rep. 558.)

In other words, our Supreme Court holds that the taxation of women without representation is in accordance with an express authority conferred by our Constitution. . . .

It may possibly be urged as "each individual of the society has a right to be protected by it in the enjoyment of his life, liberty, and property according to standing laws, and he is obliged consequently to contribute his share to the expense of the protection" that whoever is thus protected may be taxed, whether a voter or not; in other words, that taxation and protection—not taxation and representation—go together. And it is true that aliens who are not allowed to vote are, nevertheless, sometimes said to be taxed on the ground of this very protection which they receive. (Opinion of the Judges, Feb. 15, 1811, 7 Mass. 523.)

The King and Parliament also proposed to tax the colonists for their own protection; but the colonists wholly failed to see that this made any difference, or that the tax was any less tyrannical in consequence. They preferred to determine for themselves exactly how, when, and where such protection should be exerted. May not our women, properly enough, claim the same right to determine what protection they need, and are willing to pay for?

If it be argued that because aliens, having no right to vote, may rightfully be taxed, therefore native-born women who are disfranchised may also be taxed, the argument is worthless, unless we are also willing to admit that under our Constitution the property rights of more than half the citizens of the Commonwealth are no greater

than if they were aliens! Who is ready to make this admission? It
may very likely be true that women, in point of fact, enjoy no more
property rights than are accorded to aliens; but it is very far from
being true that they ought to have no greater rights than aliens
under our fundamental law, and equally untrue that they are in the
actual enjoyment of all the rights to which they are entitled, by
virtue of that law. . . .

With this I finish my statement about the taxation of women in
Massachusetts. I have honestly endeavored to state the case fairly,
and without exaggeration. The simple truth seems amply sufficient
to cause any principled man to blush for our short-comings. The
facts alone ought to be enough to arouse our sympathy, and incite us
to earnest effort to remedy the great wrong. I have proved that the
women of the State are compelled every year to pay millions of
dollars in the way of taxes. I have proved that all taxes which are
collected from them, under authority of Congress, are laid contrary
to the principles for which our fathers fought, and contrary to the
principles of the Declaration of Independence; and I hope my
readers will think I have succeeded in showing that the direct
taxation of women under our State law is not only contrary to these
same principles, but is also an infringement of our Declaration of
Rights. And may the day soon come when all of us shall be ready to
admit that taxation without representation is tyranny, and nothing
but tyranny, even if the persons taxed be women, and act
accordingly!

THE ORIGINS OF PROFESSIONAL CONSUMERISM

Maud Nathan (1862–1946) was a New York society matron who
worked to advance recognition of the fact that as consumers women
had great potential power for shaping society. To mobilize that
power she formed a consumer organization in New York that was
joined by leagues in other cities. During the 1890s, she established a
National Consumers' League, modeled on her successful New York
organizations. The following reading is her description of some of
the activities first of the New York league and then the national
league.

The original motivation of consumer leagues is very much an open question. Their initial concern for using consumer power to improve the conditions under which working-class women labored indicates a sincere interest in the welfare of other women that cut across class lines. But, except for the New York league, the more powerful concern was in guaranteeing that products would be produced under the most sanitary conditions. In both New York and the rest of the nation the consumer leagues, and the women's clubs with which they were often associated, led the movement for pure food and drug legislation, which was capped by the 1906 passage of the Pure Food and Drug Act. Furthermore, as the consumer movement progressed, the National Consumers' League received support from those manufacturers who desired higher standards of manufacture in order to enlarge their markets. Such manufacturers often agreed voluntarily to meet the criteria of production put forward by consumer leagues.

The unusual strength of the commitments of the New York league to lower-class women is difficult to explain, but a tentative explanation may rest with ethnic solidarity. Typical of the New York leadership, Maud Nathan was of a distinguished Sephardic Jewish family. As eighth-generation New Yorkers, and decidedly aristocratic in bearing, the family had a potent interest in the welfare of Jews who had recently arrived in the massive waves from Russia and the Austro-Hungarian Empire. Regardless of purpose, however, the consumer leagues demonstrated the potential power of organized middle- and upper-class women; innovated in the techniques of organizing consumer power—by developing the white list, the forerunner of the union label; and contributed significantly to the development of the markedly strengthened civic consciousness that emerged around the turn of the century.

Women and Consumer Power

. . . In the early years we were constantly called upon to explain what a "consumers' league" meant, whereas to-day it would be

From Maud Nathan, *The Story of an Epoch-Making Movement* (New York: Doubleday, Page, and Co., 1926), pp. 25–79.

difficult to find any one of ordinary intelligence who has not some knowledge, however vague or slight, of the movement.

In 1898, we considered it advisable to become an incorporated body, as other organizations with entirely different aims were using our name to further their own purposes.

This initial meeting, as I have before said, was held May 6, 1890, but it was not until January 21, 1891, that the committee had actually completed its work of organization. For during the months immediately following the mass meeting, the members of this newly formed committee had scattered for their summer holiday, and while they could not be considered hardhearted or callous, they did not feel a sufficient urge to impel them to renounce their holiday in order to hasten the instituting of contemplated reforms. The girls could swelter in stifling shops, they could pant for a cooling breath of salt air or an invigorating mountain breeze, or long to rest their tired eyes on a bit of mossy green, while we, who were enjoying all this unthinkingly, taking this refreshment of body and soul as a matter of course and as merely incident to the season, postponed all action until the bracing autumn days.

After spending many weeks in the work of organization, the committee finally elected its officers. Mrs. Josephine Shaw Lowell accepted the presidency; Mrs. Charles A. Spofford was elected treasurer; Miss Louise Caldwell secretary; while I was asked to serve on the Board of Directors.

The committee adopted a constitution which embodied the following articles:

Principles

(1) That the interest of the community demands that all workers should receive, not the lowest wages, but fair living wages.

(2) That the responsibility for some of the worst evils from which wage earners suffer rests with the consumers, who persist in buying in the cheapest market, regardless of how cheapness is brought about.

(3) That it is, therefore, the duty of consumers to find out under what conditions the articles which they purchase are

produced, and to insist that these conditions shall be at least decent, and consistent with a respectable existence on the part of the workers.

(4) That this duty is especially incumbent upon consumers in relation to the products of woman's work, since there is no limit beyond which the wages of women may not be pressed down, unless artificially maintained at a living rate by combinations, either of the workers themselves or of consumers.

Object

Recognizing the fact that the majority of employers are virtually helpless to improve conditions as to hours and wages, unless sustained by public opinion, by law, and by the action of consumers, the Consumers' League declares its object to be to ameliorate the condition of the women and children employed in the retail mercantile houses of New York City, by patronizing, so far as practicable, only such houses as approach in their conditions to the "Standard of a Fair House," as adopted by the League, and by other methods.

White List

The Advisory Board shall be required to prepare a list of retail mercantile houses which, in their opinion, should be patronized by the members of the Consumers' League, which list shall be known as the "White List," and shall be published at stated intervals in the daily papers.

Membership

The condition of membership shall be the approval by signature of the object of the Consumers' League, and all persons shall be eligible for membership excepting such as are engaged in retail business in New York (either as employer or employee).

The members shall not be bound never to buy at other shops. The names of the members shall not be made public.

The first step to be taken was to establish our White List. Our Standard of a Fair House had been drafted by the Working Women's Society and modified by us after seeking advice from those firms which had the reputation of treating their employees the most fairly.

Fourteen hundred letters were sent to all the retail dry goods and fancy goods shopkeepers in the city, as listed in the directory, with copies of the following:

Standard of a Fair House
Wages

A fair house is one in which equal pay is given for work of equal value, irrespective of sex. In the departments where women only are employed, in which the minimum wages are six dollars per week for experienced adult workers, and fall in few instances below eight dollars;

In which wages are paid by the week;

In which fines, if imposed, are paid into a fund for the benefit of the employees;

In which the minimum wages of cash girls are two dollars per week, with the same conditions regarding weekly payments and fines.

Hours

A fair house is one in which the hours from 8 A.M. to 6 P.M. (with three-quarters of an hour for lunch) constitute the working day, and a general half-holiday is given on one day of each week during at least two summer months;

In which a vacation of not less than one week is given with pay during the summer season;

In which all overtime is compensated for.

Physical Conditions

A fair house is one in which work, lunch, and retiring rooms are apart from each other, and conform in all respects to the present sanitary laws;

In which the present law regarding the providing of seats for saleswomen is observed, and the use of seats permitted.

Other Conditions

A fair house is one in which humane and considerate behaviour toward employees is the rule;

In which fidelity and length of service meet with the consideration which is their due;

In which no children under fourteen years of age are employed.

Letters were sent to shopkeepers asking them to sign an enclosed
agreement as follows:

Agreement to Be Signed by Head
of Retail Mercantile House

I, the undersigned, hereby express my desire to conduct my
business upon the principles laid down in the Standard of a Fair
House, as adopted by the Consumers' League.

I further agree to allow a committee appointed by the
Consumers' League to visit any part of my business premises and
question my employees, and I agree to answer to said committee
inquiries as to the following points (the Consumers' League
pledging itself that such information shall not be published in
detail): Rate of Wages, Holidays, Overtime, Fines, Hours
Worked, Meal Times, Sanitary Conditions.

The recipients of the letters were informed that if they felt unable
to sign the agreement in its present form, the League would be glad
to have them modify it until it met with their approval, and then
return it signed.

Thirty papers, out of fourteen hundred, were signed and returned
to the secretary of the League. Members of the Governing Board at
once visited all the stores represented by these signatures, but they
were amazed to find, after investigation, that only four of the thirty
who responded actually conformed to the League's Standard of a
Fair House. In many of the stores most of the conditions were
favourable, but one or two unfavourable ones prevented their being
included in the White List.

The principal bugbear seemed to be the nonrecognition that
overtime existed. Merchants claimed that employees were engaged
to work until 10 P.M. on Saturdays, and until the same hour for two
to three weeks during the holiday season. These hours, the
employers claimed, were taken into consideration when the wage

scale was fixed. The merchants admitted that it was often eleven
o'clock or later before customers could be coerced to leave the store,
but they saw no necessity to increase wages on that account. Finally,
after many consultations and investigations, we published our first
White List; it had but eight names:

Aitken, Son & Co., Broadway and Eighteenth Street
B. Altman & Co., Sixth Avenue and Nineteenth Street
Arnold, Constable & Co., Broadway and Nineteenth Street
Lord & Taylor, Broadway and Twentieth Street
James McCreery & Co., Broadway and Eleventh Street
E. A. Morrison & Son, Broadway and Nineteenth Street

The other two stores, to the best of my recollection, were

The New York Exchange for Women's Work, 329 Fifth Avenue
The Society of Decorative Art, 28 East Twenty-first Street

Unfortunately, the record of that first White List seems to have
been lost. The second list, published in 1892, contained eleven
additional names, as follows:

Best & Co., 60 West Twenty-third Street
Denning & Co., Broadway and Tenth Street
Mme. N. G. Felicie, 361 Fifth Avenue
Harlem Exchange for Women's Work, 40 West One Hundred
    and Twenty-fifth Street
L. P. Hollander & Co., 290 Fifth Avenue
Japanese Trading Co., 18 East Eighteenth Street
Geo. F. Langenbacher, 820 Broadway
LeBoutillier Bros., 50 West Twenty-third Street
Madison Avenue Depository and Exchange for Women's Work,
    628 Madison Avenue
F.A.O. Schwartz, 42 East Fourteenth Street
A. A. Vantine & Co., 879 Broadway

This White List was distributed by circulating it in pamphlet
form among the members, and also by paying to have it appear as an
advertisement in the leading newspapers. What was the reaction of

the shopping public and of the merchants? Many of our members who had accounts with firms whose names did not appear on the list visited them and expressed themselves as unwilling to patronize any stores not on the White List of the Consumers' League. But the White List meant little to the general public as yet. The large army of shoppers were unaffected; they continued to hunt their bargains in the same irresponsible manner. If they noticed our advertisements, it meant nothing to them. The reaction, however, of the merchants, was sharp and quick. They did notice our advertisement and resented it. They treated the matter lightly at first; they pooh-poohed the absurd attempts of a handful of "busybodies" who were trying to revolutionize business methods. It never could be done; merchants who gave their entire time and thought to their business knew better how to conduct that business than sentimental, visionary women who had no business training, and who allowed their hearts to run away with their heads. The Consumers' League, they contended, could not survive a year. Women would continue to buy where they found bargains or novelties; they would not be interested in the wages or working conditions of the store employees. Besides, what would housekeepers think if a band of men went about asking questions as to how many hours their housemaids worked, or how late at night they were obliged to continue their service, or whether they were given vacations with pay? Would housekeepers care to answer inquiries as to what kind of food they gave their servants, or what kind of beds they furnished?

These specious arguments cooled the ardour of many members of the Consumers' League. They were not so eager to have an investigation conducted of conditions for household domestics. . . .

Some of the trade unions had realized the need of a label in order that their members could distinguish articles made by trade unionists in the "closed shop," but their labels had stood primarily for the fact that all the workers employed in the making of the article were members of the union. The label did not represent necessarily a high standard of conditions, other than those demanded by unions in regard to wages and hours. This label did not guarantee a sanitary environment; indeed, much of the product bearing the union label was known to have been made in tenement rooms. The National Consumers' League felt, therefore, that what was needed was a label that would not only come up to the union standard of wages and hours, but one that would also insure to the purchaser, 1st: sanitary conditions in the production; 2d: a living wage and a fair working day to the producer; 3d: good workmanship; 4th: the elimination of child labour; 5th: the indorsement of the factory inspector; 6th: the privilege of its use by all manufacturers who could prove that they fulfilled the necessary conditions.

It required a great deal of propaganda to create a public opinion which would demand goods bearing our label, and it required as great an effort to induce the manufacturers to place such a label on their garments. The executive secretary of the National Consumers' League toured the country in order to get the label adopted. I, also, as president of the pioneer league and vice-president of the National League, was invited to address the large gatherings of federated clubs. In my capacity as chairman of the "Committee on Industry of Women and Children" of the General Federation of Women's Clubs, I had the opportunity of bringing the facts before the organized women of the country. The work was strenuous and arduous, but the enthusiastic response that we met was our great encouragement. Finally the White Label was accepted by a few of the manufacturers of women's white underwear. This branch of industry, we found, had the largest percentage of underpaid, undernourished workers, so we decided to begin our work with this particular branch of the needle trades. A contract was drawn up between the manufacturers and the National Consumers' League which covered what we considered the salient points. The first list of recommended manufacturers published contained the names of fifteen firms. During the first year, the economic value of this label was so strongly felt that other groups of manufacturers asked to be permitted to sign the contracts and use the label. These groups included makers of corsets, sheets, and pillow cases, curtains, skirt and stocking supporters, shirt waists, and children's wash dresses. The factories using the label were scattered through the following states: Maine, Massachusetts, Michigan, Pennsylvania, and Rhode Island. This product found its way into every corner of the country, and our label was found in Mexico City and in Juneau, Alaska. Our list grew rapidly; we met with the same experience with which we had formerly met in the growth of the White List of New York retail stores. Factories had to be investigated each year to see whether they maintained the required standards; a few had to be dropped occasionally; new names were added until, in 1914, we had a list of sixty-eight firms. Some of these manufacturers turned out 20,000 garments a day.[1] In 1901, there was such a variety of garments being sold which bore the Consumers' League label that Mrs. Henry B. Sleeper of Worcester, Massachusetts, conceived the idea of making a collection of sample garments which could be purchased with the label attached.

The first exhibition of labeled goods, held in Worcester, created sufficient interest to warrant its being followed by an exhibition held during three days at the Women's Educational and Industrial Union of Boston some months later, after which it was sent to Wellesley College.

This was but the beginning of a series of exhibits held all over the country, being sent actually into twenty-eight states, under the able chairmanship of Mrs. Charles E. H. Phillips. The exhibit contrasted goods made in model factories with those made in tenement sweatshops. The New York League did a large part of the work in collecting samples of sweatshop goods, and the Massachusetts League furnished many samples of labeled underwear.

Placards in the exhibits showed the wages, hours, and conditions of sweatshop workers, as well as of workers in factories.

The exhibit of the National Consumers' League was constantly being enlarged, specimens of foods being added to the list of garments and fancy articles. One specimen of so-called strawberry jam was found not to contain a single strawberry.

I must relate here two incidents which will illustrate the value that the manufacturers in general placed on our label. A firm using the White Label called our attention to the fact that one of his

1. In 1918, the Consumers' League discontinued the use of the White Label. Legislation in many states, through the pressure of public opinion, had secured standards even higher than the requirements established by the League for the use of the label.

competitors, whose standards fell far below his, was yet permitted to use the label and, because of these low standards, was able to undersell him. We investigated and found that the firm in question, not having been authorized to use the label, had forged it. A lawsuit followed, and the offending firm was forced to abandon the illegally acquired label. Another firm, known all over the world for its 57 varieties, wrote and asked why, in view of the fact that their work was done under conditions that came up to the required standards of the League, they should not be permitted to place the label on their products. The answer was obvious. Though pickles might be as dear to the heart of the American woman as white underwear, by no stretch of the imagination could even one of these 57 varieties be construed to come within the category of the needle trades! Although we treated this request as a laughing matter and were obliged to refuse it, the incident gave us a new idea of the value of the label and of its force in the economic world. We refused it to "pickles," but the time came when the placing of our label on a milk bottle was the means of saving the lives of hundreds of babies.

Two of the local leagues, one in the Middle West and one in the Far West, used their influence and the power of their organizations to compel dairymen to raise their standard of hygiene and sanitation. They conducted such a spirited and vigorous campaign that they were able to get the support of the general public. When dairymen found that the public would only purchase bottles of milk and cream which bore the Consumers' League label, they were soon impressed with the importance of cleaning up their dairies and improving their conditions. In this campaign, the Consumers' League in one city had the staunch support of one of the leading newspapers. It published an article stating that 618 babies less than a year old had died during the year, and that tuberculous or dirty milk had been the cause of nearly every death. Because of the strong public opinion aroused, a city ordinance relating to the inspection and maintenance of dairies and the regulation of the sale of milk and cream was passed, in spite of the opposition of the Dairymen's Association. Thirteen years later, there were in that city but seventeen deaths from diarrhoea and enteritis, of infants less than two years of age.

Another striking and dramatic illustration of the power of the consumer to change conditions was shown in another Western city. The telephone girls asked for higher wages, shorter hours, and better general conditions. The telephone company refused to grant their demands. The girls then went on strike. The company secured temporary help from nearby towns. The newspapers gave publicity to the working conditions of the telephone girls and to their demands. These demands appealed to the public as being just and fair. One morning, through concerted action, the telephone company received notice over the wires from one subscriber after another that, if the demands of the telephone girls were not acceded to, the subscriber wished the telephone removed and the service discontinued. The situation was so startling and unlooked-for that there could be but one response—the girls were taken back on their own terms.

Through our investigations of tenement-made garments in New York we found that not only were germ-laden garments being widely distributed, but also certain processes in food products were being carried on, to the menace of the health of the community, in these same tenement hovels. Nuts were being picked by diseased workers and piled on dirty floors; poisonous chemicals were being used to colour delectable-looking candies; ice cream was being made from impure milk in corroded tins; macaroni was being made in a small room where the worker's child lay sick with diphtheria.

Cellar bakeries, conducted at night in order that fresh loaves might be sold in the morning, were often used in winter as warm sleeping quarters, the kneading-boards serving as beds for the tired workers. While on one tour of inspection we even found a cat snugly reposing on a cushionlike mass of soft dough.

Eleven years after, a law was passed prohibiting cellar bakeries. Three thousand and seventy-seven of these were still flourishing in New York, and this number did not include basement bakeries. The legal differentiation between a cellar bakery and a basement bakery being that the former is more than half underground and the latter less than half underground.

Committees were formed in the various leagues to investigate further into the matter of prepared-food production, and these committees cooperated with other organizations which were specially interested in this branch of work. It was found that in New York City alone there were 1,360,824 pounds of food seized and condemned within thirteen weeks of the year 1904.

Up to this time, in the licensing of tenements for purposes of manufacture, only wearing apparel had been considered, but, as a result of these investigations, the New York Labour Commissioner introduced a bill into the State Legislature which included food preparations among the articles permitted to be manufactured only in licensed tenements. It was not until February, 1906, that the United States Senate passed the Heyburn Pure Food Bill, which aimed to secure to the people of the country the prevention of "the manufacture, sale, or transportation of adulterated or misbranded or poisonous foods, drugs, medicines, and liquors and regulate traffic therein."

The relating of our investigations in regard to the preparation of food products brings me naturally to the story of restaurant waitresses, who had neither the protection of the factory laws nor of the mercantile laws. In 1916, the New York Consumers' League made an intensive study of the conditions under which these girls worked. More than a thousand women were interviewed, and it was found that fifty-eight per cent of the girls employed in restaurants worked more than fifty-four hours a week, the legal hours for factories and stores. There was an extreme case in which a girl of twenty years of age worked 122 hours a week. Twenty per cent worked twelve hours a day and 4 per cent were employed at night. One-third did not have one day of rest in seven, and the majority were not allowed time off for their meals. Work in restaurants, as in stores, entailed almost continuous standing or walking, and serving many customers caused nervous strain. The waitresses began their day at 7 A.M., walked many miles during the day, carrying heavy trays, and reached their homes not earlier than 8 P.M. Usually, there was laundry work to be done in preparation for the next day's service.

Based on the findings of our investigation, we demanded legislation to protect these girls from exploitation. We carried on a vigorous educational campaign urging enactment of a measure which, through our initiative, had been introduced. In 1917, the bill passed both houses and received the Governor's signature, thus emancipating from a species of industrial slavery a group of women who, through broken-down health, would probably have been thrown upon the community for care.

The method employed by the Consumers' League to better conditions invariably followed this rule: obtain facts through investigation, acquaint the public with the facts, and after educating public opinion, secure legislation. We began by interesting ourselves in saleswomen, we enlarged the scope of our work gradually, making not only the investigations already cited, but also in the artificial flower industry, public laundries, silk factories, telephone operators, and hotel employees. The National Consumers' League also made a study of the standard of living of the average factory worker and saleswoman not living at home.

It also played an important role in preparing the defence to uphold labour laws declared to be unconstitutional. Out of fifteen cases argued before courts of last resort, there were fourteen decisions favourable to the Consumers' League. Of these, nine were in regard to hours of labour. The League had the valuable assistance of Mr. Louis D. Brandeis, who generously gave his services as counsel to the League until he was appointed to the bench of the United States Supreme Court. After that Mr. Felix Frankfurter was equally generous in contributing his services. Miss Josephine Goldmark, who was one of the staff of the National League, did magnificent work in preparing the briefs for the arguments.

The New York League cooperated with the Russell Sage Foundation in carrying on an investigation of the cannery industry. Some of the conditions were found to be deplorable: children under ten years of age shelling peas at an hour close upon midnight; in one instance, a little tot had actually fallen asleep with the peapod clutched in his little hand; abnormally long hours during short seasons of work, women sometimes working until 4 A.M. and reporting again for work at 8 A.M. the same day. The canners claimed that it was not possible to secure enough workers in order to enable them to have two shifts; they contended that, as their products were seasonal and perishable, they could do nothing to shorten hours or lengthen seasons of work. So, when protective legislation was enacted, certain exceptions were made in favour of the canning industry. Thus, rather than allow material for manufacture to deteriorate and let the manufacturing interests suffer, women and children were exploited. Dr. Abraham Jacobi, in his plea before a committee hearing in the Capitol at Albany, said sarcastically: "The freshness of the strawberry must be preserved, even if the children of the next generation perish!"

THE SCIENTIFIC MANAGEMENT OF THE HOME

As early as the 1820s, middle-class urban women had available a literature advising them on the proper ways to manage their homes. Books such as Eliza Rouch Farrar's *The Young Lady's Friend* (1836) and popular periodicals such as *Godey's Magazine and Lady's Book* instructed housewives in a variety of subjects that touched on labor-saving and nursing techniques, dress, and the preservation of health. But these subjects were often treated in a casual fashion and generally suffered in comparison with the attention given by the author to advice on the proper manners to be used with the elderly, teachers, siblings, women friends, gentlemen, party guests, and domestic servants. It was not until the last decades of the century that a serious movement developed to increase significantly the knowledge available to housewives so that they might perform their chores more efficiently and effectively.

Critical to that movement was a group of women who had just received college and graduate degrees in scientific disciplines, particularly chemistry, and had turned their expertise to analyzing systematically the problems of nutrition, sanitation, engineering, and economics faced by the housewife. To some extent, these women took up household problems because their professions discouraged them from pursuing other studies. However, their interest had far more to do with their belief that the undeveloped character of the field offered opportunities for rapid professional advancement; that the rapidly developing and amply supported agricultural sciences would contribute to the development of their related field; that the enhancement of family life was a highly moral enterprise; and that increasing the efficiency of housework would free women for greater attention to their self-improvement.

In the following reading the home economics movement is evaluated by its leader, Ellen H. Richards. Richards was the first woman to graduate from the Massachusetts Institute of Technology (in 1873); the first woman on M.I.T.'s faculty; a pioneer in water and sanitary chemistry; a leader in opening scientific careers to women; a promoter of the teaching of home economics in the public schools (partly to instruct immigrants in Yankee frugality); the leader of the first Lake Placid Conference, in 1898, designed to encourage a nationwide interest in home economics. Her definition of the field was exceptionally broad, considering it to be one sector of the "science of controllable environment," and her leadership was unquestioned. She was elected the first president of the American Home Economic Association when it was founded in 1908.

An Evaluation of the Home Economics Movement

For several reasons the house and household affairs have not partaken of the marvelous changes of the nineteenth century. Spending money and not making money was the office of the home keeper. The flow of industry has passed on and left idle the loom in the attic, the soap kettle in the shed.

The quick resource, the intelligent direction have been drafted into mercantile and manufacturing industries leaving the daily tasks relating to food and cleanliness, the dull routine work never done or only to be done over, to the less energetic and those content to drift.

Tradition has held longer sway over home life than over even religious life and probably rightly, just as the instinct for accustomed food has its justification in the vital importance of food to life, so changes in the heart of the home must be made wisely and slowly and with knowledge, lest the whole be destroyed.

Knowledge to make the necessary changes could come only from outside where investigations were being carried on and tradition

From Ellen H. Richards, "Ten Years of the Lake Placid Conference on Home Economics; Its History and Aims," *Proceedings of the Tenth Annual Conference* (Lake Placid, N.Y., 1908), pp. 19–25.

forbade the house mother to go outside to learn. From time to time appliances and suggestions were brought to her, but being alien and from without they did not fit into the general scheme and found little favor.

Ignorance was becoming exceedingly inconvenient, but alas, the great majority had not realized that the difficulty was with themselves that knowledge was to be had for the asking if they would unite in the request, that which one alone could not demand of the inventor and manufacturer, a multitude could gain. What it needed was faith.

The Lake Placid conference was a result of the faith of one woman in her sex; that if attention were called to the gaps in knowledge needing to be filled, woman would be quick to take steps towards the desired end. . . . .

Therefore first the Lake Placid conference asked questions:

What are the essentials that must be retained in a house that is a home?

What may be better done outside, what standards must be maintained inside?

What must be acquired by practice and what may be learned from books?

What must go into the curriculum for the lower schools and what is the duty of the higher education and the professional school?

Finally, what forces in the community can be roused to action to secure for the coming race the benefits of the 20th century progress?

Ten years ago one of the crying needs of the country as seen by some students of social tendencies was the appreciation of what science might do for the housewife in her daily home keeping, in making her work both easier and more efficient. But the obstacle seemed to be in the woman herself. She had not faith in the promises held out to her by the fanatical scientist. Bread mixers and washing machines were, in her experience, thrown out on the dump heap, chemical foods were a delusion, and new laundry powders a snare. How could she be induced to look with serious eyes upon the new century motor bearing down on her with irresistible power? How could she be rescued from sinking lower in the controlling plane and rise to her rightful place?

Almost all the early work in sewing as well as cooking done in the country was on philanthropic and not on ethical lines. A plea for a fuller acknowledgment of the economic and ethical was made in the name adopted by the Lake Placid conference after much thought and a full discussion—home economics; home meaning the place of shelter and nurture for the children and for those personal qualities of self-sacrifice for others for the gaining of strength to meet the world; economics meaning the management of this home on economic lines as to time and energy as well as to mere money. Lake Placid stood from the first for a study of these economic and ethical lines, let them lead where they would. And they have certainly led very far from the earlier ideals of domestic economy. Real progress is often retarded by trying to make the new fit into the old scheme of things. It has been the endeavor of the program committee to secure speakers and writers with a penetrating vision of the future as foreshadowed by the tendencies to be felt if not seen. Just as the dark end of the spectrum so long disregarded has proved to be of the greatest importance in cosmic interpretation so the obscure indication of social movements is leading us to clearer conceptions of the good whither society is tending and right in the conditions of home life is found the strongest indicator.

Such topics as the following are found in the programs of these early years: training of teachers of domestic science; courses of study for grade schools as well as colleges and universities; state, agricultural, evening, and vacation schools; extension teaching; rural school work; home economics in women's clubs with syllabuses to aid such study; manual training in education for citizenship. All these lead toward higher education in better living, the new science of Euthenics, as an essential preliminary to the study of the better race, a study to which Mr. Francis Galton has given the name Eugenics. From the very first special emphasis was laid on the educational possibilities of this work.

A classification of home economics on a working basis together with correct nomenclature and annotated bibliographies were recognized among the first needs.

Domestic science at farmers' institutes, simplified methods of housekeeping, standards of living in the conduct of the home and in relation to sanitary science, household industrial problems, labor saving appliances, cost of living, standards of wages and the ever irritating question of tips and fees have all been discussed.

Programs have included the food problem in its many phases from fads and fancies to protein metabolism and mineral matter required by the human body; nutrition, sanitation, hygiene, progress in work for public health represented by the work of the Health education league and the Committee of 100 on national health, leading to efficiency as the key note of the 20th century.

Economics in trade and professional schools, home economics in training schools for nurses, the hospital dietitian and the status of institution managers, recent dietetic experiments at Yale University, cooperation with the work of the U.S. Department of Agriculture at Washington, reports from the American school of correspondence, even psychic factors affecting home economics and cost of living have been considered.

The interest of the educator, the schoolman and the woman teacher was no less difficult to arouse than that of the housewife. The school curriculum was sacred to the usual academic subjects. . . .

The present aim of the Lake Placid conference is to teach the American people, chiefly thru the medium of the schools, the management of their homes on economic lines as to time and energy. Once the essentials of the home life are settled, they must be made a part of every child's education and the small details necessary must become so much a habit of life that no occasion will find the members of the family unprepared. Boys and girls alike should be taught how to cook a few simple foods and to keep their clothing in repair.

These ten years have seen the establishment of the Carnegie Nutrition Laboratory; the publications of Chittenden, Sager, Fletcher, and others; the establishment of a regular department of home economics literature; and a great increase in the attention paid to household sanitation. These all show the beginnings of a fundamental education along progressive lines.

THE ORACLE OF CONSUMPTION

Critically involved in the emergence of middle class women as powerful consumers were the "women's magazines." Fairly numerous and widely read even by mid-century, their period of greatest cultural impact began during the 1880s, years of rapid urbanization. Recognizing the mobility of a growing middle class, the prosperity of that middle-class, and the high level of education of middle-class women, the most successful of those magazines provided their readers with guidelines to appropriate tastes in consumption, features in home economics and child care, and fiction that was entertaining, melodramatic, and mostly middlebrow. Of all the magazines, the one that set the definitive pattern for its competitors was the *Ladies' Home Journal.* It began its leadership in 1889 when Edward Bok assumed the editorship from the magazine's founder, Louisa Knapp Curtis. A cultivated, ambitious, and shrewd Dutch immigrant, Bok advanced his concept of the ideal woman with unequaled force, reinforcing the already hardening Victorian definition. Although Bok was arrogant and not infrequently clashed with prominent women, including the leaders of the women's clubs, he did so with grace and style and these episodes did not permanently diminish the circulation built by his magazine. Apparently more central to the readership of the magazine than Bok's position on the women's movement was the formula developed by Louisa Curtis: emphasis on practical advice with respect to tastes and standards of consumption.

Through multicolored advertisements and numerous, usually sophisticated, features on home economics, manufacturers and experts told middle-class women what to buy and how to manage their households. Bok himself advised his readers on consumption, most notably through an editorial crusade for pure food and drug legislation to eliminate the sale of patent medicines. For most middle-class women, it was the *Ladies' Home Journal*, rather than home education courses, women's clubs, or consumers' leagues, that provided the links to other consumers and, of course, to the rapidly expanding, diversifying marketplace of food, clothing, and durable goods.

The year 1916 was no doubt the most prosperous year enjoyed by the American economy before the decade of the 1920s. In that year, Bok was most eloquent and persuasive in his extolling of the virtues of the high-consuming woman managing a modern household. But suddenly, in the spring of 1917, the European war that had seemed distant and insane to Bok's readership enveloped the United States. The following reading is a crucial editorial of Bok's in which he attempts to cope with the necessity for changing the tone of the *Journal* without jeopardizing the acceptance of the magazine by its readers. In so doing, in the process of indicating his appreciation of the economic power of American women, Bok reveals his underlying assumptions about the nature of womanhood. Finally, it should be noted that, after the war, after having appealed to the intelligence of women in the war effort, Bok threw the weight of the *Journal* against women's suffrage. He stated his position succinctly in his autobiography, *The Americanization of Edward Bok* (New York: Scribner's, 1922): "American women were not ready to exercise the privilege intelligently."

An Editorial: A Call to Every American Woman

May, 1917

How far the present upset condition of our peaceful country will carry us: how acute will become our state of disturbance, no one can foretell. It is a case of where "one man's guess is as good as another's." Only time can tell.

One thing is apparently certain: We are facing a time of absolute readjustment as a nation and of a sense of responsibility and cooperation that becomes personal to each one of us. Whether it was right or wrong that we should become a part of the madness that

From Edward Bok, ed., *Ladies' Home Journal* (May 1917): 8.

seems to possess a large part of the world: whether our participation could or could not have been avoided, are no longer the important questions. Nor is it a time of our personal beliefs or convictions. It is essentially, a condition and not a theory that confronts us. Yesterday ended last night. To-day is all that we have. To-morrow is our problem. And the share that the American woman will take in that problem is to count for much. Already thousands of American women are busy; thousands more will be busy when these words reach the reader. But all of us must be sure that we personally and individually *are* busy. It is a time for every American woman, of whatever station, to do her "bit." And she will. The American woman never fails to rise to an occasion: her amazing ability in time of crisis is proverbial. No picture is more stirring than that of woman in the troublous times of 1861–1865, and no picture will be more stirring than that of the women of 1917.

The American woman has been favored beyond the women of any other nation of the globe. During the past two years or more particularly she has lain on beds of ease. All the way down the line, from the high to the low, much has come to her: more than to any other woman: and the world looks for much from those to whom much has been given. The time has now come for the American woman to lay aside her dolls and playthings, as did her sisters of 1861–1865, and show the mettle that is in her. The season of play and of the lightsome mood is over: the time for sterner thought and vital work is here. From every part of the land has come the voice of complaint that the American woman has been softened by prosperity, and, to a large extent, the complaint is justified. Prosperity invariably softens a people, men and women. But that condition is over for a period. What stern realities we may face cannot be forecast. But self-denial, personal sacrifice, the thought and doing for others invariably strengthen, and if it be within the wisest necessities that we shall be hardened by adversity, it is not an experience to be dreaded. Only so is a strong people made. What the adversities of human conflict have done for the women of the warring countries across the sea is beyond human calculation. It may be so with us.

It now becomes every American girl or woman to take an

inventory of herself to see what abilities have been given her and to what service she can consecrate those abilities for the benefit of her native or adopted country. Some will work in the outer activities that the upset condition of a nation creates. Some may be called upon to send forth a husband, a father, a son, or a brother into a sea of trouble. The vast majority of women, however, will remain at home to keep the children going and the home intact. And those women must not for a moment feel that no responsibility is theirs: that no work lies at their hand. It is always the women who remain behind in the homes of a troubled nation that constitute its bulwark, whether they have the time or the ability to work outside of their homes, or fight to keep those homes intact and keep the important machinery running for the benefit of a nation's childhood. Not a woman is there to whom war does not bring its problems. Its arm reaches all, even the idle woman who sits slothfully by. Upon her womankind sets the stigma of disgrace. But there are few such, and a negligible unhealthy quantity, in any proposition, can always be ignored.

Wherever there dwells a normal woman within the confines of the land we love, from that spot in this wonderful nation of ours will come the cry for her part to do and the willingness to do it each according to her ability. With all personal interests put aside, the American woman will rise as a single unit to the call for America First!

With this woman the *Ladies' Home Journal* will go hand in hand through the future that is now veiled to us. Whatever problems there may come before her: whatever privation and self-sacrifice she may be called upon to bear, this magazine will endeavor to foresee the need and be at her side when the time is there to meet it. The most careful and comprehensive plans have been made to point the way to those outside activities that will need the help and the means of the woman who has the time, the abilities, and the means. The magazine is already in close touch with the authoritative channels of the best activities and it will be their mouthpiece and the guide of the women who wish to take part in them. With the woman in the home the magazine will likewise keep in close touch. So far as human foresight and the mechanical exigencies of a magazine that must go to press so much in advance of the time that it reaches its readers make possible, the editors will forecast the economic problems that will face the home-keeper and the mother, and show the way out. While it will seek to stimulate, to cheer, to entertain as before, more strongly than ever will the note of actual help permeate the pages of the magazine. To others will we leave the recording of the course of events. *The Ladies' Home Journal* will help in the results which those events bring to the perplexed woman.

So, hand in hand, will *The Ladies' Home Journal* and its readers meet the new situations and their resultant problems, each striving to help the other in their wisest solution. And together will the magazine and its readers face unflinchingly the experiences that may be ahead, full of courage, full of faith, full of that undaunted spirit of true Americanism that has in times gone by made the world in contemplation of it stand with uncovered head, and in which the American woman has never failed to play a large and efficient part.

CONSUMERISM IN WAR

The height of Edward Bok's influence over American households came during World War I. Although Bok's definition of a wartime purpose for his magazine and for American womanhood had been vague in May 1917, only a few months later Herbert Hoover provided him with a solution: the middle-class American woman would serve by conserving scarce resources. In the following editorial, Hoover, whom the Lever Act had authorized to buy and sell all American foodstuffs for the Allies through the Food Administration, began an extended effort to mobilize patriotism and to utilize the central consuming role of women to mitigate accelerating inflation in food prices. The *Journal* presented similar editorials virtually every month, and Bok supported Hoover with his own patronizing exhortations and detailed feature articles providing advice on menus and diets.

As a testament to the power of American women consumers and to middle-class enthusiasm for the war, Hoover's program was quite successful, despite the lack of any significant price controls. Along with increased production, consumer restraint moderated inflation significantly during the war period. This collective experience caused an increase in the clientele for the home economics movement, increased middle-class enthusiasm for household efficiency (which eventually would be focused with even greater intensity on child rearing), and lent the individual American household and housewife a sense of identity as part of larger consuming communities.

WHAT HERBERT HOOVER ASKED

August 1917

Stop, before throwing any food away, and ask "Can it be used?"
Order meals so as not to have too much.
Have a proper balance of the most nutritious foods.
Stop catering to different appetites.
No second helpings.
Stop all eating between meals.
Stop all four-o'clock teas.
Stop all refreshments at parties, dances, etc.
Stop all eating after the theater.
One meatless day a week.
One wheatless meal a day.
No young lamb; no veal; no young pigs or ducklings; no young meat of any sort.
No butter in cooking: use substitutes.
Personal marketing instead of by telephone.

Never before has the American woman faced the opportunity and the responsibility that are before her to-day. The world is short of foodstuffs, and proper distribution of existing supplies is hampered in every direction. America is in the unique position of having a surplus available for those who are in want. The final success of the war in which we are now engaged may, and probably does, depend upon our ability to produce more food and upon our thrift and self-sacrifice in conserving food products.

From Herbert Hoover, *Ladies' Home Journal* (August 1917): 25.

We are not in a position to play a large part at the present time in the actual fighting of the war, but we can play a most consequential part in caring for those who fight for us and for their women and children. To lose the war because we were unwilling to make the necessary efforts and the required sacrifices in regard to the food supply would be one of the most humiliating spectacles in history. Every effort directed toward production of food or its saving is absolutely necessary. No matter how small the attempt may be, in the aggregate the result will make a great quantity of additional food to be sent to our needy Allies.

It is of particular importance that we see that the people of France, Italy, and England receive as full a ration as it is possible for us to provide. In particular we must send those things to Europe that can be most readily controlled, most readily shipped, and that contain the most nourishment per pound of weight. Wheat, sugar, fats, pork products, lard substitutes, and margarine are the predominant European needs. Too, we must take care of the fodder requirements of the European stock, so that the horses may have grain, oats, barley, etc., and the dairy herds may have feeds that will keep up the European milk and butter supply.

Our great excess of food has led to habits of extravagance and to the setting up of ordinary eating standards that have led to the use by the average individual of from 25 to 40 per cent more food than the body actually requires in order to keep it in good physical condition. We, then, must urge upon the American people a readjustment of their eating habits in order to bring about a conservation of food and an elimination of waste, not with the idea of saving money—for there will be plenty of money and business in the United States—but to conserve food so that we may provide it for our Allies, and provide it in quantities that will make the submarine campaign a failure and will lead to tranquillity and reasonable comfort in the populations of those countries with which we are allied in this war.

There are some things that every woman can do and can do at once. Every woman should feel herself definitely engaged in national service in her own kitchen and in her own home. She should lend her active support and her influence to see that those foods obtainable near home are used freely, so that transportation is not strained. Also, she should see to it that vegetables are consumed in summer, that large quantities of perishable foods are preserved for later use and that there be a minimum use of staples. Where possible, substitutes should be used for those things than can be more readily shipped abroad.

Here are my definite suggestions:

Let the American woman stop, before anything is thrown away, and let her ask herself "Can it be used in my home, in some other home, or in the production of further food supply by feeding it to animals used also for food?"

Let her order her meals so that there will be plenty—for there is plenty—but not too much.

The intelligent woman of America must make a proper study of food ratios, so that the most nutritious foods will appear in their proper proportions on the home table.

Where there is no illness in the home, the extra energy and waste associated with the catering to different appetites and the multiplicity of foods thus occasioned should be done away with. This food problem is not a matter of a few months, but will be with us every day for the next ten years.

All second helpings should be discouraged, and where the number of courses in formal meals is reduced the tendency to overeat should not be encouraged by a return of the plate for further additions.

Eating between meals is not only unnecessary and often harmful but it leads to excessive eating and should be discouraged.

Four-o'clock teas and late suppers may be all right in peace times, but there is no occasion for adding to the burden already so great upon our food supply by this additional strain.

In the aggregate the amount of food consumed for refreshments at parties, dances, etc., is very great. Certainly we should be willing to give up such indulgences for the great cause in which we are engaged. The same thing applies to the eating of meals at unusual hours by those not engaged in productive labor. In particular this applies to eating after the theater.

We hope soon to be able to indicate clearly the amount of bread and rolls that is sufficient for good nourishment for the adult and for the body building of the child, and then to request that no more be consumed.

The voluntary establishment of a meatless day a week, and of one or more wheatless meals a day by substitution of other cereal breads, will go a long way, even in this early stage, to make our savings for export considerable.

We must look ahead and stop consuming young lamb and veal, young pigs and ducklings, in order to allow our food animals to grow to that stage of maturity found most economical.

Although the telephone has brought many wonderful things to American life, it has separated the American woman from the market to a large extent and has increased enormously the expensive delivery service now thought requisite for the local handling of food. When the man power of the country has been reduced by establishment of the great armies now being organized, there will not be the same opportunity for urban delivery that now exists. The American woman should reestablish the old habits of personal marketing, so that by actual knowledge of prices and of abundance or scarcity of foods she may purchase more easily for herself and in the interests of the whole food supply question.

Great world decisions may follow upon a multiplicity of comparatively minor acts of large groups of our people. The American woman and the American home can, by voluntary act and by thrift, by good will and by patriotic devotion, bring to a successful end the greatest national task that has ever been accepted by the American people.

Index

Abbott, Edith, 187

Adams, Abigail Smith: biographical note, 78; recommends limits on legal power of husbands, 79–81; letters from, 79–81, 83–87; letters to, 81–83; reply of John Adams to request for new code of laws, 81–83; informs Mercy Otis Warren of her request for a new code, 83–85; on dangers of absolute power, 85–87

Addams, Jane: influence of on Alice Hamilton, 284–85; on prostitution, 244

Adkins v. *Children's Hospital,* 185

Agricultural labor: and family units, 9, 17–18; women's role in, 43, 91–92; slave women, 92–93; Rose Williams, 95–98; of New York farm wife, 110–19; Wisconsin, 127–30

American Federationist, excerpts from, 213–16

American Federation of Labor (AF of L): attitude of toward women, 216; Samuel Gompers and, 216, 227; William Green and, 224, 226; opposition of to Communists, 227

American Home Economic Association, founding of, 328–29

Antenuptial contracts: in colonial America, 42

Apprenticeship, contracts of. *See* Indentures

Ayscough, Richard, will of, 71

Bagley, Sarah G.: organizes workers in Lowell Mills, 159; reports on factory hours, 162–63

Baker, Sarah, indenture of, 74–75

Barry, Leonora M.: organizer for Knights of Labor, 209–11

Bassett, Francis, indenture of, 77

Beaulieu, Sarah E., Wisconsin farm girl: biographical note, 126; diary of, 127–30

Beecher, Catherine: *The American Woman's Home,* 309

Benevolent societies: role in Philadelphia poor relief, 148–49

Berry, Mary, indenture of, 77

Blackwell, Elizabeth: biographical note, 272–73; *Pioneer Work in Opening the Medical Profession to Women,* 273–82; evaluates European medical cures, 277; on need for knowledge of obstetrics, sex, and women's diseases, 278–79; on sex discrimination as a medical student, 279–81; on aid for Marie Zachrzewska in securing medical degree, 279, 282

Black women. *See* Agricultural labor; Civil War; Domestic service

Bok, Edward, 333–34

Bowditch, William I.: *Taxation of Women in Massachusetts,* 310–14

Bradley, Martha: recalls life as field hand under slavery, 93–95

Bradwell, Myra Colby: biographical

343